American Institutions, Political Opinion, and Public Policy

American Institutions, Political Opinion, and Public Policy

Robert G. Lehnen
University of Houston

The Dryden Press
Hinsdale, Illinois

Copyright © 1976 by the Dryden Press
A Division of Holt, Rinehart and Winston
All rights reserved
Library of Congress Catalog Card Number: 76–3085
ISBN: 0–03–013906–6
Printed in the United States of America
6789   038 987654321

**To Sandra,
Laura Catherine
and John Frederick**

Preface

In our concern about the serious problems facing political leaders today—economic stability, world peace, hunger, material shortages, integrity in government—we all too often lose sight of the political activity of average people. The activities of the typical American doing his routine work and play are no match for the attention-catching business of political decision makers. Although concern with novel and dramatic events is not unusual, such concern can draw attention away from an important part of political activity in the United States—the political participation of individual citizens. Unfortunately, politics is often equated with the behavior of public leaders. Somehow, we have lost sight of the millions of citizens who will never hold (or desire to hold) an elected or appointed public office. I have always found this a curious position, because what the average citizen feels, thinks, cares, and does about public matters, in my mind at least, is the ultimate yardstick by which elites may be judged and societies evaluated. To concentrate on elite political behavior to the exclusion of mass political behavior seems a ludicrous state of affairs. Yet the manner of instruction in many classrooms today comes close to this situation. Short of some material about how voters behave in presidential elections, there is little concern about mass political behavior in general.

This book is an attempt to summarize a wide range of literature on the political involvement of individuals with the institutions of government. It is directed both to the college undergraduate and to the reasonably informed reader who has an interest in political affairs. It focuses on three main themes.

The first theme concerns the ability of citizens to engage in political affairs. It seems ironic that the late Professor V.O. Key, Jr., began a recent book by stating, "Voters are not fools." He did so because the capacity of average people to form and organize their political thoughts and values has been the object of a wide-ranging scientific debate. This debate has raised serious questions concerning the competence and rationality of citizens in regard to political affairs.

The second theme is how and why people perceive and evaluate institutions and their incumbents. Although many summaries of public opinion poll findings are readily available, few of these summaries concentrate on the public's views on specific policy concerns of the day and, at the same time, relate these views to particular political institutions. The existing literature leaves the distinct impression that most people are so uninformed and have political views so unfocused that they cannot differentiate various aspects of political activity at the federal and state levels. Yet material presented in Part II will suggest the contrary. People have rather specific political concerns; they may not follow foreign affairs, but prayer in the public schools may be an important political issue for many of them.

The final theme concerns the place of active citizens in politics. I shall look at those actions taken by citizens that assume political relevance (such as acquiring information, voting, contacting an official). Citizens have different ways of becoming politically involved. These different styles will be illustrated, and the causes and consequences will be explored.

A premise underlying the organization of this book is that to understand political opinion and behavior, one must appreciate the scientific procedures used to study them. Some knowledge of questionnaire design, sampling, and data analysis is essential for evaluating facts produced by opinion studies. Scientific findings are not simply discovered; they are the product of conscious (and unconscious) decisions of every researcher. Unfortunately, these decisions often determine the scope and compromise the integrity of scientific findings. Part I, which summarizes the basic steps of sample survey methodology, is designed to make the reader skeptical of some research yet appreciative of the power of the generalizations derived from properly conducted studies.

There is no single theory of public opinion. Rather, partial theories of public opinion phenomena abound. We have theories on attitude formation and change, social integration, political participation, and support for governmental institutions, to mention just a few. The literature is incomplete with respect to these theories, and many of them have little or no evidence to confirm or disconfirm their predictions. Part I defines some important ideas pertaining to mass political behavior and provides a framework for organizing the substantive material that follows. It is a synthesis of commonly recognized approaches for organizing the complex aspects of public opinion research. This framework provides a rationale for why some comparisons—say, between social status and voting—were made and others were not.

The analysis presented in this book is selective, representing what I judge to be the most relevant material with respect to the framework provided in Part I. Because the scientific literature is incomplete on many topics, the finding of a single national sample survey of mass political behavior conducted in 1969 have been used to supplement the literature and data from various survey organizations. This survey data is from the Southeast Regional

Survey I Project, which was funded by a "science excellence" grant awarded to the University of North Carolina by the National Science Foundation.

There are many people to whom I owe an enormous debt for aiding me at various stages in the preparation of this manuscript. Dr. Thad L. Beyle of the Department of Political Science at the University of North Carolina and I worked jointly during the academic year 1968–69 to design and conduct the Southeast Regional Survey Project. The staff of the Institute for Research in Social Science at the university provided critical assistance in the design of the survey and the coding and processing of data. Angell Beza, associate director of the Institute, was especially helpful at this critical stage of the research project. At the risk of omitting the names of many people who contributed in various ways to the design of the survey and the processing of data, two former graduate students at the University of North Carolina, Laura Irwin and Ken Hardy, deserve special recognition for their contributions.

The analysis and writing of this manuscript occurred on the campus of the University of Houston. I have received considerable support and encouragement from members of the Department of Political Science, who provided essential support for the successful completion of the work. I am also grateful to the Director of the University Computing Center, William Rowley, and Ric O. Stewart for the unsponsored computing time and programming assistance they provided. In addition, two former undergraduates at the University of Houston, Robert Barr and Robert Downing, helped immeasurably with data processing problems. I am indebted to the Office of Research and Sponsored Activities at the University of Houston and its director, Francis Smith, for generous support of various aspects of this research through two Limited-Grant-in-Aid-Awards. Finally, I wish to acknowledge the useful criticisms of early drafts of the manuscript by Professor Dan Nimmo of the University of Tennessee, Knoxville.

R.G.L.
Houston, Texas
March, 1976

Contents

Part One
An Introduction to the Study of Public Opinion and Political Participation

Chapter 1	**Attentive Publics and Responsible Citizenship**	**3**
	The Case against Mass Political Participation	**5**
	The Common Man's Role Is Re-evaluated	**9**
	Mass Participation: An Expanded Role for the Common Man	**13**
	The Importance of Citizen Participation in Classical Theory	**15**
	Attentive Publics: A Model for Citizen Participation	**17**
	Two Explanations of Participatory Behavior	**19**
	An Overview of Things to Come	**22**
Chapter 2	**The Study of Political Opinions**	**25**
	What Are Opinions?	**26**
	Individual Opinions and the Political Process	**28**
	A Macro-view of Political Opinion and Process	**31**
	The Continuity of Political Opinion and the Macro-process	**34**
	A Micro-view of Political Opinion	**35**
	An Overall Model: Combining the Micro- and Macro-models	**37**
Chapter 3	**How to Study Political Opinions: The Genealogy of a Research Project**	**41**
	Posing a Question and Reviewing Past Research Findings	**42**
	Types of Questions Used on Surveys	**44**
	Some Limiting Effects of Survey Costs	**49**
	The Importance of Probability Sampling	**50**
	Area-probability Samples	**52**

The Role of Sampling Error   53
Processing the Completed Interviews   55
The Presentation of Data in the Text   60

Part Two
Citizens and Their Political Institutions

Chapter 4   **Support for Political Institutions**   67
Diffuse Support and Political Culture   67
Diffuse Support for Public and Private Institutions   70
Citizen Attention to Levels of Government   72
Specific Support for Public Institutions   79
The Relationship of Diffuse and Specific Support   80
Citizens' Perceptions of Governmental Power   85
Popular Commitments to Grass-roots Democracy   88
The Effects of Social Background on Some Aspects of
    Political Culture   91
Social Background and Perceptions of Power and
    Effectiveness   98
Some Summary Observations   100

Chapter 5   **Public Views of Chief Executives:**
Comparisons at the National and State Levels   103
Public Opinion and Chief Executives: An Overview   103
The Salience of Executive Activities   106
Political Knowledge and Perception of Executives   111
Partisanship and Policy Evaluations   115
The Role of Long-term Psychological Attitudes on
    Perceptions of Executives   119
The Role of Social Background on Perceptions of
    Executives   131

Chapter 6   **The Supreme Court and Political Opinion**   135
The Salience and Perception of Court Activity   136
Political Knowledge and Perceptions of the Justices   140
Partisanship, Ideology, and Evaluations of the Court   141
Long-term Attitudes and Evaluations of the Court   143
The Role of Social Background on Perceptions of the
    Court   150

Chapter 7   **The Congress and Public Opinion**   153
The Responsible Party Model and Public Opinion   154
Citizens' Perceptions of Congress between Elections   156
The Salience of U. S. Senators   157

The Content of Senatorial Perceptions   **160**
Partisanship and the Salience of Senators   **163**
Public Evaluations of Congress   **164**
Partisanship and Evaluations of Congress   **168**
Public Expectations about Congressional Performance   **170**
The Effects of Social Background on Perceptions   **171**

Chapter 8   **Political Action: Modes of Overt Citizen Participation**   **177**
Some Types of Participation   **179**
The Degree of Participation   **181**
Styles of Participation   **190**
Some Causes of Political Participation   **192**
Some Consequences of Participation   **199**

Part Three
Some Concluding Observations

Chapter 9   **The Citizen and Participatory Democracy**   **207**

Appendices   **213**

Bibliography   **223**

Index   **231**

List of Figures

Figure 2–1   A Macro-Model: Political Attitudes and Beliefs in the
             Political System   32
Figure 2–2   A Micro-Model: Factors Affecting Public Policy
             Opinions at the Individual Level   35
Figure 2–3   An Overall Model Combining Individual Political
             Attitudes and Beliefs with the Macro-Political Process   38
Figure 3–1   Flow of "Party Identification" Question Sequence   45
Figure 3–2   Sort Board Used in the Southeast Regional Survey   46
Figure 4–1   The Distribution of the Number of Specific Mentions to
             Four Institutions   75
Figure 4–2   Trends in Questions Asked by the Gallup Poll during the
             Watergate Affair   84
Figure 4–3   The Effects of Institutional Saliency on Perceptions of
             Governmental Power   87
Figure 5–1   The Effects of Events on the Public's Evaluation of the
             Nixon Presidency   110
Figure 5–2   Political Knowledge and Response to Policies of Chief
             Executives   113
Figure 5–3   The Effects of Partisanship on Response to the
             President's Activities   116
Figure 7–1   The Public's Evaluation of Congress, 1963–1975   165
Figure 8–1   Hypothetical Patterns of Political Participation   182
Figure 8–2   The Effects of Age on Political Participation with Status
             Controlled   197

List of Tables

Table 3–1   The Relationship of Sampling Error to Sample Size   **54**

Table 3–2   Codes Used to Summarize Responses to Question about the Supreme Court: Now, Thinking about the Supreme Court in Washington, Is There Anything the Supreme Court Has Done Lately That You Don't Like? What Is That? Is There Anything Else?   **56**

Table 3–3   Record of Gallup Poll Accuracy, 1936–1974   **59**

Table 3–4   A Summary of Table 5–1   **62**

Table 4–1   Distribution of Diffuse Support for Public and Private Institutions   **72**

Table 4–2   Citizen Attention to Levels of Government: A Comparison of Findings   **73**

Table 4–3   The Salience of Institutional Politics and the Level of Political Knowledge   **76**

Table 4–4   The Relationship of Education to the Saliency of Political Institutions   **77**

Table 4–5   Distributions of Specific Support for Three Public Institutions   **79**

Table 4–6   The Effects of Diffuse Support on Net Specific Support for Three Public Institutions   **81**

Table 4–7   The Effects of Perceived Power on Attitudes toward Specific Governmental Performance   **88**

Table 4–8   The Effects of Sex on Diffuse Support for Selected Institutions, Controlling for Education   **94**

Table 4–9   The Effects of Race on Diffuse Support for Selected Institutions, Controlling for Education   **96**

Table 4–10   The Effects of Sex on Perceptions of Power in Seven Institutions, Controlling for Education   **98**

Table 4–11   The Effects of Race on Perceptions of Power in Seven Institutions, Controlling for Education   **99**

Table 5–1	Favorable and Unfavorable Responses to the Policies of the President	107
Table 5–2	Favorable and Unfavorable Responses to the Policies of State Governors	108
Table 5–3	The Effects of State Party Identification on Perceptions of Governors' Policies	118
Table 5–4	Strength of Attitudes toward Foreign Affairs and Perceptions of Presidential Foreign Policy Activities	121
Table 5–5	The Relationship of Criticism of Executive Tax and Spending Policies to the Ordering of Spending Preferences	126
Table 5–6	Some Indicators of the Dimensions of the Law and Order Issue	127
Table 5–7	The Effects of Attitudes toward Law and Order on Response to Governors' Policies on Law and Order	129
Table 5–8	The Effects of Sex on Policy Perceptions of Chief Executives, Controlling for Socioeconomic Status	131
Table 5–9	The Effects of Race on Policy Perceptions of Chief Executives, Controlling for Socioeconomic Status	133
Table 6–1	Favorable and Unfavorable Responses to the Policies of the United States Supreme Court	138
Table 6–2	Supreme Court Justices Identified by National Sample (1969)	141
Table 6–3	The Effects of National Party Identification of Response to Supreme Court Policies	143
Table 6–4	The Effects of Attitudes toward Law and Order on Response to Supreme Court's Decisions on Law and Order	144
Table 6–5	Effects of Religion and Religious Practice on Religious Belief and Attitudes toward School Prayer Decisions	145
Table 6–6	Effects of Attitudes toward Law and Order on Response to Supreme Court's Decision of School Prayer	147
Table 6–7	Effects of Religion and Religious Practice on Attitudes toward Law and Order Decisions	148
Table 6–8	Effects of Race and Stereotyped Racial Attitudes on Response toward Civil Rights Decisions	149
Table 6–9	The Effects of Sex on Policy Perceptions of the Supreme Court, Controlling for Socioeconomic Status	150
Table 6–10	The Effects of Race on Policy Perceptions of the Supreme Court, Controlling for Socioeconomic Status	151
Table 7–1	Proportion of National Sample Identifying Selected Members of the U.S. Senate	159
Table 7–2	The Salient Characteristics of Selected U.S. Senators	161
Table 7–3	Effects of Party Respondent's Identification on Perceived Characteristics of Selected Senators	164

Table 7–4	Comparisons of Level of Public Confidence in Selected Institutions, 1966–73	165
Table 7–5	The Effects of Respondent's Party Identification on the Approval of Selected U.S. Senators in 1969	169
Table 7–6	Institutions from Which the Public Would Seek Assistance in Solving Selected Problems	171
Table 7–7	The Effects of Sex on Salience and Approval of Selected U.S. Senators	172
Table 7–8	The Effects of Race on Salience and Approval of Selected U.S. Senators	173
Table 7–9	The Effects of Status on the Salience and Approval of Selected U.S. Senators	174
Table 8–1	Description of Selected Types of Political Participation	180
Table 8–2	Selected Indicators of Citizen Involvement in Politics	181
Table 8–3	Report of Electoral Participation (1968)	184
Table 8–4	Summary of Turnout and Voting in 1972 Presidential Election	184
Table 8–5	Rates of Citizen Interaction with Selected Public Agencies and Officials	187
Table 8–6	Distribution of "Most Important" Contacts by Citizen Role in Contact	188
Table 8–7	Distribution of Styles of Participation	192
Table 8–8	The Effects of Sex on Political Participation with Socioeconomic Status Controlled	193
Table 8–9	The Effects of Sex on Style of Political Participation, with Socioeconomic Status Controlled	194
Table 8–10	The Effects of Race on Political Participation, with Socioeconomic Status Controlled	194
Table 8–11	The Effects of Race on Style of Political Participation, with Socioeconomic Status Controlled	195
Table 8–12	The Consequences of Differing Styles of Political Participation on Levels of Political Knowledge	200
Table 8–13	The Consequences of Differing Styles of Political Participation on Evaluation of Governmental Performance	201

American Institutions, Political Opinion, and Public Policy

Part One

An Introduction to the Study of Public Opinion and Political Participation

Chapter One

Attentive Publics and Responsible Citizenship

The moral foundation of a democratic society rests on a faith in the common man's dignity and in his potential for functioning as a responsible individual in a free society. E. E. Schattschneider characterizes this moral foundation as "an attitude toward people"; as a system of government where "Men are equal in the dimension that counts: each is a human being, infinitely precious because he is human" (1969, chap. 3). From this belief in the inherent worth of the individual comes the challenge of democracy: to organize and perpetuate a working, practicable system of governing that confronts the hard realities presented by a large, industrial society. The challenge is to translate a moral proposition into a functioning governmental structure, to find a means of governing whereby the common man may play a meaningful, participatory role. The objective is to have government that not only recognizes the value of the individual citizen but also incorporates him into the ongoing process of public affairs.

For most Americans—who have been reared on a steady diet of Fourth of July rhetoric, American history, and electioneering—an assertion concerning the worth of the individual is neither novel nor controversial. Such phrases as "we, the people" and "government of the people, by the people, and for the people" are almost second nature to them. Yet such statements do not reflect the substance of American government in action as we know it today. The moral system of democracy is not now realized as democracy in action because the participatory political role of the common man does not conform to the moral standards of classical democratic theory. In fact, the basic moral theory of American democracy has been substantially altered to conform to the current system of governance. The dominant intellectual interpretation of American democracy presently reflected in both theory and practice has been labeled by Peter Bachrach as the theory of *democratic elitism* (1967). Democratic elitism, like many bodies of theory and practice, has no single interpretation, but all variations share several common themes. The beginning axiom is that even in democratic societies, some men will have the ability to provide political leadership and organization for the greater number of citizens, who on the whole have lesser political abilities and little political cohesion (cf. Prewitt and Stone,

1973). The first group can be called political "elites" or "leaders" and the second group are called "masses" or "followers."

The central premise of classical democratic theory has been a general belief in the capability of the average citizen to be a political participant. It affirms a general confidence in the decisions citizens make about political matters. Democratic theorists assert the right, indeed the *necessity*, to involve the followers of a political system in the important decisions made by the leaders. It is repugnant to suggest that leaders know "best" and that citizens should simply leave important political matters to them. Traditional democratic theorists recognize the importance of democratic procedures (e.g., one man, one vote; majority rule) but assert the need to evaluate the system according to its consequences for its individual members. One consequence of principal importance to democrats is the acknowledgment of the beneficial consequences of citizen participation—the enhancement of the individual's self-esteem and the development of favorable individual qualities. Thus, the democrat recognizes the benefits that accrue to the participant because of his involvement in politics. Finally, classical democrats are not content to look at a political system only in terms of its "outputs." The masses must play a role in formulating the alternatives on which decisions are made (the "inputs") also. Thus, Bachrach observes that the central theme of classical democratic theory "is based on the supposition that man's dignity and indeed his growth and development as a functioning and responsive individual in a free society, is dependent upon an opportunity to participate actively in decisions that significantly affect him" (1967, p. 98). To have a stable and prosperous system is not enough; the measure of the society is the political and social well-being of the individual citizen.

Democratic elitism is both an intellectual and a practical response to the complexities of governing large, industrial societies. But in attempting to find a workable system of political organization, it has redefined, in fundamental ways, several central premises of classical democratic theory (Bachrach, 1967). Democratic elitists start with the notion that the common man (the follower) has, at best, only a limited ability to become involved in public decisions that concern him. Thus, the participation of the masses must be limited and structured to prevent breakdowns in the operation of the political system. A second premise of democratic elitism is the reliance on elites to set the standards and direct a course for achieving the best decisions and a good society. To keep the society based on popular rule, however, democratic elitists acknowledge the need to have democratic procedures for the exercise of political power; otherwise, the system could become totalitarian and elites would cease to be representative. As a result, every citizen must have an equal opportunity to achieve the exercise of power, and therefore many democratic elitists would support the principle "one man, one vote." Every qualified citizen would in theory have an equal opportunity to select (or recall) elected political leaders. Finally, the democratic elitists evaluate the soundness of the political system they govern by the consequences of its "outputs"—the security, stability, and prosperity of the society.

The dilemma posed by the redefinition of classical democracy in terms of democratic elitism is that classical theory summarizes a set of values endorsed by many Americans but presents a system that appears unworkable in a large, industrial society. Democratic elitism, a practical and apparently workable response to the problems of modern government, has subtly but fundamentally changed the moral basis of democracy to the point that one might charge, "The baby has been thrown out with the bath water."

In the past twenty-five years, modern social scientists have added a new chapter to the discussion about the common man's role in politics. During this period, in-depth scientific studies of how people in fact behave, what they feel and think, and why they act have provided a unique form of evidence to supplement, the moral assertions of the elitists that the common man does not deserve our confidence. This merging of moral assertions with scientifically determined generalizations has produced a serious argument that cannot be ignored, for the decisions made in pursuance of the argument will shape the kind of political society that we live in. The conclusions one makes about citizen participation will have direct implications for determining who shall vote; how public programs—such as urban renewal, welfare assistance, and protection of the environment—shall be administered; and in general, how individual citizens as well as political elites view the political role of the citizen in mass society.

The question under debate can be stated in a deceptively simple way: Does the typical American citizen have the ability to undertake the responsibilities of citizenship? The hidden complexity of this question lies in the definition of slippery terms such as "the responsibilities of citizenship" and "ability." Just what are a citizen's "responsibilities"? What does one mean by "ability"?

The Case against Mass Political Participation

In interpreting scientific evidence on how people behave, social scientists have painted a dark picture of the common man's capacity to play a meaningful role in the politics of large and complex societies. Both by inference and by direct conclusion, many studies have supported the view that the average person is not really capable of undertaking the burdens of citizenship. The implications for electoral reform are profound. Why expand the suffrage when reputable scientific evidence suggests that expanded participation increases the risk of "irresponsible" citizenship? What if the "irrational" electorate began to participate in political decision making at an abnormally high rate?

Most of the research leading to the conclusion that the typical American citizen was not well equipped to handle the responsibilities of citizenship have arisen from the intense study of a relatively restricted form of mass political participation—electoral behavior. The notion of the ability of a citizen to participate has been defined in the context of presidential election studies to mean the level of information a person had about candidates and issues, whether he had formed opinions on public issues, and the degree to which the researchers viewed these opinions as correct or sound. The principal data supporting their conclusion on citizen participation have come from opinion polls conducted during electoral campaigns, from major electoral studies done by social scientists in the 1940s and 1950s, and from voting records.

Probably the best known statement of this pessimistic position comes from the authors of *Voting* (Berelson et al., 1954; Berelson, 1952). They defined a standard of citizen behavior called the rational-activist model (cf. Luttbeg, 1968). The rational-activist model of citizenship assumes that people will be interested and actively engage in political matters. They will be knowledgeable and informed about political controversies. Based on this knowledge, they will not make political decisions frivolously, impulsively, or habitually, but they will arrive at decisions about political principle by reason and deliberation.

When social scientists compared their empirically based findings with the rational-activist standard, the citizens studied in *Voting* failed to measure up to the standards of behavior postulated by the model. Rather than being interested, knowledgeable, and informed, many voters were ignorant of the candidates, issues, and basic facts of the election. People rarely weighed issues and seriously balanced the competing arguments of the two parties before deciding how to vote. More often the case, most voters could not articulate clear reasons for making their choices, and when they did, these choices were based on liking the candidate or support for a political party rather than on knowledge and issues. In the study *Voting*, the authors tried to reconcile their scientific evidence with certain values they held toward participation. Although the best scientific evidence of the day did not support hopes that citizens were, or could become, active and involved in the electoral process, the authors of *Voting* suggested that all was not lost; they argued that a strong and stable democracy could still be built on such patterns of citizenship. Apathetic and uninvolved citizens were good for the stability of the political system: they would not "rock the boat." If too many of these attitudinally unstable and unknowledgeable citizens became actively involved, political elites could neither meet the expectations of these citizens nor govern effectively.

The American Voter (Campbell et al., 1960), a major voting study conducted during the 1952 and 1956 presidential elections, tended to confirm the overall findings of *Voting*. *The American Voter* concentrated more on the factors best explaining the decision to vote and the choice between candidates. The "funnel of causality," the underlying theoretical model of voting behavior used in *The American Voter*, postulated that psychological conditions close in time to the voting decision would be most influential in determining the individual choice. Three key variables were found to play a central role in shaping electoral choice: the party identification of the respondent, his perception of the candidate's qualities, and his position on the dominant issues in the campaign. Although other factors contributed to the voter's decision-making process, these three influences were by far most important. Of the three, party identification was the dominant cause, and the respondent's attitudes on the issues was the least important. Since party identification proved to be a stable, continuing attitude showing little change over the course of a respondent's lifetime, the single major cause of voter decision making was a long-term condition not greatly affected by short-term influences arising during the campaign. In sum, people's votes were most influenced by a condition—party identification—that generally was not reflective of the issues and problems arising during an election period. This finding implied that voters tended to be more habitual than deliberative in casting their votes.

The comparison of party with issue influences further contributed to the debate surrounding the principal question: can the voter meet the requirements of citizenship? People did not form precise or strong attitudes about current affairs. The studies further demonstrated when such issue-attitudes existed, that they were of little or no importance, relative to party loyalties, in predicting how people would vote. Many analysts saw *The American Voter* as additional evidence confirming beliefs about the voter's inability to be the rational-activist citizen. The average voter was most influenced by his party loyalties, an attribute acquired early in life and remaining relatively unchanged despite the ebb and flow of political events. The issues of the day, a better barometer of the current state of political controversy, had only a small influence on voter choice.

The American Voter also explored a respondent's ability to conceive and articulate issues and political philosophies in a meaningful way. In an in-depth analysis of responses to a series of questions about the good and bad points of the two parties and the two candidates, the respondents were classified according to four categories characterizing the "level of conceptualization" about political matters expressed by the respondent. The respondents who spoke in terms of a liberal-conservative dimension and tended to structure their political comments with respect to some political philosophy were called "ideologues." These individuals came closest to realizing the rational-activist standard. Respondents who spoke of the parties and candidates in terms of group interests were treated as a second level of conceptualization below the ideologues. These respondents saw politics in terms of population groupings and not so much in terms of programs and policies. They spoke of the Democrats as helping the "poor people," or Republicans as being "good for business," rather than Democrats "having a social welfare policy" or Republicans "supporting low inflation at the expense of more unemployment." A third group was classified by "nature of the times" responses. These respondents may have mentioned a specific issue but could not relate their comments either to a broad philosophy (ideology) or to a group interest. These respondents tended to speak in vague and less precise terms about how things were. Finally, the fourth category of respondents failed to mention any issues in their open-ended responses. They often spoke in terms of "mudslinging" by the candidates or of their personal characteristics ("nice person," "honest," etc.).

This classification was used to divide a representative sample of the 1956 electorate into the following categories (Campbell et al., 1960):

Type of Response:
Ideological or near-ideological	12%
Group interest	42
Nature of the times	24
No issue content	22
	100%

Since the ideological category best approached the ideal of the rational-activist model, the analysis from *The American Voter* has further added to the already weighty evidence against the model. Only 12 percent of the sample could be classified as ideological and an additional 42 percent made issue-type comments in terms of group interests. Thus, a total of 54 percent of the sample was classified as barely conversant in the bases for electoral conflict. The remaining 46 percent was almost totally uninformed or sufficiently inaccurate, fragmentary, and misinformed so as to clearly fail the rational-activist test of citizenship.

Related research on the structure of attitudes held by respondents toward major political issues of the day also has contributed to the belief that theoretical expectations about the levels of mass political participation were too high. Philip Converse (1964a) analyzed how respondents in national surveys felt toward a series of issue questions on foreign affairs, civil rights, and other current topics. He postulated that should a system of beliefs concerning public questions exist for the average voter, then question responses would be interrelated. If, for example, respondents favored the government providing jobs for people who needed them, then they would probably favor government efforts to provide a minimum income. Similarly, a respondent opposing trade agreements with the Communist nations would probably oppose attempts to secure disarmament agreements as well. The first pattern might be predicted based on an underlying social-welfare philosophy whereas the second would arise from anti-Communist or isolationist attitudes.

Converse found little pattern among public responses to policy questions. "Agree" responses to one social-welfare question did not coincide with "agree" responses to another social-welfare item. Converse concluded that most citizens did not cluster their political values into "belief systems" but rather held these opinions in isolation from and often in contradiction to each other. Axelrod (1967) also confirmed Converse's research conclusion, although he found some clustering of attitudes around a populism dimension. On a related piece of research, Converse (1964b) also suggested that respondents did not always give meaningful responses to broad policy questions administered in public opinion studies. He found logically inconsistent patterns of change in responses to the same questions repeated over a period of four years. An example of such change is a person giving a strongly favorable response to public school integration at one time, then becoming strongly opposed at a later time, and finally becoming strongly in favor at a third point in time. Such changes as a general pattern would be difficult to explain, since attitudes toward public policy are thought to be rather deeply grounded in one's personality. Converse was able to explain changes toward two policy questions by assuming a random pattern of change. In this context, "random" can be thought of as meaning "unpredictable" for the individual case, in the same sense that the outcome of a single coin toss is unpredictable. The outcome of many tosses of a coin is entirely predictable, however, and our intuition tells us what the theory of probability confirms: that a large number of throws is likely to produce about one-half "heads" and one-half "tails." Converse used a similar logic to explain how large numbers of citizens changed their responses to certain policy questions. The implication was that for certain policy questions, citizens' responses to opinion questions were as random as the toss of a coin.

The issues in this scientific debate are complex and extend beyond the discussion presented here. They are further complicated by the fact that subtle questions of how the findings were derived—questions about research methodology—are interlaced with the substantive issues. The critique of the rational-activist model of citizen participation, however, can be oversimplified to the following main points. First, the citizen is not as highly informed as the model suggests he should be. His information is incomplete and often inaccurate. His choices appear shaped by long-range considerations, such as his party identification, as much as by his responsiveness to the issues of the day. In fact, the research summarized here suggests there is almost no role for issues in the decision making of the average man. What issue-attitudes that exist are unstructured and often unstable. For a small proportion of people with much higher education and awareness than most, issues may be more structured into belief-systems and play a more central role in shaping political choices. But for the typical person issues and current controversies have little impact on his political choices. Furthermore, these issue-attitudes have little to do with explaining the vote. Party identification is the single best predictor of how people vote. Party loyalties, however, are formed early in life and are greatly influenced by parents and in the home. In addition, these loyalties change little over the course of a person's life. Thus, the typical voter makes his choice based on long-standing partisan loyalties and is only weakly influenced by short-term forces such as issues and candidates.

The Common Man's Role is Re-evaluated

Science rarely provides answers that are totally consistent with one point of view and the debate over the correct model for citizen participation is no exception to this rule. Most of the counter evidence to the pessimistic interpretation of the rational-activist model emphasizes a modification of extreme conclusions about citizen participation and usually suggests an improvement in the way the initial conclusions were derived.

Probably the most well-known single work providing counter evidence is V. O. Key, Jr.'s *The Responsible Electorate* (1966). Because it was published posthumously, this book raises almost as many questions as it answers. Two key sections—the introductory materials and concluding chapter—were reconstructed from Key's notes. It is from the introductory material that the rallying statement of the counter movement appears. Key wrote in his notes on the introduction, "The perverse and unorthodox argument of this little book is that voters are not fools." He arrived at this conclusion by analyzing "standpatters" and "switchers" across presidential elections from 1936 through 1960. These two types of voters were, respectively, people who voted for the same party between two presidential elections, and people who changed from one major political party to another. Key analyzed the patterns of change and stability with respect to attitudes toward important issues of the time and found logical and reasonably coherent patterns of behavior. Thus, Key's research gave re-emphasis to the role of issues in presidential voting and also suggested that under certain conditions, large groups of voters changed patterns of past voting behavior in a manner consistent with the dominant issues of the campaign.

RePass (1971) has also helped re-establish the role of issues by showing for the 1964 election how issues and party identification are interrelated (see also Leege, 1972; and RePass, 1972). RePass argued that some issues were more salient to the citizen than others, and that "salient issues had almost as much weight as party identification in predicting voting choice."

Boyd (1972), using data from the 1964 and 1968 presidential elections, determined that attitudes toward such policies as the Vietnam War, race relations, and urban disorders caused large deviations in the traditional voting patterns of Republicans and Democrats. These traditional voting patterns are the "normal" levels of voting expected if the effects of these issues are not present. Feelings that the movement toward improved civil rights had gone too fast and that more force should be used to maintain law and order depressed the actual Democratic vote from its expected levels. Almost all salient opinions about Vietnam policy—whether escalation versus de-escalation or withdrawal versus military victory—reduced the expected level of Democratic voting. Thus, current issues contributed to how people decided to vote. Boyd argued that these issues had such profound impact because of three characteristics. First, a substantial number of people had intense views about specific policy alternatives. Second, information was readily available about the positions of competing candidates and parties on these matters. Finally, these attitudes were not readily manipulated by elites; rather, they were relatively deep-rooted and not greatly subject to change. The trend of these studies done in the middle and late 1960s suggests that, under certain conditions, issues play an important role in citizen participation in elections. These dominant issues characterized the current political conflicts—civil rights, law and order, and Vietnam. Thus, the common man was not as "issueless" as first thought. He was able instead to respond to selected contemporary issues and base his vote on the judgments he formed.

The structuring of attitudes into belief-systems also came under re-examination. Field and Anderson (1969) found a substantial increase in the proportion of ideologues in the 1964 electorate. They attributed this change to the increased differentiation made between the parties and candidates of that period. During the Eisenhower years, when *The American Voter* was written, there was little to differentiate the parties. Barry Goldwater's candidacy though created "a choice, not an echo" for the voter. With meaningful distinctions presented by the candidates, voters perceived the candidates in more ideological terms. Pomper (1972) expanded this theme by showing that from 1956 to 1968 voters had substantially increased their differentiation of the party positions on such key issues as school integration, fair employment laws, foreign aid, and programs of public medical care. Voters perceived the political parties as offering different alternatives on these policies. Furthermore, they applied the terms "liberal" and "conservative" in a consistent manner to the parties to characterize differences in position on issues. Thus, the voters began to reflect a more structured and issue-oriented approach to electoral contests, which in part reflected the different conflicts present in the 1960s and absent in the 1950s. We thus see the argument that good citizenship also depends on the political environment. Citizens failed the rational-activist test in the 1950s as much because of the style of politics as because of inherent shortcomings.

The coherence of political attitudes was also re-examined. Brown (1970), for example, conducted an experiment to compare the consistency over time of political articulates and inarticulates to determine whether Converse's thesis (1964a)—that the inarticulates would be less consistent—applied. He found no significant differences over periods of two, four, and six weeks in the stability of attitudes held by articulates compared to inarticulates. Lehnen (1971–72) also has provided evidence that variations in question-wording and respondent unreliability account for the lack of a consistent pattern of belief-structures among masses. When the question wording and unreliability were controlled, average respondents not only demonstrated consistent patterns of response to policy questions on civil rights, open housing, law and order, and foreign aid, but also showed coherent belief-systems.

In the face of the heat, smoke, and confusion surrounding this scientific controversy, several findings are clear. Retesting of early hypotheses based on data collected in the 1940s and 1950s has re-established the importance of attitudes toward issues in shaping political perceptions and actions, particularly as they pertain to voting choices. Some recent interpretation now centers around the question of whether people behave differently today than twenty years ago, suggesting that both the early findings of the 1950s and more current research of the 1960s are essentially correct. The studies of Field and Anderson (1969), Pierce (1970), and Pomper (1972a) give direct evidence to support the argument that the Eisenhower years of the 1950s created a politics characterized by muted public opinion, whereas during the turbulent decade of the 1960s issues became more salient, and Americans perceived greater political differences.

Much of the evidence regarding the capacity (or inability) of citizens to govern has been overinterpreted. The extreme ends of the debate about citizen participation, on one hand, find the Pollyannaish rational-activist model, and on the other, reputable empirical investigators who paint a dark and gloomy picture of citizen participation. A recent essay by Hennessy (1972) suggests the extremes to which reputable scientists have demoted the citizen's role. Hennessey states in the essay, "A Headnote on the Existence and Study of Political Attitudes":

> I advance the proposition that political attitudes are an elite phenomenon. Most people do not have political attitudes. . . . When we accept that fact, and accept the epistemological and research implications that flow from it, we will be able to make more sense of attitude formation and change, of leader-follower relationships, and of the public policy-making processes.

After summarizing some arguments and evidence, Hennessy concludes:

> We are naive and inconsequential if we waste time with mass belief systems and mass attitudes. Beyond the concern for some outer cultural limits to what elites may do, we should not try to investigate that which isn't.

As one might suspect, the resolution of this matter falls somewhere between these extremes. "Votes are not fools" but neither are they civics-book models of behavior. They are influenced by issues, knowledge, and common sense, but they are also directed by prejudice, misinformation, and ignorance. If this controversy has contributed anything, it has probably forced a more realistic, and empirically based, understanding of citizen participation.

Many of the underlying assumptions about political participation are unfounded. The rational-activist model represents too much of the civics-book answer to a complex set of normative and empirical questions. The documentation of the foundations of the rational-activist model—the assumptions underpinning much of the controversy—is in many respects a response to a straw man. According to some theorists, the rational-activist model is a construction of contemporary social scientists without explicit foundations in the writings of classical democratic theorists (cf. Pateman, 1974). Thus, the empirical attack is directed at an ill-defined question, a question that no one, except possibly the researchers, has asked in the form presented. In this context it is easy to understand why the American citizen has been successively demoted and promoted. A more comprehensive and realistic formulation of an empirically based citizenship model is needed to better understand how the common man is involved in political affairs.

Mass Participation: An Expanded Role for the Common Man

Americans have many more opportunities than presidential elections to exercise citizen responsibilities. Presidential campaigns, though important, are but episodes in the ongoing processes of politics. During forty-two out of every forty-eight months, no candidate is actively campaigning for the presidency, and the media are not totally possessed by politics. During this period many important political events occur that are not major elections. Congress will hold two sessions; the Supreme Court will have four nine-month terms; the governors and state legislatures of the fifty states will be elected or serve out their terms; and thousands of elected and appointed officials—county officials, large and small city mayors, city councils, school boards, and state and local judges—will conduct the public's business. In this context, the question of citizen involvement in governmental affairs takes on a new emphasis. To consider electoral behavior as the primary gauge of mass participation at the expense of this broader picture is to "miss the forest because of the trees."

Three forms of citizen behavior occurring between elections have particular relevance to the day-to-day business of politics. These three general forms of behavior are support, evaluation, and political action. Supportive citizen behavior constitutes activities which have the effect of maintaining a stable political system and of providing a context in which governing elites may plan and implement policy decisions. We experience direct manifestations of political support almost on a daily basis. Driving to work, one sees an American flag decal pasted on a car window or a bumper sticker proclaiming "America the Beautiful, Don't Litter." Most public events start with the national anthem and a flag ceremony; our children say the pledge each morning before class. Decals, bumper stickers, flags, songs, and pledges are not the same as support; these activities are but material representations, often used in conjunction with certain rituals, which symbolize an underlying conformity in attitudes and feelings regarding political institutions. The rituals and their accompanying symbols merely serve to teach and to reinforce these political attitudes.

Since the study of support is relatively new, social scientists do not know the precise importance of various kinds of supportive behavior. In theory, supportive behavior is the political "glue" that holds complex, heterogeneous societies together; it permits them to achieve some sort of collective political action. In small homogeneous societies, such as tribal orders, kinship, a common culture, and similar social ties provide cohesion. In complex, heterogeneous industrial societies, the situation is quite different. Besides the difference in scale, there is specialization of work and play and the lessening of social and cultural bonds that provide a common identity. What does the Chicano living in the Rio Grande Valley share with the urban black living in Chicago, the Swedish farmer in South Dakota, and the Irish Catholic factory worker in Boston? In spite of the many differences in race, language, culture, and social status, these people have one strong bond: they are all American. They would not find it unusual to work for the same presidential candidate, join the armed forces, or pay taxes to the same government. The common political identity is one consequence of supportive behavior—that is, they have common loyalties to certain politically relevant institutions. Such behavior does not deny the real and fundamental differences among these citizens in social and cultural matters; it only means that these Americans have a common political basis from which to work.

A second form of politically important citizen behavior is evaluative. Evaluative behavior can be subdivided into two major opinion processes: the formation of opinion and the development of some political judgments. The first process—opinion formation—involves the study of saliency, whether citizens are aware of the political activities of elites and the dominant issues of the day. It also involves the formation of politically oriented desires, goals, or wants that may or may not receive any recognition from some governing elite. The second process—the formation of judgments about policy—pertains to how and why people form evaluations. The study of these opinion processes also focuses on how and why people change their evaluations of political events. For example, one can examine whether citizens find the national debate about foreign aid a salient issue (awareness). If so, what opinions, favorable or unfavorable, do they have on the subject (judgment)? Finally, are these opinions likely to change, and if so, why (stability versus change)?

The social scientist uses the term "behavior" differently from common usage. In normal speech, "behavior" usually refers to overt actions, such as running, throwing, or talking. Political actions are behavior in the layman's sense of the term—namely, overt actions such as voting, talking politics, and contacting public officials. In the scientist's use of the term, however, "behavior" also includes attitudes or opinions. No one has ever seen or heard an "attitude," but he has observed certain representations of attitudes. Thus, one infers that a person is angry if he is red in the face (involuntary behavior) or yells obscenities (voluntary behavior). These acts are manifestations of attitudinal conditions known by the scientist as behavior. But a scientist might consider the attitudinal behavior to exist even if the person sat absolutely still. How might the scientist infer that such attitudes existed? If he did not observe overt acts (yelling, a red face), he might measure a suitable bodily condition, such as heart beat or blood pressure. Clearly, heart beat and blood pressure are not anger, but symptoms of anger. The scientist might also ask, "Are you angry?" or "Do you feel mad?" and depending on the response, conclude that the subject was or was not angry.

The distinction raised here concerns the differences between supportive and evaluative behavior on one hand and overt behavior on the other. The first two behaviors are thought important enough for the operation of the political system and for the health and well-being of a citizen to measure their existence by inference. Thus, the scientist often must ask a question—say, in a research study—to ascertain the attitudinal condition of the citizen.

In the case of political action, a third type of citizen participation, one studies actions easily observed and recorded. They are of interest because of their consequences both for the political system and for the people who engage in them. These overt actions include such election centered behavior as voting and campaigning. Actions such as talking politics with others and writing letters to elites are also thought to be important. Having interpersonal contact with public officials represents another activity occurring between elections, when voting and campaigning are irrelevant. In contrast, supportive and evaluative behaviors are of most concern because of their more direct consequences for the individual, although such behavior produces latent consequences for the political system.

To summarize, support, evaluation, and political action are all forms of behavior known as political participation. These forms of citizen behavior are thought important in shaping politics both between and during elections. The fact that some forms of participation are only indirectly observed or difficult to measure does not make such behavior any less relevant for study and interpretation. The problem then is to examine what behavior does occur and for what reasons. Finally, it will be important to speculate about the observed and supposed consequences of mass political participation.

The Importance of Citizen Participation in Classical Theory

In a democracy the role that citizens play in relationship to public authority takes on special significance. There are several reasons why citizen involvement is believed to be important for the functioning of a healthy society. One of the dominant themes of the literature on political participation stresses the need to maintain and increase control over the actions of elite decision makers.

Various forms of political participation contribute to the masses' control over elite actions. For some theorists elections are the critical institutionalized activity for extending popular control to elites (see Pomper, 1968; also see Luttbeg, 1974). Although there is some disagreement about the precise way in which this electoral model serves as a mechanism for controlling elites, the selection and recall powers of the vote are seen as restraints on elite power. Others see elections as providing "mandates" or directives for more specific courses of action on broad policy questions. No theorist believes that elections exercise a continuing, day-to-day directive; rather, the influence is general and episodic, coming only during campaign periods.

Because most writers recognize that the electoral mechanism cannot provide continuous input of public needs and wants, other structures that provide control have received some attention. One is the organized political party at the grass-roots level. The party organization is largest and most organized during electoral periods, but it tends to atrophy afterward. The lines of communication once alive with activity break down, and party regulars cease to interact. For this reason, the political party is thought to be a suitable mechanism for control through political participation in electoral periods, but it fails to serve as a *continuing* structure for communicating public wants and needs to elites and informing citizens of elite activity. To the extent that it does, it provides communications from an unrepresentative and atypical public.

Another formalized structure thought to provide opportunities for political participation, and thus communication and supervision of elites, is the organized interest or pressure group. These are organizations of people based on common interests—often a single one—devoted to communicating their desires to public authorities, to attempting to influence favorable legislation or bureaucratic action, and to reporting on activity of public officials pertinent to their interests. Not all citizen interests are represented by interest groups, and those interests that are organized do not have equal influence. Two of the most well-organized and successful interests are farmers and veterans. Most scholars believe that these two groups, because of superior organization, are exceptionally successful in promoting their position on Capitol Hill and securing favorable legislation. Other interests, such as the poor and elderly, have not been as successful in influencing elite decision making. The two major criticisms of interest group representation are (1) not all citizens are represented, and (2) there is great disparity among represented interests in terms of the power to influence decisions and to command the resources of government.

The first problem arises from the fact that some people, by virtue of their lifestyle and resources, are difficult to organize. Migrant farm labor is a well-known agricultural interest that has defied past attempts to organize into a political interest group. The high mobility, poor education, and low income of these workers are contributing causes to this situation. In contrast, the Farm Bureau and National Farmers Organization are highly organized pressure groups representing farm owners.

The problem of resources greatly affects influence. Clearly, the milk industry, oil industry, and Teamsters Union are examples of organized, well-financed groups. Organizations such as AIM—the American Indian Movement—and civil rights groups have sought to make up with publicity and moral persuasion what they lack in financial resources. At best, the record of pressure group representation is uneven. Some interests have used this device with success, but the interests of most Americans remain effectively unrepresented by them.

Another form of citizen participation, which has received increased attention, is administrative representation. An important source of citizen information about government comes from interaction with government on a daily basis. A person who is stopped for a traffic violation and goes before the local court for a hearing obtains information, admittedly involuntarily, about this aspect of government. He also may express his feelings about the fairness or suitability of the government's actions, which serves as low-level input about what citizens like and dislike. A parent may call the principal of his child's school about the English textbook and not only learn about school board policy but communicate his opinion on the matter.

Most people would consider such interactions routine, of little significance, but from the standpoint of political participation, interactions arising from the normal service functions of public officials provide a means of communication for public wants and needs and for evaluations of existing policies. These interactions also give the agency an opportunity to provide information about the reasons for public policies and the objectives of the program.

Administrative representation is important because it gives a more continual reading of public conditions. Because much of it is based on agency initiation rather than private action, the public agency also has the opportunity to contact many who would not act voluntarily. There are limitations though with this form of contact. Public agencies often operate in narrowly defined functional areas. Much information collected through contacts with individual citizens, which is not relevant to the agency's functions, is probably lost. A parent who complains to the school principal about traffic speeding through the school zone may not receive much satisfaction, unless the principal takes the initiative to call the city police.

The various models for communication of public demands and supervision of elite behavior all fail to provide a comprehensive view of the wide range of citizen participation. The electoral, party, interest group, and administrative representation models each deal with a selective aspect of mass participation. At some given point in the political process and for some selected group, the models may provide a partial explanation of how participation acts as a brake on elite misconduct or serves to direct elite decision making to some public needs. From the standpoint of a more comprehensive model of citizen participation, which realistically captures the range of citizen activity, these four explanations must be subsumed under a more comprehensive view of the citizen's participatory roles. That model is called the "attentive publics."

Attentive Publics: A Model for Citizen Participation

Several writers have used the notion of attentive publics in recent years. Almond (1950) used the idea in the context of a study of public opinion and foreign policy. More recently, Devine (1970) and Rosenau (1974) have treated the concept in some detail, and many others have contributed to the meaning of the phrase (cf. Devine, 1970; Rosenau, 1974). Because many people have called similar phenomena by different names or identified different phenomena by similar labels, it is necessary to clarify the use of the term here.

A principal idea inherent in the concept attentive publics is that of differential participation. There is a utopian view of political participation called "democratic egalitarianism" (Devine, 1970) that views all citizens as having equal participatory behavior. Most empirical studies, however, have demonstrated the selective and limited characteristics of mass involvement. The average citizen is necessarily selective about what political events to follow. Competing non-political information and conflicting demands of work and leisure reduce the importance of politics for the average person. Thus, a more realistic approach requires some recognition of this selective or differential participation.

It is established that supportive and evaluative attitudes and certain political actions are significant forms of participation, but what is the object of this participation? Toward what is it focused? Attentive publics direct their political participation toward the behavior of institutions and the actors who hold positions in those institutions. Institutionalized politics means the behavior of elites, which has a systematic and continuing pattern of activity and relationships. For example, most Americans understand the concept of the presidency. It is an idea presented in the constitution and defined by the behavior of many actors across time. The presidency is not simply Gerald Ford, Richard Nixon, or Lyndon Johnson, but these men and their predecessors, by their words and deeds, contributed to the definition of the presidency. The presidency is also the Cabinet, staff, and activity associated with the office. Particular actors come and go, but the presidency continues.

There are many public institutions in the United States—Congress, the Supreme Court, the governor, judges, to name a few—and corresponding to each of these institutions is an attentive public. Because there are many institutions, there are many publics. Members of these publics may engage in supportive, evaluative, or action-oriented behavior—that is, various forms of mass participation. The major portion of the chapters that follow explore this political behavior in the context of four dominant political institutions: the presidency, state governors, the Senate, and the United States Supreme Court.

Since there is more than one dominant institution, it follows that more than one public exists—hence, the idea of many publics. Citizens may have no memberships, which would imply little or no institutionalized political participation, or they may have one or many. Their participatory style approximates the notion of rational-activist citizen raised earlier. One should distinguish an important difference in the notion of attentive publics, however; the citizen engaging in participatory behavior directed at one or two institutions is involved politically, though his involvement is selective. Because few citizens are totally involved across the broad range of institutional activity, there is no justification for concluding that they fail the expectations of a participatory model. Rather, the issue centers on the questions of the how many memberships a citizen has and the nature of his participation.

Participation in institutional politics varies with time and circumstances. A person securely employed probably will not find the economy much of an issue. Let recession threaten his job security, however, and suddenly the president's proposals for full employment take on new meanings. I shall explore who finds the president a salient political elite. Also, I shall examine what is salient and consider some of the causes for this behavior. In sum, I shall look at institutionally directed publics.

Membership in a public is not a matter of joining, paying dues, or registering.

In other words, the idea of publics is a construct of the scientist to help understand the complex world of mass political behavior. For example, a city planner might use the concept of a "communications artery" to refer to the main corridors for the movement of people and goods. Thus, highways, railroads, rivers, and canals, are representations of the phenomenon he is interested in. The key test is whether the idea helps simplify and illuminate the problem under study. Hopefully, the idea of attentive publics will serve this function for understanding mass political participation.

Two Explanations of Participatory Behavior

Although I have established the idea of possible membership in several publics I have done little to elaborate on the possible patterns of participatory acts that members of each public might engage in. There are two major explanations of how people organize and mix their participatory acts. These two explanations are known as the hierarchical and the multi-system approaches.

The Hierarchical Approach

Early empirical studies of political participation produced a hierarchical theory of political participation. In a study of how and why people become involved in politics Lester Milbrath (1965) postulated a hierarchical ordering of participatory activities. Milbrath introduced a colorful metaphor, based on the Roman arena, to characterize different modes of participation. He called the four levels of political activity "gladiatorial," "transitional," "spectator," and "apathetic." Gladiators were at the center of the political arena—the most active and the focus of attention. People in transitional activities were less active but could become gladiators. Spectators were passive participants minimally involved in politics, and apathetics were uninvolved citizens having few political interests.

The primary emphasis of the Milbrath work was on participatory actions associated with election campaigning and voting. Milbrath classified such political activity as the holding of public office, candidacy for public office, and attendance at party caucases and conventions as gladiatorial activities. Transitional activities included attending political rallies and contacting public officials. Spectator participation would be characterized by discussing politics with others, wearing a campaign button, voting, and seeking out political information in the media. Apathetics were citizens without any of these activities. Thus, Milbrath's work is focused primarily on overt participatory behavior during elections.

The difference between gladiators and apathetics was one of degree. Gladiators were involved in political activity that was more public and conflict-ridden. These actions also required considerable initiative on the citizens' part. As one moved down the hierarchy, the activities became more private, consensual, and passive. Voting, a minimal form of political activity in the Milbrath hierarchy, was a relatively private act requiring little initiative and producing few consequences affecting the individual specifically. Making a campaign speech, in contrast, was a highly public event producing direct consequences, both good and bad, for the individual involved. It required considerable initiative and persistence. One implication of the Milbrath theory of participation was that people rarely moved from a lower to a higher level of participation without moving through intermediate steps. Thus spectators rarely became gladiators without first engaging in transitional behavior.

Several major studies of political participation have used the Milbrath scheme. Matthews and Prothro (1966) studying black political participation in the South found a hierarchy of campaign-related activities, but in several critical respects the order (hierarchy) of black political participation was different from that of white citizens. Voting, for example, was less common than expected, even though discriminatory legal constraints on black registration had been removed. Matthews and Prothro attributed these depressed rates of voter turnout and different patterns of political involvement among Southern blacks to a combination of economic conditions and social relations predominating in the South. In related studies of voter registration, the pattern of race relations, economic conditions, and educational levels, as well as legal constraints, were demonstrated to have important effects on voter registration and electoral turn out for whites as well as blacks (cf. Matthews and Prothro, 1963a, 1963b; Kelley et al., 1967). In sum, the notion of hierarchy was retained; only the sequence was changed. Different groups had different sequences, and most people did not move "up" or "down" the participation hierarchy except by following the appropriate sequence.

The Multi-system Approach

In another major study of political participation Verba and Nie (1972) introduced a multi-system approach to political participation. They expanded the range of participatory activities to include much more than voting and campaign activity, which was the primary emphasis of the research summarized by Milbrath. Verba and Nie also examined contact behavior and memberships in political and quasi-political groups. Contact behavior represented the interaction of citizen with government. Thus, they expanded Milbrath's work to include nonelectoral behavior.

Verba and Nie came to the conclusion that there are not so many hierarchical patterns of political participation as there are multiple patterns. They identified six types of participatory styles (Verba and Nie, 1972):

	Population
Inactives	22%
Voting specialists	21
Parochial participants	4
Communalists	20
Campaigners	15
Complete activists	11
	93%
Unclassified	7
	100%

The inactives were similar to Milbrath's apathetics, people taking virtually no part in political life. Voting specialists did not participate in campaign activities, contact officials, or work at community activities. Their participation was confined to voting in major elections. In Milbrath's terms, voting specialists would be called low-level spectators. Campaigners were also involved in campaign type activity as well as voting. They came closest to approximating Milbrath's transitional participant. Complete activists and Milbrath's gladiators also were similar.

Two of Verba and Nie's participatory systems—parochial participants and communalists—have little precedent in Milbrath's work. Parochial participants have few political involvements other than contacting public officials and agencies. This activity requires considerable initiative, which in Milbrath's scheme would be a higher form of participation, but parochial participants do not engage in the lesser activities—voting and campaigning. Communalists are people who vote but avoid partisan campaigning yet are actively involved in community affairs. This type also is mixed in terms of the initiative required and, therefore, does not readily fit into Milbrath's hierarchy.

The main difference between Milbrath's four types and Verba and Nie's six systems is the lack of hierarchy implied by the latter. Verba and Nie do not intend any order to their six categories and do not suggest that citizens move through intermediate systems when moving from one system to another. As Verba and Nie observe:

> Our analysis of the nature of participation suggests that there are not merely gladiators, spectators, and apathetics (to use Milbrath's metaphor). Rather, activists differ among themselves in how they engage in political life.

Some people have campaign interests; others, community-oriented values. One group is not less active than the other; it is just active in a different way.

The Verba and Nie multi-system approach provides a means for clarifying how attentive publics behave. In the context of institutional behavior, a citizen may be totally involved with the affairs of the president concerning civil rights and be completely unaware of the Supreme Court's decision on school integration. Thus, he would be an activist in one context and an inactive in another. A realistic approach requires one to conceive of participation as varying in style by the context in which the participation occurs. Institutional contexts vary for two reasons. First, they have different functions and responsibilities and thus provide different content to their actions. Legislatures, for example, have bill-making responsibilities; courts are concerned with conflict resolution (adjudication). Second, institutional elites have some ability to change the context of their behavior. Thus, different institutions present varying circumstances that affect the patterns of mass participation. Even if the institutional context should be the same across institutions, there are still enormous differences between citizens.

In sum, one must consider the political or institution context and also the social and political characteristics of the citizen to adequately understand participatory behavior. The actors are citizens as members of attentive publics. These individuals, as members of various publics, engage in selected patterns of participation directed toward and in response to institutional elites. They hold supportive beliefs and evaluative attitudes; and they engage in politically relevant actions. The overall consequences result in the articulation and focusing of mass wants and needs, supervision of elite behavior, and responses to elite decision-making initiatives.

An Overview of Things to Come

The chapters that follow have been designed to briefly provide a summary of the scientific knowledge about how the average citizen is involved in public affairs. Because the evidence is derived from a set of procedures called "science," chapters 2 and 3 give some background for appreciating the difficulties in studying political behavior and for evaluating conclusions based on these procedures. In chapter 2, the theory and language of opinion science is defined and explained. I shall look at the meaning of such words as "opinion" and "attitude," as a scientist uses them, and at a general overview of a model for political behavior. Chapter 3 tells how opinions are studied and illustrates both the strengths and weaknesses of opinion methodology. It will be shown that all polls are not "created equal" and that some polls are "more equal than others."

Part II begins the first of five substantive chapters designed to summarize the state of the art regarding knowledge about mass political involvement. Specifically, chapter 4 examines diffuse support for political institutions—the so-called "glue" that facilitates political organization, compromise, and consensus among heterogeneous American publics.

Chapters 5, 6, and 7 explore the day-to-day reactions of Americans to their key political institutions. In these chapters, I shall explore what attentive publics perceive about the major political actors, how they evaluate their actions, and finally some causes and consequences of those evaluations. These chapters tell why citizens are enraged, euphoric, or indifferent to politics by revealing some of the content about what Americans think important. Chapter 5 compares some of the more visible political actors—the president and the state governors. From the executive branches of government, I move to an exploration of public attitudes toward officials in the judicial process. Chapter 6 provides an overview of what Americans think about the United States Supreme Court and ongoing legal controversies of the decade. The legislative process is examined from the attentive public's viewpoint in chapter 7.

Chapters 4 through 7 provide information about relative passive forms of participation—how people feel, think, and react to politics. Chapter 8 explores the modes of political activity most commonly engaged in by Americans and some consequences of this behavior for the individual citizen.

Finally, chapter 9 presents a brief summing up. What has the scientist to contribute to an understanding of how people behave politically? What do these conclusions suggest for the application of classical political values to today's circumstances?

Chapter Two

The Study of Political Opinions

In chapter 1, we learned of the range of conclusions and the degree of disagreement among scientists regarding man's capacity for political involvement. The basic human phenomena measured by these scientists have been the opinions of citizens about key components of the electoral process (parties, candidates, issues) and selected political actions reported by them (whether they voted and whom they voted for). Although scientists have reasonable success in communicating to each other what they are referring to when they speak of attitudes and opinions, conversations among laymen often become arguments arising from definition of terms. Usually, discussions between scientists and laymen are hopelessly confused. How can we agree that Americans are becoming more conservative in attitude unless we define what a conservative attitude is? To illustrate the potential problems of communication, here are a few of the terms and distinctions commonly made by opinion scientists: cognitive versus evaluative; subjective versus objective; and political versus public. To avoid unnecessary confusion in later chapters, I will define terms such as these.

A second problem that laymen interested in public opinion and behavior often encounter, even after they have learned the special language of opinion analysts, is why some attributes are used to explain behavior and others are not. Take the simple act of voting—why do people decide to take the time to vote? Consider all the reasons that facilitate or hinder the act of voting—interest in politics, concern for the issues, liking a candidate, free transportation to the polls, bad weather, and illness. All of these and many others are potential reasons for voting or not voting; yet a scientist tends to focus on only selected attributes. It is an exceedingly rare voting study that concentrates on the role of weather as a cause of voting, but one can find hundreds of studies on the role of social characteristics. The reason is simple—the scientist's informed guess was that social characteristics were more important than the state of the weather in the respondent's neighborhood, and empirical results confirmed this guess. How does the scientist decide which attributes are most important and which are relatively unimportant? Since no scientist has the resources to study every potential cause, he must necessarily be selective. One guideline for selecting potentially important explanatory variables is the theoretical perspective he holds. A theoretical perspective is nothing more than an informed guess about what is important for explaining behavior. Theories are judged by their internal consistency and comprehensiveness in explaining phenomena. Applied theories already have some evidence to confirm the predictions derived from the theory. Social science has few complete theories, but one general theoretical framework described below has shaped the choice of phenomena that opinion scientists have selected for study.

What Are Opinions?

The term "opinion" is used rather loosely in everyday speech.[1] One often hears of the opinion of the American people concerning the likelihood that a candidate will win an election. We are told about public opinion regarding the acceptance or rejection of some recent governmental decision. Newspapers speak of the opinion of Congressman X and of the Congress regarding a foreign aid bill. Each of the above examples uses the term "opinion" in a somewhat different way.

In scientific language, the term "opinion" is a general one referring to the mental predispositions or states of individuals toward some referent. A referent is simply the object to which the predisposition is directed. Since the definition of "opinion" encompasses so much, it is easier to clarify the term by distinguishing two types of opinions: beliefs and attitudes. Beliefs are mental states held by individuals representing conditions of knowledge, learning, or cognition. Thus the statement "The United States Congress presently has a Republican majority" is an example of a political belief. Beliefs are by definition subjective conditions —that is, they are "facts" thought to be true or correct by the individual holding them. The existence of two individuals holding mutually contradictory beliefs is not inconsistent with the definition. Nor is the fact that one can demonstrate the other's belief to be false inconsistent with the definition. To take the example of the number of Republicans in Congress, it is relatively easy to demonstrate that there are more Democrats than Republicans in the Congress, but such information, though interesting, is not essential to the study of beliefs. It is the existence of beliefs as much as whether they are true or false that is important. For example, many Americans believe (incorrectly) that the United States Supreme Court is opposed to the Bible and religious practice. Newspapers broadcast the "banning of religion" in the schools and similar sorts of misinformation. Any examination of the decision of the Court, however, will show that the Court has never banned the Bible; in fact, it has steadfastly defended the right of citizens to practice their religion (but not with the support of state and federal governments). This illustration shows that even if beliefs are incorrect in an objective sense they nevertheless can be critical pieces of information for explaining political behavior.

Attitudes are distinguishable from beliefs because they represent mental predispositions that require judgment, affect, and evaluation. The existence of an attitude implies a feeling that the referent is good or bad, desirable or undesirable, or positive or negative. Attitudes, then, are evaluative as opposed to cognitive. Attitudes imply the holding of value judgments, which may or may not be based on beliefs. Studies of grade school children, for example, show that they form favorable attitudes toward the president but have no understanding of what the president is or does. They have formed an attitude, a positive judgment about the president, without supporting beliefs.

The measurement of attitudes requires that two questions be considered: Does the attitude exist? If so, what is its valence or direction? Terms such as "valence" and "direction" refer to the type of evaluation—favorable or unfavorable. Attitudes may or may not exist with respect to a given referent—say, the need for "foreign aid payments to underdeveloped countries"—depending on the salience of the referent to the individual. For many Americans, questions of foreign policy do not hold their attention. Thus foreign policy questions would not be salient. Issues involving the pocketbook—jobs, prices, taxes—are often highly salient problems, and most people have formed attitudes regarding these issues.

Given that an issue is salient, one must establish the direction of the attitude. This is accomplished by using a scale such as follows:

Meaning	*Scale Categories*
Most favorable	Strongly agree
	Agree
. . .	Depends (agree and disagree)
	Disagree
Least favorable	Strongly disagree

This type of attitude scale permits statements concerning the amount of an attitude—in other words, whether one is more or less favorably predisposed toward the referent. Thus, if the referent is "trust the president to do a good job," one could make an inference, according to the response category selected by the individual, about the amount of trust in the president held by the subject.

Some opinion analysts also distinguish the valence of an attitude from its centrality to an individual's personality needs. These researchers have found that respondents many times answer "strongly agree" or "strongly disagree" to an issue they have little concern for. This seeming contradiction in the concepts valence and centrality may be clarified by an example. Suppose that a respondent agrees strongly to the following statements:

> The government should take diplomatic steps to avoid atomic war.
> The government should make sure everyone who wants a job can get one.

If one also were to ask, "What day-to-day problems do you worry about most?" few respondents would ever mention the threat of atomic war, but many of them would mention jobs and the economy. This example shows that both attitudes have the same valence, but one referent (jobs) is more central than the other.

Should an international event such as the Cuban Missile Crisis of 1962 occur, then the centrality of the atomic war issue would most certainly change. Because the centrality of attitudes is extremely difficult to measure, the problem of centrality of an attitude will be discussed in this text in terms of its salience.[2]

Attitudes are distinguishable from beliefs with respect to the question of their truth-value. Although subjective beliefs are potentially amenable to verification by reference to the objective world, attitudes are not. There is no answer to the question, "Is a respondent correct for disliking the president?" because one is dealing with an attitude, not a belief. One might probe the respondent's beliefs about the president and appeal to them by presenting certain facts to change the respondent's perceptions. But one is now dealing with the problem of persuasion or attitude change, the relationship of attitudes to each other, and the association of beliefs with attitudes. The belief, "The president supports the Equal Rights Amendment," is subject to verification, provided that terms such as "supports" are defined adequately and the kind of evidence needed to prove or disprove the statement is agreed to. The purpose of the subsequent chapters is to show what beliefs and attitudes Americans have and why they hold them. It is not the purpose of this text to show that some beliefs and attitudes are better than others.

People hold opinions directed toward a wide range of phenomena: the relative merits of Fords and Chevrolets, of long and short hair, of Democrats and Republicans. Certainly not all opinions are relevant to the study of politics. The focus of this text is on those opinions that pertain to political referents. They are called political opinions. For example, Americans have strong feelings about the importance of praying from the Bible. As such, these opinions are not considered political opinions because religious values are not generally considered to be political in nature. But the attitudes of citizens toward the importance of praying from the Bible in a public school classroom is very much a political opinion, because the opinion is now related to an important political referent: the First Amendment to the Constitution prohibits the establishment or support of religion or religious practice by the government. For well over fifteen years now, the United States Supreme Court, the United States Congress, local school boards, and state boards of regents—to mention just a few governmental agencies—have been involved in controversy over this question. In sum, the nature of the opinion referent is the basis for classifying opinions as either political or public. Although it is probably impossible to define precisely what "political referents" are in general, the scope of the referents used in this text can be specified: they include opinions toward public institutions, public figures holding elected or appointed office, and the policies (and decisions) attributed to these political actors.

Individual Opinions and the Political Process

Attitudes and beliefs are phenomena related to the behavior of individuals. Groups, societies, organizations, or any other collectivity do not have opinions

—only individual members within those aggregate groupings do. Thus, the Republican party does not have an opinion about Big Government, but many Republicans do. The party's opinion is nothing more than an average based on some of the individuals, who actually may not be typical of Republicans in general. Thus the party's platform committee at the national convention makes summary statements (called the party platform) which characterize the Republican position on selected issues. But who in fact does the platform represent? Certainly, most candidates either disavow specific platform provisions or reinterpret vague phrases to suit their own needs; and the average Republican would find much of the platform of little interest. In sum, aggregates do not hold opinions, and group statements purporting to represent the aggregate usually have little or no relationship to the attitudes and beliefs of the individuals composing the group. There are noteworthy exceptions, however. A single purpose interest group may have a specific limited statement of objectives. In this context, the opinion of the group may be synonymous with the opinions of individual members. The emphasis on the individual as opposed to the group nature of opinions make one fact clear: the phrase "political opinion" is a shorthand expression for talking about the net effects of individual opinions on the political process.

Elections are an important example of how individual opinions are institutionally related to collective decisions. One can view voting in an election as an organized process by which millions of individualized beliefs and attitudes are translated into legally binding collective choices regarding who shall govern. When one speaks of the "decision of the electorate," this phrase is only a figurative expression characterizing individual decisions. Elections are unique opinion events in the sense that the rules for determining how these millions of opinions will be transformed into only *one* decision are fixed and well specified. Thus electoral laws determine such matters as who shall vote, when and where; who can be a candidate; and how individual votes shall be used to decide the winner. This latter rule is quite complex for presidential contests. For state and local elections, the rules vary from state to state and from contest to contest.

Even though elections represent the most highly institutionalized method for transforming individual opinions into collective decisions, the outcome of elections is still ambiguous. In a narrow sense election outcomes are quite clear: candidate X was elected and the others were not; in the broader sense, candidate X will try to claim a mandate for certain policies and decisions. Even losing candidates may attach certain meanings to the collective outcome. Thus, Eugene McCarthy took his strong showing in the 1968 New Hampshire primary as evidence that the American people opposed the Vietnam War. Most poll results showed, however, that many supporters of the war voted for McCarthy for other reasons, and still others who voted for him were not aware of his antiwar position (Converse et al., 1969).

If one finds the outcome of elections ambiguous at the collective level, then consider the problems of relating public opinion to the political process in a nonelectoral situation. Contrast an electoral contest with a not-too-hypothetical situation: the United States Congress is considering legislation to implement a system of national health care through the federal government. A respected pollster systematically determines that an overwhelming majority of American citizens strongly desire such a service and are willing to pay the taxes for it. Even though the public support exists, such results do not mean that the Congress will pass a national health care bill.

There is another approach to the importance of citizen participation in public affairs that has little to do with how elites behave. This position is not so much concerned with the direct or indirect consequences of mass involvement on elite behavior as of such behavior on citizens themselves. From this viewpoint citizen participation in public matters is beneficial to the citizen himself and, therefore, to the society. A person who learns to control his own destiny and to act with a community interest is a better person. This theme—the fulfillment of the citizen—has received renewed emphasis with the revelation that modern complex societies are producing generations of citizens with a sense of powerlessness, apathy, disinterest, and alienation from self and community. Although most social theorists believe these conditions are morally objectionable, they also point to the social, economic, and political consequences of such behavior—reduced production, poor quality workmanship, increased crime, disinterest in governmental affairs, or in general, a pervasive callousness toward life, one's fellow man, and public responsibility. Since most ideas about responsible government are also based on the notion of a responsive citizenry, the quality of life in the society has ominous implications for "good" government. The quality of individual political life cannot be separated from the quality of governance.

The major forms of institutional participation—support, evaluation, and political action—are all components contributing to the development of citizen potential. Supportive behavior provides the common denominator for political involvement—a sense of belonging and worth. It is essentially a latent force setting limits on action and reaction.

Evaluative behavior is especially important because it represents one form of interface between citizens and governmental activity. The use of the term "interface" does not necessarily imply interpersonal contacts between citizens and officials. A broader notion of interface is congruence—whether there is some correspondence between what people know, feel, and desire and what governmental officials believe, perceive, say, and do. Thus, it is not necessary to show that a citizen talked to his congressman about cutting taxes, but it is fundamentally important to know what the citizen values and the forces that shape his judgments.

The study of congruence, then, is dependent on several prior steps. First, it requires knowledge of public opinion processes—the evaluative attitudes of citizens and their causes. Next, one needs to understand the behavioral context in which relevant elites—congressmen, city aldermen, judges, appointed officials—form judgments about policy and about what citizens think. Finally, the processes that aid and hinder congruence—sometimes called the linkage problem—must be examined. Within the scope of this text on public opinion, only the first step will be considered. In part, this is a practical division to make the material manageable. In another sense, it is a response to the study of public opinion that concentrates on the last two questions without any working knowledge of the first.

It is important to understand what citizens feel and want regardless of what elites do. To focus only on the problem of congruence often means that one asks, "How does citizen opinion agree with elite opinion?" By implication only the set of citizen opinions held by elites is relevant for study. Stating the question in this form is, in my opinion, backwards. The more appropriate question is, "How accurately, if at all, do elites perceive mass opinion?" This question now shifts the burden to the study of citizen behavior. We must know something about public opinions before we can consider the problem of congruence. There is an implicit value question in this approach. It ultimately requires that the reader decide for himself what are "good" opinions and what consequences are "good." There is more to be said about this in later chapters, but at this point, the reader should ask himself, "What kind of political participation do I want in my society? What kind of citizen involvement do I desire?"

A Macro-view of Political Opinion and Process

Once every four years the country engages in a national election which mobilizes mass opinions and heightens the level of political awareness. For the remaining three and one-half years, mass political activity is essentially dormant, with some stimulation coming from state and local elections in the interim period or from special public controversies. It is during this three and one-half year period that most of what is called politics goes on. Yet simple questions about what average citizens feel and think about ongoing political affairs are left unanswered, except possibly for the occasional Harris or Gallup polls on some current event.

To appreciate how political opinion plays a role in the political process during nonelectoral situations, one needs to define an overview of the process. This overview is called a macro-theoretical model. It is theoretical in the sense that it attempts to generalize across many diverse political situations. The price of this generality is its failure to precisely describe any particular political situation. It is called a macro-model because it deals with institutions and collectivities of people—opinion aggregates—rather than with specific, political decision makers and individual citizens. It is the difference in generality which arises from discussing the behavior of the "neighborhood" as opposed to a "neighbor." Regardless of individual consequences, one must also inquire about the collective or societal impact of public opinion.

Figure 2-1
A Macro-Model: Political Attitudes and Beliefs in the Political System

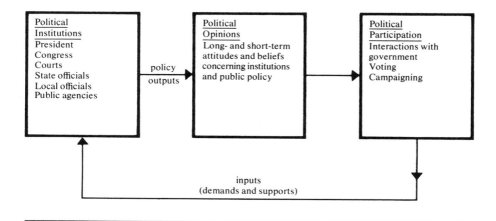

Figure 2–1 pictures the three basic components comprising the political process: political institutions, political opinions, and political participation. Citizens hold a complex array of political attitudes and beliefs. Some are relatively stable or long-term while others are more momentary or short-term. The interplay of these opinions comprises what is often referred to in popular usage as public opinion. These political opinions form the essential conditions for affecting the average citizen's interaction with political institutions. This interaction is called political participation. The most widely understood forms of participation occur during elections, when people form judgments, acquire information, campaign, give money, attend rallies, watch political news on television, talk politics with family and acquaintances, and vote.

Since elections are episodic, the more sustained channels of participation center on organized and individual interactions with governmental representatives. At the organized level, interest groups and, to a lesser extent, political parties provide vehicles for interaction with governments. Pressure groups and parties, though an important aid to participation, provide access for relatively few citizens—usually the well-educated, white, and economically secure.

Individual participation is probably the most frequent and broadly based. It takes place as citizens interact with government on a routine basis. Parents attending school meetings, having conferences with teachers, or calling the principal; citizens called for jury duty, arrested for speeding, or filing a legal paper at the courthouse are participating. Using the city park, calling the local alderman, and writing one's congressman also are political participation. These interactions have one thing in common: they provide a means for communicating citizens' wants and needs to public officials—elected and appointed. If there are problems in the schools, teachers and principals probably hear about it first and become vehicles for aggregating and communicating to other officials in the school hierarchy—school board officials, state and federal officers, state representatives and congressmen. Voluntary and involuntary consumption of legal services will shape how the police, courts, and correction agencies do their job. Flagrant disregard for speed limits on a residential street may cause stricter enforcement. The willingness and availability of jurors shape the outcome of court trials. Even increased use of the city park may foster discussion about improved recreational services.

These examples illustrate that so-called normal behavior has political consequences because it shapes the kinds of inputs experienced by institutionalized decision makers. Evaluative behavior forms the basis for communicating public needs and wants to decision makers. Overt action often coincides with evaluative behavior and therefore provides important cues about public aspirations. The decision maker may play an active or passive role in determining these aspirations. He may solicit opinions in a systematic or unsystematic way, or he may receive communications and other information involuntarily. Much of overt political action is a blend of passive and active communication. Sometimes the citizen is the initiator; sometimes he is a respondent.

Supportive behavior is important also in the ongoing macro-process. It provides a basis for compliance with elite actions, acceptance of controversial decisions, and the development of consensus. If the federal income tax did not have support from most Americans, the costs and difficulties in collecting it would become so great that one of two things would happen: either restrictive laws and practices would be administered (at great expense) to collect the tax or an alternate method of collecting public revenues would be found.

Complex political processes within and among political institutions determine the policy-decisions of government. It is one purpose of college courses on the president, the Congress, the courts, or state and local government to describe and explain how these institutions make decisions. The decisions take the form of policy outputs and outcomes that eventually have consequences for political opinions. A 1954 Supreme Court decision (*Brown* v. *The Board of Education of Topeka, Kansas*) has had profound effects on primary and secondary education: forced integration, busing, the equalization of educational opportunity, different textbooks, altered teacher assignments. President Nixon's decision to sell millions of bushels of wheat to the Soviet Union has created profits for some businesses, increased the production of wheat, and raised the price of meat. Although the effects of specific decisions may be either wide-ranging or limited, they form the means by which political opinion often is shaped and new participation occurs. These effects may cause changes in opinion states—the predisposition of citizens toward governmental policy—and they may also serve to stimulate a different kind of political participation—thus affecting public support, evaluation, and action. The key concept is process—actions today affect reactions tomorrow and actions the day after that.

The Continuity of Political Opinion and the Macro-process

Conceiving of the role of time is an important part of appreciating the political process. Events around which attitudes are focused are limited to specific situations and occur at certain times. In one sense, these acts of circumstance are distinct from events preceding and following. For example, in election campaigns the opposing candidate pairs are obviously specific to particular elections: Truman versus Dewey; Johnson versus Goldwater; McGovern versus Nixon. Each candidate brought to the election contest a unique set of factors (candidate image) that influenced the vote. Similarly, issues have their own special effect on voting. The 1952 election presented Korea and 1968 presented Vietnam as issues, but each war had its special impact on the vote. The 1952 election did not have a law and order issue as the 1968 election did, but corruption in government was a consideration in 1952. Thus the combination of candidates and issue events can create special effects that influence opinion.

In another sense, attitudes and beliefs represent continuing forces, called long-term forces, that have transcended the specific short-term circumstances causing them. The Great Depression, for example, caused a realignment of political groupings that even today has relevance for voting. The Cold War of the 1950s still affects how many Americans now feel about the Communists, although Joseph McCarthy is almost forgotten.

The Watergate affair represents a contemporary example of the mixture of short- and long-term themes in American political opinion. It is a short-term set of events where particular personalities are concerned—by removing the principal actors from the scene, much of the intensity of opinion dissipated. Americans have had scandal in their governments before; Truman, Eisenhower, Johnson, among the postwar presidents, had to face charges of corruption, fraud and/or irregularities high in their administrations. But who remembers Alger Hiss, Sherman Adams, and Bobby Baker today? Who will remember Mitchell, Ehrlichman, and Haldeman tomorrow?

Such an argument does not suggest that Watergate has no long-term effects. It no doubt will affect the distribution of Republican and Democratic office holders at the state and national levels for some time to come. Although these effects are important, there are also more subtle nuances to a Watergate that probably cannot be answered in the short run. How will Americans feel about their public leadership in the future? When a president needs to rally national support at some critical time, will the residue of cynicism reduce his ability to lead? How many people will give up hope where public life is concerned?

To begin to assess the impact of day-to-day events as well as dramatic ones such as Watergate on political opinion, one needs a perspective on the continuity of mass opinions. Long-term, more so than short-term, attitudes and beliefs shape the course of political opinion. Short-term opinions only serve to redirect politics momentarily and may leave a residue that becomes part of the broader trends of opinion.

A Micro-view of Political Opinion

Understanding the interplay of long- and short-term opinions and their effects on the political process focuses attention on another level of political behavior: a micro-model of political opinion. This model, unlike the macro-model, concentrates on the forces affecting individual opinions. Both long- and short-term factors play an important role in shaping individual political opinions. The most stable of the long-term forces is the social and political environment in which politics occurs (Figure 2–2). Some scholars have labeled one

Figure 2-2
A Micro-Model: Factors Affecting Public Policy Opinions at the Individual Level

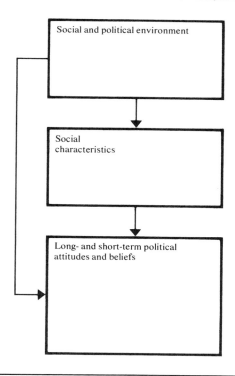

aspect of this environment "political culture." Donald Devine, for example, argues that Americans share a distinct political culture based on the political ideas of John Locke, an eighteenth century English theorist. These political values are best articulated in the United States Constitution and Bill of Rights. Public leaders and average citizens even today adhere to these values and share a common understanding of their importance (Devine, 1972).

Other long-term factors include the economic and demographic conditions that shape political needs and wants. The South in comparison to the North remains economically poor, just as it was in the nineteenth century. These economic conditions—reliance on agriculture, low wages, land ownership patterns—give rise to distinct patterns of politics. To be absolutely correct, one should distinguish the economic and social conditions that give rise to opinions from the opinions themselves. Since these conditions are essentially stable over an individual's lifetime, they do not cause short-term change. Rather, they serve to provide continuity from generation to generation by providing a constant set of conditions.

Whereas influences from the social and political environment are shaping forces removed from the individuals, social characteristics are conditions associated with the individual that affect political behavior. They vary from person to person and give rise to distinct opinions. Such factors as a person's social class, race, sex, and education play important roles in the formation and maintenance of political opinions. These conditions are stable in a relative sense: they are set at birth or early in life—usually by adulthood—and affect an individual's life chances for the remainder of his life.

There is some confusion, however, regarding the nature of the effects these variables have on attitudes and beliefs. When the social scientist refers to the role of sex in shaping political opinions, he does not literally mean the effects of biological distinctions between male and female. The emphasis, rather, is on the social implications of being male or female in this political culture. Males learn different values from those females learn. These differences in learning often have political ramifications. Females, for example, were much less supportive of the Vietnam War than males. One study has attributed these differences to the social roles (and associated values) each sex has (Verba et al., 1967). Women, on the average, have values more oriented toward preserving the house and supporting life than men do; men, in contrast, are more aggressive and competitive. Thus, social characteristics imply the learning of attitudes and beliefs, usually early in the life cycle, that affect political behavior throughout adulthood.

The third kind of long-term variables are psychological. Psychological factors are attitudes arising from individual personality needs and from associated experiences (Katz, 1960). Thus some men went to Vietnam and came back convinced that the war was justified, while others made the opposite conclusion. Such differences in attitude are undoubtedly based on differing personalities and the interaction of experience with these personality needs. People who fear a Communist conspiracy usually have had little experience to support such fears, but the fears are real to the person involved and shape at least some of his political choices. Understanding the psychological needs of individual respondents will not be the purpose of this book. Instead, the emphasis will be on the effects of such attitudes on other political behavior. It is important, nonetheless, to recognize that political attitudes and beliefs may be tied to nonpolitical causes.

Short-term political opinions are mostly based either on social characteristics or on psychological experiences. Some social characteristics are short-lived, and their impact strong though momentary. When a student goes away to college, he usually adapts his lifestyle to his new role: college student. It is a period when he is more free to experiment with his ideas and behavior than at almost any other time. Many students experience significant changes while on campus—changes ranging from superficial ones (dress and grooming) to more profound ones (attitudes and beliefs). Behavior that would never be attempted or tolerated at home becomes routine on a campus.

By assuming the role of student and living on campus, the individual has significantly altered his own expectations and especially his social environment. When a student leaves campus for vacation or because of graduation, things do not always seem the same. His parents remark that he has changed and friends who stayed behind are not always as interesting. Clearly, home has not changed as much as the student has. Graduation and the assumption of a new role (a job!) usually bring a new environment and new attitudes. Campus radicals become middle-class job holders. Suits or dresses replace jeans and sweatshirts. In sum, the assumption of responsibilities in a different social environment changes behavior. Students differ politically from nonstudents of the same age and social class, and college students differ politically from college graduates. For some political attitudes, such variations in social characteristics produce important variations in political behavior.

Finally, current events create political attitudes with short lives. The political hero of today is the forgotten person of tomorrow. For the most part, these attitudes are more akin to fads in popular taste. They are of interest only so far as they affect long-term attitudes. Otherwise, they are responses to current affairs having little relevance, other than as historical curiosities, to the ongoing process of political opinion. These attitudes are usually strongly influenced by long-term conditions rather than vice versa. For example, to fully appreciate why there was such an extreme outpouring of national grief over the assassination of John Kennedy, one needs to understand the depth of support most Americans have for the office of president (cf. Greenberg and Parker, 1965).

An Overall Model: Combining the Micro- and Macro-models

Figure 2–3 represents an overall theoretical view of individually based and system-oriented political opinion. The connecting lines show the main flow of events, both within and around the individual citizen. There are undoubtedly lesser connections between the components, but Figure 2–3 presents a simplified picture of the more important relationships.

Figure 2-3
An Overall Model Combining Individual Political Attitudes and Beliefs with the Macro-Political Process

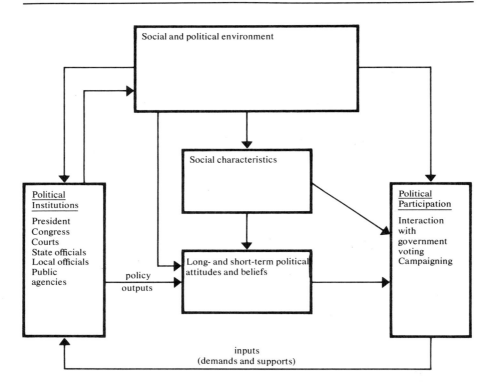

The overall model suggests that political participation is influenced primarily by three causes: the social and political environment, the social characteristics of the individual, and long- and short-term attitudes. A number of recent studies of voter registration in the South illustrates how the first two conditions affect one form of political participation—voter registration (Kelley et al., 1967; Matthews and Prothro, 1963a, 1963b). Environmental factors depressing the level of black registration in Southern counties include literacy tests, restricted registration times, residence requirements, racial violence in the community, and the lack of competitive political parties seeking black votes. Social characteristics such as age, sex, income, and education also have important effects on voter registration. Individual political attitudes including interest in politics and sense of citizen duty are a third major cause of voter registration. As *The American Voter* has shown, increased interest and a heightened sense of citizen duty increase registration and voting (Campbell et al., 1960).

Political participation in its many forms serves to influence political decision making by inputing demands and supports. The overall model shows that in addition to this input from mass political participation, the social and political environment can shape institutional decision making and in turn be affected by political institutions. To take the case of voter registration in the South again, the existence of a climate of racial violence and legal restraints on black voter registration probably caused the cautious application of civil rights laws in the 1960s. Yet the actions of the Supreme Court, several presidents, and the Congress have directly affected these conditions. Poll taxes, for example, have been made unconstitutional, and the national guard has been used to enforce court decisions in many communities. Certainly, such outputs have also affected long- and short-term attitudes, as will be demonstrated in subsequent chapters.

In conclusion, it is important to realize the interplay between forces around the individual citizen and forces within him on political opinions. These macro- and micro-processes may not always produce compatible consequences. In other words, the collective and individual consequences may not be equally desirable. Consider, for example, the "problem of the Commons." In the early days of Boston, a common green area (the Commons) was set aside for public use. Many citizens took advantage of this free land to graze sheep. Since it cost nothing, it was reasonable for each farmer to add more and more sheep. At the individual level, this policy made sense; collectively, it was a disaster. Ultimately, the Commons was grazed bare, and many sheep died for lack of grazing land.

The authors of *Voting* raised a "problem of the Commons" too. Since they concluded that the individual citizen failed the rational-activist "test," they had to confront the question, "What are the collective consequences?" Their answer was essentially as follows: At the individual level, the apathetic, uninvolved citizen is a disappointment to those who aspire for more citizen participation. One need not despair though, since collectively the political process worked well. The political system was stable and elites could govern. Given the known capacities of citizens to participate, it is probably better, in fact, that they do not participate any more than they do. Otherwise, elites would be overloaded with conflicting demands, confronted with an unmanageable electorate, and in general be unable to govern effectively (Berelson et al., 1954; Berelson, 1952; see also Pateman, 1970). Although the empirical evidence leading to these conclusions has now been modified, one can never avoid the potential problem of the Commons: what may be good for the individual may not always be good for the society, and vice versa. The implication drawn from the evidence presented in *Voting* is that one can safely ignore the shortcomings of the individual because the collective society works satisfactorily.

This argument is precisely the kind that classical democratic theorists find repugnant. In fact, we must ask: Do the conclusions of social science necessitate a reformulation of the ideals of classical democracy toward a model proposed by democratic elitists? The answer in part depends on a further examination of the scientific evidence presently available for evaluating the components of the micro (individual) behavioral model. From this examination, we shall be able to confront the dilemma of the Commons more directly. Must we accept the conclusion that citizens are apathetic and without requisite skills to be actively involved in politics? If so, the collective consequences of individual irresponsibility could threaten the very foundations of government.

Notes

[1] A useful summary of various meanings of the term "opinion" and related concepts is found in Hennessy (1970).

[2] The critical reader may note that the presence of an attitude may be taken as evidence of the centrality of an attitude. This approach appears defensible in the case of open-ended questions where no prompting of response is attempted. Closed questions often stimulate response. In general most opinion analysts have had little success measuring the centrality of an issue as distinguished from its salience; thus the latter has come to represent a shorthand for the former.

How to Study Political
Opinions: The Genealogy of a
Research Project

The results of empirically based research are often reported in today's introductory textbooks. Although the tendency to incorporate the latest research knowledge of the discipline into teaching materials has contributed to an upgrading of the educational process, many textbooks based on evidence obtained from empirical methods have failed to communicate to the reader the strengths and weaknesses of such information. As a consequence, the student must rely solely on faith and the author's judgments for an evaluation of the scientific conclusions.

It is surprising to many students to learn that science is a process that rarely produces absolutely certain and unqualified statements. Rather, the methods available for studying behavior are only inexact and expensive, and scientists when communicating with each other implicitly understand the limitations inherently contained in their conclusions and findings. This is not the case with laymen—nonscientists—however, who demand to know what is true and "the answer." Since the subsequent chapters are based largely on current and past studies of the political behavior of Americans, the student must have some appreciation of the ways and means of scientists to critically undertsand what is known about political participation. He needs some knowledge of the tools of science as applied in opinion research studies and, most of all, he must develop a critical attitude that avoids either of two extremes—one, that human behavior cannot be studied scientifically, and the other, that scientists, the new gods of knowledge, are always correct.

In this chapter, a brief introduction to one kind of empirical method regularly used in opinion research—sample surveys—will be presented. Sample surveys have provided the principal source of information about human political behavior, and the original data reported in the subsequent chapters are also from a national survey. By my discussing how this particular survey was conducted, the student may acquire some perspective on the range of decisions required to conduct even the simplest form of opinion research. Furthermore, he shall see some of the many problems that every competent researcher attempts to control in order to improve his answers to scientific questions. His success in controlling these problems will determine the correctness of those answers.

Posing a Question and Reviewing Past Research Findings

Every scientific research project begins with a problem or set of questions. This project—called the "Southeast Regional Survey Project" (SERS)—began in the summer of 1968 to conduct research on political attitudes and behavior of continuing significance.[1] Since "political attitudes and behavior" emcompasses too wide a range of phenomena to investigate in a single study, the first major objective was to narrow and refine the statement of the overall purpose of the study and to clarify the major questions of interest. It was agreed that an omnibus survey of political attitudes and behavior should be conducted that covered the following areas:

1. the measurement of what citizens knew or perceived about the activities of government.
2. the measurement of how citizens evaluated these activities.
3. the collection of information on how and why people used governmental goods and services.
4. the collection of data relevant for explaining these perceptions, evaluations, and behavior.

Since most of the existing research results pertaining to this focus were based on data collected during electoral campaigns, it was decided to conduct the survey during a period when no major election was being contested.

The initial project was to study citizen interactions with government at all levels—not just with the federal government. Because of the many different kinds of governmental authorities across the nation, it was judged necessary to select people from all sections of the United States rather than confine the research to one city, state, or region. In addition, a parallel study on the attitudes of officials in the governmental process would provide useful information about the context surrounding citizen interaction with public officials, and thus provide valuable data for answering the questions of interest.

One of the principal reasons for selecting a nonelectoral period and a national sample was to replicate past research. Replication is an important part of any scientific process. No single research effort can give exacting and final answers to scientific questions. Although some of the reasons for this situation will become clear later in this chapter, most scientists accept the necessity of qualifying their conclusions and repeating (replicating) their research in various contexts and conditions. If two scientists, working independently of each other, find approximately the same results, one is more certain that the results are correct than if conclusions are based only on one study. Ten studies, each showing similar conclusions, are rather compelling evidence that the scientific conclusion is sound.

Most scientific research is not overwhelmingly consistent. Five studies may show black people are alienated, but two of them may indicate blacks are no more alienated than whites. In this context, most scientific inquiry focuses on the conditions surrounding the research to identify factors that may influence the research conclusions. These influencing factors may include, among other things, how the research was done—its methodology—or unmeasured and un-controlled causes. For example, one might find that a person's sense of personal achievement shaped feelings of alienation and that the five studies showing a relationship between race and alienation involved people with a low sense of achievement. In contrast, the two studies showing no relationship involved people with a high sense of achievement. Scientists would call "sense of achieve-ment" a confounding cause or condition. Unfortunately, most scientific prob-lems do not simplify so readily. Rather, they present complex causal fabrics that must be separated thread by thread.

One means of sorting out and imposing some order on a complex problem is to identify the key conditions and variables of a problem and hypothesize how they work together to produce the behavior under study. This imposing of order on phenomena is called theory building. The explanation of how condi-tions and variables are connected is called a theory of behavior. Social science differs from physical science to the degree that its theories are much less de-veloped and complete than those of physics or chemistry. The social sciences are young members in the family of sciences—the oldest social science, psychol-ogy, being only 100 years old. The merging of scientific methods with the study of social and political phenomena is a relatively new occurrence.

Part of the process of replication in science is to examine what other scientists have done. By doing this, one not only learns of their explanations of the behavior but also of the methods used to arrive at the conclusions. Social scien-tists call the conditions and factors affecting the behavior "concepts." Some ex-amples of concepts are political party identification, educational achievement, and race. Concepts are complex ideas that are never directly observed. Take, for example, the concept political party identification. A political party is an ab-straction used to describe how groups of people interact to conduct political business—say, electing a candidate to office or communicating political wants to officials. One abstracts this behavior by summarizing one set of interactions as the Republicans and another as the Democrats. Of course, the Republican and Democratic parties are much more than a group of people electing can-didates. They are also policies, programs, philosophies, social organizations, and recreational bodies. Thus, a political party is an abstraction summarizing complex social andpoliti cal behavior. What, then, is "political party identifica-tion"? Political scientists define it as an evaluative attitude toward the complex phenomenon called party. The attitude implies a sense of belonging, association, and self-identity.

Concepts are not directly observable. Rather, one constructs measures to get at the complex political characteristic. In the case of party identification, the standard question used in many previous surveys is:

Regardless of how you vote, when it comes to national politics, do you usually think of yourself as a Republican, a Democrat, an Independent, or what?

The question represents an established means for classifying a person either as a Republican, Democrat, or Independent. It measures an attitude for which a scientist may see many manifestations—attendance at a party meeting, voting for the party's candidate, or verbal expressions of favorableness toward a party program.

The particular behavior one observes to decide whether a person is, in fact, a Republican, Democrat, or Independent is based on a restricted but precise criterion: how he responds to the survey question. The logic behind this method is for each person under study to have the same question read to him. This question-reading is sometimes called the stimulus, and one goal is to find a neutral wording that is uniformly administered to all subjects. For obvious reasons, one does not phrase the question, "What are you, a Democrat, or one of those crooked Republicans?" Questions used on surveys are designed not to be leading, and interviewers are trained to read the question and provide no encouragement or other aids if the respondent says, "I don't know; what do you think . . . ?" What the respondent says to the stimulus is called a response. The job of a trained interviewer is to record it "in the words of the respondent"— that is, verbatim. One does not use a smile resulting from a reference to President Ford to indicate Republican in one case and a verbal comment about those "damned Democrats" in another case. The decision to classify a person is based solely on the survey question response and not on ancillary evidence— smiles, shrugs, coughs, or other verbal comments.

Types of Questions Used in Surveys

Part of the process of scientific replication is to review the types of questions used to operationalize concepts. Party identification has been measured in different ways with somewhat different results. An important step of any research project is to examine the available literature on the general topics and begin a file of questions used in previous surveys to measure the attitudes and behavior of interest.

There are two broad kinds of attitude questions used in most surveys—open and closed. The closed-ended question asks a question or presents a statement to the respondent and has him select a category of responses that best describes his reaction. For example, each respondent was read the statement: "The government in this state capital wastes a lot of the money we pay in taxes." Then he was asked to either agree or disagree, depending on which answer most closely described how he felt.

The question on national party identification presented three categories— Republican, Democrat, and Independent. Since many respondents say Independent, a follow-up question is necessary to separate the party leaners from the true Independent. In the case of the party identification question, one follow-up question was: "Do you usually think of yourself as closer to the Republican or Democratic party?" Past surveys have shown that many respondents are not true Independents, and this follow-up question permits further classification. In addition, those respondents selecting Republican or Democrat were asked the follow-up question: "Would you call yourself a strong [Republican, Democrat] or a not very strong [Republican, Democrat]?" Thus, a series of structured closed-ended questions, such as those used to measure national party identification, permit the classification of respondents into one of the categories listed in Figure 3–1.[2] Previous research has adequately demonstrated that this series of questions efficiently classifies people according to their party preferences. The most compelling proof is the many forms of political behavior correctly accounted for by this single variable.

Figure 3-1
Flow of "Party Identification" Question Sequence

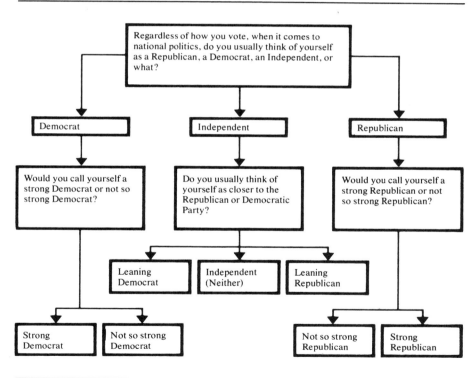

Most closed-ended questions either ask a question and present categories of response, as is the case with the party identification questions, or present statements eliciting agree and disagree responses. Sometimes the amount or degree of agreement valence is measured by providing more categories, such as agree strongly, agree, not sure, disagree, disagree strongly. These five categories not only classify the respondent with respect to the question asked but order him on an "agreement continuum":

Strong
Disagreement   ⟵———————⟶   Strong
Agreement

Some respondents do not immediately recognize the *order* implied by the five agreement categories and thus are more likely not to report their feelings accurately. There are several methods to reduce this error and give the respondent a better understanding of how the categories describe his feelings about the statements read. One method is the card sort technique. It was used in the Southeast Regional Survey to measure attitudes toward approximately ninety-seven statements.

The interviewer gave the respondent a sort board similar to that pictured in Figure 3–2. The interviewer explained that the seven boxes represented seven categories of agreement and disagreement and that those farther to the left and right represented "stronger" feelings than those closer to the middle. The middle box was described as the neutral box for people who had thought about the statement and had an equal amount of agreement and disagreement. The box above the other seven was defined as the "have no opinion" box for people who really did not have an opinion and therefore could not agree or disagree. The sort board then presented a number of visual cues to the respondent which helped him define the order and distance between the various categories of agreement.

Figure 3-2
Sort Board Used in the Southeast Regional Survey

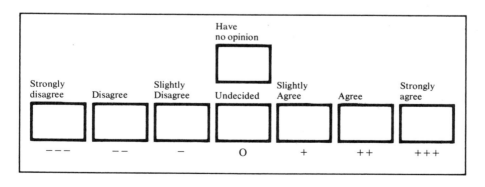

At two different points in the interview, the respondent was given a set of about fifty cards with single statements printed on each. For example, one card measuring the concept "diffuse support for the president" had the statement: "The president can be trusted to do what is good for people like me." Respondents read each card to themselves and placed it in the box best describing their first reactions to the statement. To insure that the subject understood the use of the sort board, two trial questions were introduced to explain its use before the respondent sorted the first deck of statement cards. The first trial statement was, "I like hamburgers." The interviewer had the respondent place the card in the box on the board that described how he felt about hamburgers. Then the reasons for the choice were discussed to insure that no misunderstanding occurred. The second trial statement, "President Nixon likes hamburgers," was placed on the board, and if the respondent did not pick "have no opinion," the interviewer asked whether the respondent actually knew about Nixon's preferences. Since one can assume most respondents did not, this card was used to illustrate the differences between "no opinion" and ambivalence ("not sure"). The interviewer explained that he did not know about Nixon's preferences and would have placed the card in the "have no opinion" box. After this initial instruction, the interviewer gave the respondent the first deck of forty-eight cards and sat quietly and unobtrusively while the subject sorted the deck. After the sort was completed, the interviewer recorded the question numbers in the appropriate place on the interview schedule.

This method of attitude measurement has several advantages and disadvantages. Since respondents often tire of listening to questions read to them, this card sort was treated rather enthusiastically by respondents. Although the card sort takes time to explain, it is a faster means of collecting data if a large number of items are sorted. Furthermore, respondents are less influenced by the interviewer, who when reading the same questions to a respondent can introduce variations in tone, emphasis, and pronunciation which influence the response. One commonly recognized problem with interviewer pronunciation occurred in the 1960s with the word "Negro." At that time many pollsters sought information about attitudes toward race relations, but the variations in the pronunciation of "Negro" ("Nigro," "Negra," "Nigra") often provided clues to the respondent about the feelings of the interviewer and, therefore, influenced the response. Ultimately, the phrases "colored people" and "black people" were used in many surveys in place of the term "Negro." The difference in language, pronunciation, and meaning among social classes and regions of the country contributes no small part to the error found in normal survey procedures.

Some of the disadvantages of the card sort included the cost of the materials and extra training required to administer it. Some interviewers found the board cumbersome and a nuisance and would have preferred the usual read-and-record-response approach. The card sorts greatly added to the complexity of the questionnaire and permitted interviewer error (in administration) on occasion.

Also, some respondents were nearly illiterate or had sufficiently bad eyesight so that reading the cards was difficult for them. In this situation, the interviewer read the card to the interviewee and placed it where he directed.

The other major type of question format is the open-ended question. This question does not structure the response but rather permits the subject to reply in his own words. Therein lies the advantage and disadvantage of the open-ended question. The respondent may not always stick to the question asked or he may make references that are insufficiently explained. Thus, much information obtained in this manner is either extraneous or incomplete. A well-trained interviewer will record the responses verbatim and give gentle probes such as, "How's that," which often cause the respondent to clarify and direct his comments to the question of interest. Without well-trained interviewers, the material from open-ended questions is often nearly useless, but with sufficient probing, the answers can provide a wealth of information. The problem partially avoided by open-ended questions is the solicitation of responses that are created only by the interviewer asking the question. These reponsenses pose the problem of "meaningless" attitudes. There is some evidence that respondents often try to answer questions, when they really have no opinion, in order to help the interviewer out and hide their ignorance. These types of responses are called "nonattitudes." The open-ended question is an expensive check on this problem.

Since a key part of the research design was to collect information about what respondents perceived about governmental activity and how they evaluated it, a number of open-ended questions were used in the interview schedule to study attitudes toward the president, the governor of the state, the Supreme Court, and a U.S. senator. An example of the questions used to measure dislikes and likes about the Supreme Court was:

> Now, thinking about the Supreme Court in Washington, is there anything the Supreme Court has done lately that you *don't* like? What is that? (Probe:) Is there anything else?

for unfavorable responses, and

> Is there anything the Supreme Court in Washington has done that you liked? What is that? (Probe:) Is there anything else?

for favorable responses.

In addition to the closed- and open-ended questions designed to measure attitudes and feelings, two other types of questions were included in the instrument—social background questions and items soliciting reports on political activity. In a strict sense, these questions did not measure attitudes but conditions related to attitudes. The social background questions solicited information about occupation, education, income, place of birth, father's and mother's political activity, and similar characteristics. The items on political activity asked whether the respondent had voted or had contact with a certain public agency—say, the public schools. This information might be obtained at great expense and effort through other means—for example, checking public records or observing the respondent secretly. The book *Unobtrusive Measures* (Webb et al., 1966) is a delightful inventory on ways to collect such information without doing a survey, but the survey method provides a relatively inexpensive means to collect a large amount of data quickly.

Sometimes the information is not completely accurate. If used with discretion, however, it may serve the purposes of the study. Most respondents, for example, cannot report their income correctly, not so much because they do not desire to or because they lie, but because they do not know. Checks of census reports by the Bureau of the Census against income records show that people often miss their true income by several hundred dollars. If the researcher is only interested in approximate categories, such as "less than $10,000" and "greater than $10,000," recall information on income is still useful, but if the information must be accurate to the nearest $100, then other methods must be used. Accuracy is a relative need—the degree of accuracy required depends on the research questions to be answered.

The income question is one type of "recall" question often used in surveys. Other attributes measured by recall questions include the number of years of education, parents' political activity, and past voting behavior. This last question is subject to known biases. In addition to the respondent's failure to remember, there is social pressure to say one voted even if he did not or can't remember. Most people believe a "good" citizen should vote and, therefore, it is embarrassing to admit not voting. Evidence of this bias is found in every presidential election study, which consistently report a greater proportion of voters who said they voted than, in fact, did.

Some Limiting Effects of Survey Costs

Many long hours were spent analyzing questions and researching how other survey studies had asked questions. It was not difficult to find good examples of questions used in previous surveys and to add to this list new questions of original design. On topics where little is known, open-ended questions are better choices because they do not prompt the respondent as much and because such questions do not prematurely limit the categories of possible response. Unfortunately, open-ended questions take much more time than other question forms. Time is a problem in sample surveys, where one equation holds: time = money.

Costs more than anything else serve to limit the scope, accuracy, quality, and hence generality of research projects. Cost restrictions played a critical role in limiting the scope of the SERS project. The standard industry practice is to provide a one-hour interview with two call backs. This simply means that the pollster will provide information that can be obtained in a one-hour interview where the interviewer will contact the household and select the respondent. If the respondent is not available, the interviewer will make attempts at two later times to interview the respondent before selecting another household and respondent. One hour is the approximate upper limit of attentiveness that a respondent will give to an interviewer.

Any pollster will provide higher quality polling, if one has the money to pay for it. The main cost of interviewing is the time the interviewer spends getting to the interview site, finding the proper respondent, then setting up the interview and completing it. The per interview cost bid on this study by reputable survey firms using the industry norms for quality control were in the range of $30 to $40. Thus, for a national sample of 1,500, one has data collection costs of between $45,000 and $60,000. Of course, there are ways to reduce costs, some of which do not sacrifice the quality of the sample and its information. But, no matter how one economizes, sample survey information is expensive.

The primary compromises made in the Southeast Regional Survey Project to obtain a national sample of sufficient size and quality were to eliminate all interviews with governmental elites and reduce the number of questions, especially open-ended ones, in the interview schedule. This latter decision forced us to obtain less complete information about how citizens interacted with government and to eliminate questions about their evaluations of many state and local officials. Thus, the final product was a compromise between the goals of the overall research project and the limitations imposed by the research budget. It would be an unusual research project that did not face such compromises.

The Importance of Probability Sampling

One can spend months in the design of a questionnaire and fail to collect meaningful data unless equal care is taken to select the appropriate respondents. It was decided that a national sample of adult Americans of voting age would be our subjects for study. The technical term for this total group of possible subjects is a research population. It would have been easy to go to different parts of the nation and find a few adults of voting age in each area who would answer our questions, but such information would have been next to useless because one could not have made broad statements about the population of Americans of voting age.

The methods used to select respondents are called survey sampling, and the group of people actually selected is called a sample. There are two kinds of samples—good ones and bad ones. Good samples use the rules of probability to select people who are representative of the population. Without these rules, one cannot select a representative sample no matter how careful, objective, and fair one tries to be. Student reporters often make this mistake when they conduct a campus poll—say, interview twenty students about the increase in food prices in the campus cafeteria. The reporter will write about student opinion because he purposely chose students with different sexes, majors, and other characteristics. In fact, all the reporter can say is what twenty particular students think, because the reporter has drawn a nonprobability sample, a sample not representative of the student population.

A probability sample insures that all people in the research population have an equal chance of being selected. One method for implementing this requirement is to place the names of each student on slips of paper, place them in a large urn, mix them thoroughly, then select twenty names. If followed correctly, this procedure should produce a sample that is representative of the research population (students). This type of sample is called a simple random sample. Our student reporter violated the first rule of a simple random sample: equal chance of selection. He never gave students who go to night school, who were sick that day, or who attend classes on the other side of campus a chance to be interviewed.

Since our reporter saw the error of his ways, he went to the college registrar for his next survey, obtained an official list of all students, 30,000 in number, and selected every 1500th name to interview. (Since 30,000/1,500 = 20, the reporter would obtain a sample of twenty students.) This is a substantial improvement over his first selection method and represents a minimally acceptable approach. It is not an ideal method, however, because it violates the principal of equal selection in minor ways. Since the registrar's list would be ordered alphabetically, relatives with the same last name could not appear in the same sample. Jim Smith and John Smith, brothers, would appear on the list at an interval which was less than 1,500 names. Hence, the selection of one brother guarantees that the other cannot be in the reporter's sample. If the registrar produced a list that was randomly ordered—that is, names appeared in no predictable sequence—our reporter would have an acceptable sample.

Several conclusions should be emphasized at this point. First, it is impossible for a person to select a simple random sample without some guidance from the rules of probability. Our reporter is not a "random device" able to make selections free from his own preferences. Such methods as randomly ordered lists of students or thoroughly mixed urns full of names are "random devices" free from such systematic selection biases. The second point is that failure to select a probability sample means that the sample represents only the opinions of those interviewed and nothing more. Without use of some random method, one cannot have any assurance that the sample reflects the research population.

Public opinion pollsters such as George Gallup and Louis Harris, academic research operations such as the Survey Research Center (University of Michigan) and National Opinion Research Center (University of Chicago), and many market research firms use probability sampling methods to select respondents. Although the cost and effort are greatly increased, the payoffs in terms of the ability to generalize from a sample to a large population more than outweigh the costs. The Gallup and Harris polls regularly report the attitudes of over 140 million adult Americans based on samples ranging from 600 to 3,000, and the typical sample is between 1,000 to 1,500 respondents. By using probability samples, Gallup and Harris are able to generalize to the entire population because the sample is representative in all respects of the characteristics of the population. Without probability selection, the sample only represents the opinions of those interviewed.

Area-Probability Samples

As mentioned above, an ideal method for selecting a national sample of 1,500 adult Americans would be to write the name of everyone who fits the definition of adult American on a separate piece of paper, put them in a barrel, mix them thoroughly, and then select 1,500 names. Although this procedure is theoretically desirable, the chance for its practical application is nil. For one thing, no one could assemble an up-to-date list of all adult Americans residing in the United States. Names compiled from telephone books from every city, town, and village would systematically exclude people of lower incomes who could not afford telephones, and people who had unlisted numbers. The Army, Internal Revenue Service, and Social Security Administration would not, and could not, provide a complete list. Even if such a list could be provided, it is impractical to put all the names in a barrel and mix them up thoroughly. Imagine the size of the barrel! Obviously, the survey sampler must find a procedure that is sufficiently analogous to the ideal that it will provide a probability sample. The method most commonly used by survey organizations is called area-probability sampling.

An area-probability sample is generally accomplished by the following steps. First, find a good map of the area where the people in the population live, in this case, the United States. Divide it into a grid of small areas having nearly equal population. Give each of the areas, called sample points, an equal chance of selection and pick the required number of points. Select five households in the area at which to conduct interviews. The typical number of interviews clustered at a sampling point is five but may vary as high as ten. Be sure that each household has an equal chance of selection. If an apartment building or other multihousehold dwelling is present in the area, be sure to give each apartment the same chance of selection as a single family dwelling.

After a household is selected, it is important to determine how many individuals live in the households that are included in the research population. Children, for example, would not fall in the research population, nor would visiting relatives who are not residents of the household. Once the names of permanent, adult residents has been determined, one should be selected in a systematic manner. In the early days of polling, good samples were drawn to the household level but few controls were placed on the selection of a respondent within the household. As a result, too many housewives, elderly and retired people, and unemployed persons were interviewed. Since these characteristics are related to most social behavior of interest, the result was highly biased samples that did not always reflect the research population.

One surprising fact about survey sampling is that the size of the sample is not as important as how it is selected. The now famous poll of the *Literary Digest* is a perfect example of a large sample—over 3 million—that did a poor job of providing information about the preferences for voters in the 1936 presidential election. (It predicted that Langdon would win.) The weakness of the poll was not its sample size or question format but the fact that its respondents were selected in an unrepresentative—that is, nonprobabilistic—manner. The *Digest* had a subscribership with high socioeconomic characteristics and above average education, two factors associated with Republican voting. The magazine solicited the opinions of its readers by inserting a ballot to be returned in each copy of the magazine. As a result, low income voters (Democrats) were systematically excluded from the sample.

A typical sample of adult Americans of voting age is, in practice, not exactly representative of the research population. Certain groups are systematically excluded for one simple reason—the inordinate cost required to obtain interviews with them. The Southeast Regional Survey, as most national surveys, excluded people living in Hawaii and Alaska. Most national surveys are confined to the "Lower 48." Also, institutionalized people are excluded. These include respondents living on military reservations, in hospitals, in nursing homes, and in prison. Since households are selected, certain groups of mobile and homeless people are excluded by the sampling process because they have no permanent residence. Itinerant or migrant workers, inner-city poor, and college students living in residence halls, fraternities, and sororities are systematically excluded. Students living at home and in apartments are more likely, however, to be interviewed in the typical national survey.

Each of those compromises in procedure is a concession to the restrictions imposed by cost. They introduce a certain amount of unknown error, but it is usually not critical. Of course, if the research population were all college students, excluding students in residence halls, fraternities, and sororities would be a serious omission and would invalidate the sample.

The Role of Sampling Error

If a sample is selected properly, statements based on it can be made about the population with a known degree of certainty. Using a national sample of only 1,500 voters which shows the following results

	Preferring
Candidate A	60%
Candidate B	40
	100%

one can be 95 percent certain that in the research population of over 140 million potential voters, 60 percent favor Candidate A, give or take 4 percent. The phrase "give or take 4 percent" represents the error known to exist in our statement. This error is called sampling error and results from the fact that one only interviewed 1,500 carefully selected people instead of many millions. Phrased another way, one can say with 95 percent certainty that Candidate A actually has between 56 percent (60 percent − 4 percent error) and 64 percent (60 percent + 4 percent error) of the voters' preferences. Sixty percent represents the best guess given the sample information, but one never knows exactly what the correct value is.

The main point to understand about sampling error as it relates to published poll results is that no poll is exactly correct. Properly conducted polls are close— that is, they have a known range of sampling error. Table 3–1 gives the sampling error for various sample sizes. It demonstrates that sampling error gets smaller as the number of people selected (observations) gets larger. Unfortunately for commercial pollsters, doubling the sample size does not halve the error. To reduce the sampling error ten times, a pollster must increase his sample size 100 times. This means that should a pollster decide on a sample size of fifty and then choose to reduce his sampling error by a factor of ten, he must increase his sample to 5,000 observations (see Table 3–1).

Table 3–1
The Relationship of Sampling Error to Sample Size

Sample Size	Sampling Error*
50	±13.86
100	± 9.80
250	± 6.20
500	± 4.38
1000	± 3.10
5000	± 1.39

*The estimate of sampling error is based on the assumption of a simple random sample and a test of the hypothesis that the proportion in the research population equals 0.50. The reported errors are at the 95% level of confidence—that is, there is a 5% chance that the population value is not in the range specified by sampling error. The formula for computing the sampling error is

$$\pm \text{ Sampling Error} = \pm 1.96\left(\frac{.5}{\sqrt{N}}\right).$$

This simple fact explains why most samples fall in the range of 1,000 to 1,500 interviews. The enormous cost of doing interviews prohibits increasing sample size beyond this point, because the improvement in accuracy is more than offset by the tremendous increase in costs. Only in situations where more precise estimates of the population are required—say, in a close election such as 1960—will pollsters invest the necessary dollars to obtain the needed precision.

The data used in this text came from a national sample of 1,500 one-hour interviews selected by area-probability methods. Approximately 300 sample points with clusters of five interviews at each point were used. The decision to cluster five interviews at a sample point rather than requiring a smaller number reduced the field costs of the survey. A sample with 500 sample points and clusters of three at each would be more expensive, but more precise, since interviewers must travel to 500 areas, as opposed to 300, to obtain the same number of interviews. An additional amount of sampling error is introduced as clustering around sample points increases from three to five, and thus one loses some precision in exchange for reduced costs.

Processing the Completed Interviews

The completed interviews, which had already been checked for authenticity and accuracy, were returned to the offices of the Institute for Social Research at the University of North Carolina. Students were trained to check the interviews as they arrived for accuracy and completeness and "code" the information from open-ended questions into a set of content categories. The coding process is a critical step in any research project and is one where enormous bias may enter. The problem associated with the coding of open-ended questions is to provide the coder with a set of categories summarizing possible responses—these categories are called codes—and have him record the category that best characterizes the response. For example, Table 3–2 lists the code categories used to characterize the responses to the question:

> Now, thinking about the Supreme Court in Washington, is there anything the Supreme Court has done lately that you *don't* like? What is that? (Probe:) Is there anything else?

The problem facing the coder is to find the two codes in the list in Table 3–2 that most closely summarize the verbatim answers recorded by the interviewer.

Coding is a difficult job requiring many subtle decisions. To insure reliable coding, coders were trained and tested at various times for their inter- and intra-coder reliability. Inter-coder reliability simply means that two coders, working independently of each other, will code the same information in the same way. Intra-coder reliability means that a coder will consistently record the same information in the same way. The minimum level of inter- and intra-coder reliability for this study was 80 percent—meaning that there was 80 percent agreement in coding decisions between two coders and for a given coder with himself. Whenever unreliability occurred, the inconsistencies in the coding were discussed with the coders to clarify the instructions and the meaning of the various code categories.

One task of the coder was to check the interviewer to determine if sample selection instructions within the household were carried out. This point in the interview process is probably one of the weakest points in the entire selection process. Interviewers are anxious to complete their interviews and sometimes help out by interviewing the wrong person in the household. This practice

Table 3–2
Codes Used to Summarize Responses to Question about the Supreme Court: Now, thinking about the Supreme Court in Washington, is there anything the Supreme Court has done lately that you don't like? What is that? Is there anything else?

Cols. 60–61: code first mention or most important if so indicated
Cols. 62–63: code second mention

PERSONAL CHARACTERISTICS OF THE SUPREME COURT
01. . . general dislike category: "I don't like it"
02. . . has done a lot of things I don't like (unspecified)
03. . . any mention of *other* specific dislikes about the Supreme Court (personal reference only)

PARTY AFFILIATIONS
04. . . any negative mention of political parties and the Supreme Court

POLICY (ISSUE) POSITIONS
General
05. . . dislike of Supreme Court's policies (unspecified)
06. . . *other* mention of issues not elsewhere coded

Specific—Economic
07. . . dislike of its regulation of private enterprise and industry
08. . . *other* mention of economic policies not elsewhere coded

Specific—Tax Policy
09. . . decisions on taxes (any mention)

Specific—Civil Rights or Integration
10. . . support of open housing
11. . . opposition to (or lack of support of) open housing
12. . . support of equal employment opportunities
13. . . opposition to (or lack of support of) employment opportunities
14. . . support of school integration (including bussing of children)
15. . . opposition to (or lack of support of) school integration (including bussing of children)
16. . . support of civil rights—general mention
17. . . opposition to (or lack of support of) civil rights—general mention

Specific—Social Welfare
18. . . decisions on poverty programs
20. . . support of education and schools (not integration or school prayer)
21. . . opposition to (or lack of support of) education and schools (not integration or school prayer)
22. . . decisions on welfare programs
23. . . decisions on *other* social welfare programs

Specific—Functioning of Supreme Court
24. . . increasing government activity, size, power
25. . . decreasing government activity, size, power
26. . . dishonesty relating to the justices
27. . . appointments to the Supreme Court

28. . . handling of its duties
29. . . decisions overriding other courts
30. . . *other* dislikes referring to functioning of Supreme Court

Specific—Law and Order
31. . . support of the police; giving the police more authority
32. . . restriction of the police; ending police brutality
33. . . crackdown on criminals
34. . . leniency toward criminals
35. . . restriction of riots and violence (including student protestors but not draft)
36. . . leniency toward riots and violence (including student protestors but not draft)
37. . . enforcement of safety in the streets
38. . . inaction on the problem of safety in the streets
39. . . decisions contributing to general permissiveness of society (unspecified)
40. . . *other* mention of law and order

Specific—Other
41. . . decision restricting use of Bible in schools (school prayer ban)
42. . . lenient decisions on draft protestors (anti-war also)
43. . . strict decisions on draft protestors (anti-war also)
44. . . decisions on Communists and left-wingers
45. . . reapportionment decisions (one man-one vote)
46. . . lenient decisions on obscenity and pornography (dirty books, words, and movies)
47. . . strict decisions on obscenity and pornography (dirty books, words, and movies)
48. . . decisions on electoral laws (voter registration)
49. . . any mention of any *other* specific issues not elsewhere coded

POPULATION GROUPS
50. . . against "all the people"; the common man, etc.
51. . . for "all the people"; the common man, etc.
52. . . against labor; unions; the working man, etc.
53. . . for labor; unions; the working man, etc.
54. . . against business, businessmen; industry, etc.
55. . . for business, businessmen; industry, etc.
56. . . against farmers; rural areas
57. . . for farmers; rural areas
58. . . against the poor
59. . . for the poor
60. . . against Negroes; minorities
61. . . for Negroes; minorities
62. . . against *other* population groups not elsewhere coded
63. . . for *other* population groups not elsewhere coded

SPECIAL CODES
64. . . destroying (deviation from) Constitution and/or goals of founding fathers
65. . . old (aged) judges remaining on Supreme Court
66. . . Fortas nomination as chief justice
67. . . Warren as liberal chief justice

96. . . any answer not elsewhere coded
97. . . answer cannot be ascertained
98. . . respondent refused to answer
99. . . question is applicable, but no answer is given

typically results in too many housewives. One particular survey suffered from such wholesale abuse of the household selection process that the final representative sample had over 60 percent female respondents—many of whom were housewives or elderly.

Many humorous occurrences revealing the human element in a rather technical process come to light when processing interviews. One interviewer was given a sample point requiring five interviews in the Roxbury section of Boston, a low-income section of the city. The interviewer was kind enough to write a note on the questionnaire to the effect that the she did not enjoy working in that neighborhood. To help out, however, she completed five neatly done interviews with residents of the Beacon Hill section of Boston and was thoughtful enough to comment about how nice the homes were, even though the interview had not called for such information. These five interviews were discarded, of course, since they did not meet sampling requirements, and replaced with five correctly selected ones.

After the interviews had been checked and the open-ended questions coded, the information was punched onto computer cards and processed by means of an electronic computer. The final data set contained over 300 separate pieces of information for each of the 1,504 respondents, or over 450,000 separate pieces of information. With this large amount of data at hand, an electronic computer becomes an essential tool for rapid, accurate processing and analysis.

This detailed account of how one research project was done should demonstrate one conclusion clearly. Every research project involves many decisions that compromise and limit the scope of a project and introduce error into the information collected. To summarize, some of the possible sources of error compromising research conclusions include the following:

1. sampling and selection error
2. interviewer-induced biases
3. poor questionnaire construction
4. mistakes by the field staff
5. coder unreliability
6. key punching and other processing mistakes.

Every research project is a struggle to maintain the quality of the information collected and still meet objectives within the limitations of a research budget. This account is designed to provide the reader with a realistic understanding of the limits of any scientific study of public opinion and instill a sense of caution when reading about research conclusions.

Many people upon learning of the compromises and mistakes inherent in a research project become quite skeptical about the ability of polls to report anything that is true. The experiences of the Gallup Poll in predicting such complex events as the outcome of presidential elections demonstrate the validity of survey research. Table 3–3 summarizes the experience of the Gallup Poll. The Gallup Poll substantially improved its predictive abilities after the 1948

Table 3–3
Record of Gallup Poll Accuracy, 1936–74

Year	Gallup Final Survey*		Election Result*		Error on Winning Candidate or Party, Based on Major Parry Vote	
1936	55.7%	Roosevelt	62.5%	Roosevelt	−6.8%	Roosevelt
1938	54.0	Democratic	50.8	Democratic	+3.2	Democratic
1940	52.0	Roosevelt	55.0	Roosevelt	−3.0	Roosevelt
1942	52.0	Democratic	48.0	Democratic	+4.0	Democratic[1]
1944	51.5	Roosevelt	53.3[2]	Roosevelt	−1.8	Roosevelt
1946	58.0	Republican	54.3	Republican	+3.7	Republican
1948	44.5	Truman	49.9	Truman	−5.4	Truman
1950	51.0	Democratic	50.3	Democratic	+0.7	Democratic
1952	51.0	Eisenhower	55.4	Eisenhower	−4.4	Eisenhower
1954	51.5	Democratic	52.7	Democratic	−1.2	Democratic
1956	59.5	Eisenhower	57.8	Eisenhower	+1.7	Eisenhower
1958	57.0	Democratic	56.5	Democratic	+0.5	Democratic
1960	51.0	Kennedy	50.1	Kennedy	+0.9	Kennedy
1962	55.5	Democratic	52.7	Democratic	+2.8	Democratic
1964	64.0	Johnson	61.3	Johnson	+2.7	Johnson
1966	52.5	Democratic	51.9	Democratic	+0.6	Democratic
1968	43.0	Nixon	43.5	Nixon	−0.5	Nixon
1970	53.0	Democratic	54.3	Democratic	−1.3	Democratic
1972	62.0	Nixon	61.8	Nixon	+0.2	Nixon
1974	60.0	Democratic	58.9	Democratic	+1.1	Democratic

Source: The Gallup Opinion Index

*The figure shown is the winner's percentage of the Democratic-Republican vote except in the elections of 1948 and 1968. Because the Thurmond and Wallace voters in 1948 were largely split-offs from the normally Democratic vote, they were made a part of the final Gallup Poll pre-election estimate of the division of the vote. In 1968 Wallace's candidacy was supported by such a large minority that he was clearly a major candidate, and the 1968 percents are based on the total Nixon-Humphrey-Wallace vote.

[1]Final report said Democrats would win control of the House, which they did even though the Republicans won a majority of the popular vote.

[2]Civilian vote 53.3, Roosevelt soldier vote 0.5 = 53.8 Roosevelt. Gallup final survey based on civilian vote.

presidential election, when the poll incorrectly predicted Truman's actual vote by more than 5 percentage points. For the congressional and presidential elections held since 1950, however, the average error in prediction has been only 1.4 percent, whereas the average error for the period through 1948 was over twice as high (3.9 percent). One can see that in spite of the many sources of error and bias discussed above, the Gallup organization has with few exceptions an excellent record in predicting the political behavior of millions of Americans. Yet the picture would not be complete without some recognition of the failures of modern polling.

Undoubtedly, the most notable failure in recent years was the prediction of a Labour Party victory in the 1970 British Parliamentary election. Every major polling organization failed to predict the Conservative Party plurality (cf. Abrams, 1970). In the United States, the record of many state and local polls is less than commendable. In the 1974 congressional elections, many of these polls made incorrect predictions of electoral outcomes (cf. *Congressional Quarterly*, 1974). In sum, the validity of a poll prediction must be critically examined. The general reputation of the pollster, the time of the field work, the size and type of sample, and the design of the questions can give the reader some basis for evaluating its published predictions.

The Presentation of Data in the Text

One underlying policy guiding the preparation of this text is that the reader should appreciate how data were obtained and have available to him the information on which conclusions are drawn. It would be too cumbersome and tedious to list the responses to a question for over 1,500 people, but one can accomplish these same ends—the presentation of information—and economize on space. Two forms of presentation, tables and figures, provide information from the sample. Descriptive statistics summarize the responses of the sample for a specific characteristic. The most common descriptive statistic used here is the percentage. A percentage is nothing more than a proportion of a total number who hold some characteristic. Thus, the statement, "Forty percent of the sample gave favorable responses to the question . . . ," means that *on the average* forty people out of every 100 sampled responded "agree" to the question, and sixty people out of every 100 said something else (disagree, not sure, etc.). Although this percentage is the best guess one can make about how the population feels about the question, it is subject to sampling error and to other unknown sources of error. As a consequence, one can be certain that the 40 percent estimate is not exactly correct but is close to being a true estimate of the population percentage.

Other statistics regularly used in the text are as follows:

frequencies (f): A frequency is a count of the number of people who fall into a particular category (for example, the number of males).

net percentages: This statistic is the difference between "Percentage Agreeing" and "Percentage Disagreeing." A net percentage of "+100 Percent" means that everyone agreed to the question; a net percentage of "−100 Percent" means that everyone disagreed to the question; and a net percentage of "0" means that an equal proportion agreed as disagreed. The formula is Net Percent = Percent Agreement − Percent Disagreement.

mean score: A mean score is also called an "average" and is computed by adding together the values for each person surveyed and dividing by the total number surveyed. Sometimes the average or mean score can be thought of as the "typical" score. For example, if one finds the average American family has 2.2 children, one does not mean that everyone has 2/10 of a child in addition to two whole ones. Rather, this statistic means that the typical family has between two and three children and more families are likely to have two children instead of three.

The statistics described above are presented in tables of three different kinds: univariate or one variable tables; bivariate or two variable tables; and complex or tables with more than two variables. A univariate table simply summarizes how many or what percentage of people studied have each value of the characteristic studied. For example, a table on the distribution of the sample by race would show:

White	90%
Black	10
	100%

Table 4–1, labeled "Distributions of Diffuse Support for Public and Private Institutions," summarizes, among other things, the univariate distributions for seven "trust" questions. In addition, the last column of the table lists the net percentages, called Net Diffuse Support, for each of the seven variables.

Bivariate tables show the relationship between two variables—that is, whether one variable is associated with the other. The first variable is called the independent variable and in some cases may be thought of as the cause or antecedent to the second variable, which is called the dependent variable. By convention, the independent variable is placed across the top of a bivariate table and defines the columns of the table. The dependent variable forms the rows of the table. Table 5–1 is an example of a bivariate table comparing whether the respondent was favorable or unfavorable (independent variable) with the content of the responses (dependent variable). The percentages in a bivariate table will sum to 100 percent down each column. Thus, one can read, "Fifty-four percent of all favorable responses were about the 'Trip to Europe' while only 11 percent of unfavorable responses were about the trip." One can conclude that some topics receive unusually favorable treatment (foreign trips) and others do not (taxes and spending). The basic rule is to percentage down the columns, summing to 100 percent in each, and compare the resulting percentages across the rows.

One special form of the bivariate table is the collapsed bivariate table. The collapsed table uses a category of the dependent variable that is of interest—for example, those who commented about Vietnam (see Table 5–1)—and summarizes the entire table as shown in Table 3–4. Since everyone falls into the categories Mentioned Vietnam Policy or Did Not Mention Vietnam Policy, the entire table can be further simplified to

	Favorable	*Unfavorable*	*Total*
Mentioned Vietnam policy	8% (65)	17% (61)	11% (126)

since the Did Not Mention Vietnam Policy category is implicit. Table 7–4 on "Comparisons of Level of Public Confidence in Selected Institution, 1966–73" follows this summary format. Each row of the table is a bivariate

Table 3–4
A Summary of Table 5–1

	Favorable	Unfavorable	Total
Mentioned Vietnam	8%	17%	11%
policy	(65)	(61)	(126)
Did not mention	92	83	89
Vietnam policy	(733)	(302)	(1035)
	100%	100%	100%
	(798)	(363)	(1161)

table (time x level of confidence) in summary form. The dependent variable is the summary variable, the percent responding "great deal" to the confidence question; and the independent variable is the year of the survey. There are four bivariate tables summarized, one for each institution.

Complex tables are extensions of the bivariate table to more than two variables. Table 5–2, entitled "The Effects of State Party Identification on Perceptions of Governors' Policies," is a complex table because it contains three variable comparisons. The first row of Table 5–2 shows the effects of the combinations of the respondent's party and the governor's party (independent variables) on the net percentage approval of a governor's tax policies. The negative sign indicates disapproval, and the magnitude of the number indicates the degree of disapproval.

The final mode of presentation is the figure or graph. Figures and graphs are pictures of the relationships of two or more variables. At times, complex relationships can best be presented as a picture instead of a table. Take Figure 4–2, "Trends in Questions Asked by the Gallup Poll during the Watergate Affair," as an example. By convention, the independent variable (time of the survey) is placed on the horizontal (x) axis and the dependent variable (percent giving a certain response) on the vertical (y) axis. The general decline of the two lines indicates that as the Watergate controversy proceeded, the rates of response (e.g., percent approval) decreased. Since the lines do not decline at a fixed rate, one can learn from a quick inspection of Figure 4–2 when the most rapid rate of decline occurred and for what question the decrease in response was greatest.

To gain full value from the text, the reader should not rely wholly on the discussion to interpret each table presented. A table or figure can summarize much more than can be fully discussed. The reader should develop the habit of studying each table with some care and summarizing the relationships and other information presented in addition to the highlights discussed in the body of the text. A good habit is to read the title of a table first to establish what variables are summarized and what, if anything, is being compared with what. Is it a univariate, bivariate, or complex table? What descriptive statistics are used— percentages, frequencies, net percentages, means? For additional help, two books that provide excellent treatments on how to construct and read tables and figures are Zeisel (1968) and Anderson and Zelditch (1975).

Notes

[1]The name "Southeast Regional Survey" arose from the general title given in the research award. The National Science Foundation awarded the University of North Carolina a general "science excellence" grant to conduct continuing research on problems of regional and national concern. Three surveys were funded as part of the overall grant. SERS was the first study to be undertaken. Other projects in later years also had the title "Southeast Regional Survey" but, except for name and common funding, they had no connection with this project.

[2]Since the survey went into the field the year after Governor George Wallace ran for the presidency, the party identification sequence also included questions to determine whether "Independent" meant "American Independent Party" or just "Independent."

Part Two

Citizens
and
Their Political Institutions

Support for Political Institutions

Most Western governments are based on the feelings of loyalty and acceptance held by the citizens they represent. As a moral issue, these governments need such acceptance; as a practical matter, it is essential to the existence of the governments. The problems encountered by contemporary governments lacking public acceptance from a significant sector of the population are well documented. The Protestant-dominated government of Northern Ireland must confront the challenge of dissident Catholics. Israel faces the claims of disposed Palestineans. Even English Canada must contend with a secessionist French Quebec, while the United States fought the Civil War over the withdrawal of support to the central government by eleven states.

In less extreme situations where active, armed resistance is absent, governments still cannot enforce laws and regulations solely by the threat of force. Consider the number of police and national guardsmen used during the 1960s to enforce civil rights legislation and campus order. The routine application of force to gain compliance with the law is simply not a workable alternative. In ongoing political systems, not only do most citizens support the government, they also willingly comply with its laws and policies (cf. Wahlke, 1971).

Diffuse Support and Political Culture

Political scientists have begun to explore the nature of this bond that allows the political system to operate effectively. David Easton has suggested the concept "support" as the key ingredient contributing to the cohesiveness of a political system (1965). Support is a network of attitudes and beliefs held by individuals toward the political community, political regime, and political authorities. Support is both a long- and short-term attitude. Long-term support is called diffuse support; short- term support is known as specific support. Diffuse support is relatively stable over a person's lifetime and not easily changed. It is more closely tied to an individual's personality, social needs, and political values than specific support. Day-to-day events, even of the most dramatic kind, do not immediately affect diffuse support.

Americans learn strong positive feelings of diffuse support toward political community and political institutions early in life. Studies of American school children show how young people learn attitudes of positive diffuse support. By the second grade, many children know that "the president" is good, but they are not sure what exactly he does. They have developed strong, positive feelings toward "the president" without having any information (beliefs) about the president. Support toward other institutions, such as the Congress and the Supreme Court, comes in later years, but it too is positive and precedes established beliefs. Aging brings some diminishing of these Pollyannalike feelings, but even by adolescence, diffuse support for regime and institutions, though diminished, is highly favorable (cf. Hess and Torney, 1967; Easton and Dennis, 1965, 1967, 1969; Greenstein, 1965). Children also learn quickly about the symbols of American greatness—the Constitution, the Bill of Rights, the flag, Washington, Jefferson, Lincoln.

The American federal system of government is a complex, and often confusing, structure of interrelated and interdependent public authorities. The collection of public money through taxes is a perfect example of the complexity. Similar governmental functions are performed by national, state, and local authorities. It is not uncommon for a citizen to pay federal income taxes to the Internal Revenue Service, state income taxes to a state department of revenue, property taxes to a school district and county, and sales taxes to the city. Any taxpayer who has worked or owned property in more than one state knows the difficulties in determining what fair share of tax money is owed to which government. Most public functions—even public education, which is traditionally a locally based governmental activity—involve local, state, and federal governments. Local school boards may set policy regarding teacher salaries, selection of textbooks, and tax rates on property, but state departments of public instruction also supervise the selection of books, certify teachers, and monitor curricula, to mention only a few functions. Then the federal government requires certain standards to be met for a school district to receive such aid as school lunch assistance or school construction money. In the face of this governmental complexity, it would not be suprising to find that the average citizen is ambivalent about the attention paid to governmental activity.

Such complexity poses an interesting question: What levels of government and which institutions become the primary foci for support? The diffuse support of citizens toward specific levels of government or particular institutions is a major component of a more general set of psychological orientations toward political objects. This total collection of fundamental cognitions, feelings, attitudes, and beliefs held by citizens toward objects of the political system is called political culture (Almond and Verba, 1963; Devine, 1972). Political culture has intrigued many authors for one basic reason. They hope that by determining the key elements of political culture, one gains a better understanding of why some nations are stable and continuing and others are always on the verge of collapse or chaos. Devine (1972), for example, explains the continuity of American politics over 200 years by arguing that Americans have a commonly held and persistent set of beliefs and values best articulated by the eighteenth century political philosopher John Locke and later incorporated in the Constitution. Devine argues that Americans have a cohesive political culture because for generations they have readily understood and endorsed certain symbolic political values. Most Americans would name Lincoln and Washington among the two or three greatest men in the history of the United States; they readily recognize the American flag and the "Star Spangled Banner" and have deep respect for them; they trust their governments and believe they work for the best interests of the nation; and finally, they endorse broad constitutional guarantees such as freedom of the press, religion, and speech, as well as such concepts as equality and liberty (Devine, 1972; see also Prothro and Grigg, 1960).

Another perspective on the importance of understanding political culture is given by Almond and Verba (1963). They compared the psychological orientations of citizens in five modern nations—the United States, Great Britain, West Germany, Italy, and Mexico—toward political authority and individual participation. These authors found significant differences not only in the mode of individual interaction with government, but also in citizens' attitudes toward the suitability and consequences of such interactions. Americans differed substantially from citizens in other countries both in their belief that they should be active and in the frequency of times they actually attempted to influence governmental action.

The definition and identification of the elements of political culture are necessary to highlight the political orientations accounting for how and why citizens relate toward government. This relationship of citizen to government institution is called political participation. Political participation takes many forms, from strictly psychological behavior to overt action. Political participation may constitute nothing more than being interested in politics, acquiring information, and forming a judgment about some political event. Or it might involve attending political meetings, calling on a city official, or demonstrating in front of the federal building. Thus, participation varies from essentially passive behavior to active involvement. In the day-to-day affairs of most citizens, diffuse supportive attitudes would fall more toward the passive end. There are exceptional periods, however, when the full meaning of supportive attitudes is manifest.

Diffuse support for political institutions is especially evident during crisis periods. External threats often bring societies together. The British had "their finest hour" during the Battle of Britain; Americans rallied behind President Roosevelt after the Pearl Harbor attack. But war is not the only crisis situation that can reveal the full intensity of supportive attitudes. One particular event of the past fifteen years has demonstrated the depth of diffuse support for a man and a political institution: the assassination of President John Kennedy. In unemotional terms, Kennedy's death was a straightforward act of homicide, and homicides unfortunately are routine daily occurrences. The murdering of a president, however, was an event that prompted a deep, emotional response from an overwhelming number of Americans. Studies of individuals' reactions to the news showed a profound national response (cf. Greenberg and Parker, 1965; Greenstein, 1966). The news of Kennedy's death spread instantaneously. Adults reacted with symptoms of emotional stress such as crying, fatigue, irritability, and depression. They expressed fear about the future of the country and world. School children became unruly, listless, noisy, and hard to manage. Accidents of all kinds, job absenteeism, hospital admissions, and doctors' visits increased, and the stock market plummeted. As much as six months later, mental hospitals revealed increased admissions directly resulting from people who still could not cope with the knowledge of the president's death. Earlier, less detailed studies of the public's reaction to the sickness of President Eisenhower (1955) and the natural death of President Roosevelt (1945) suggest similar public reactions. In sum, the death of a president, any president, offers the opportunity to see the depth of affective attachment to the man and the institution held by the American people and the resulting fear and uncertainty about the future.

During more settled times, there are many opportunities for observing manifestations of diffuse support. Phrases such as "My country, right or wrong" and "Love it or leave it" represent the sentiment in blunt terms. More subtle manifestations of the existence of diffuse support are the public singing of the national anthem, standing when the flag goes by, and the use of the colors red, white, and blue for political purposes. Consider also a typical scene: 100,000 people jammed into the Rose Bowl stadium on New Year's Day at considerable expense and some discomfort for one purpose—to see a football game. But every year at the height of excitement, the moment before kickoff, the crowd quiets to a whisper, stands, faces a tri-colored piece of cloth, and sings a song! And they all know the words (more or less). The fact that most Americans would find nothing unusual about a patriotic ceremony before a football game demonstrates clearly how deeply held and broadly based such feelings of diffuse support are. If one doubts this fact, try an experiment. Engage in behavior that is not in compliance with expectations. Sit down, talk loudly, and generally ignore the flag during the flag raising (but please do not send me your medical bills).

Diffuse Support for Public and Private Institutions

A range of studies have focused on the nature of diffuse support for other political institutions in addition to those mentioned on the presidency; among the institutions examined are the state legislature (Boynton et al., 1968; Patterson et al., 1969); the criminal justice system (Murphey and Tannenhaus, 1968; Walker et al., 1972); and the political party system (Dennis, 1966). These studies have found a generally high level of positive diffuse support in the United States. Because the various studies have used different measures at different times on different study populations, direct comparisons are difficult. Although diffuse support is a generalized feeling toward political referents, the variations in the composition, behavior, and output of political institutions most likely create differences in public evaluations from institution to institution. Most research on adult feelings shows the relatively special positive feelings directed toward the president. In contrast, an institution such as the United States Supreme Court does not gain the public's awareness as much as the president; as a result, one would expect important differences among institutions in the presence of support as well as in the direction of the feelings.

Another area where our knowledge of the levels of support is minimal relates to nongovernmental institutions. The concept of support has been discussed only in terms of political institutions, mainly because they are assumed to have the power to enforce binding decisions on society. Many private institutions—namely, large business corporations and labor unions—exercise a public power also. Corporations and unions have influence through wage, production, and price decisions to affect employment, fiscal, and monetary policies of the federal government. Thus it is logical that support for major private institutions having potential or real *political* power be considered in this analysis.

To provide a basis for comparing the levels of diffuse support for both private and public institutions, all respondents were asked seven common questions of the form: "[Institution] can be trusted to do what is good for the people."[1] The seven institutional referents were "The president," "The governor of the state," "The Supreme Court in Washington," "United States senators," "Local judges," "Business and industry," and "Labor unions." The purpose of the question was to measure the level of unqualified acceptance of the actions of each institution. The statement was not explained or restricted in any way. Thus, an "agree" response would represent an almost unreserved acceptance of the institution. "Disagree" responses represent a withholding of this unqualified commitment. Such a response need not represent anti-institutional sentiment, although that possibility is present.

Table 4–1 summarizes the responses to these seven trust questions. The over-all positive feelings toward public institutions is evident from the high percentage of the sample, always more than half, that give a supportive response. There are dramatic differences, however, between the levels of support for public and private institutions. Over half of the sample expressed a "disagree" response to the trust questions about private institutions.

The contrasts among institutions are best shown by the Net Diffuse Support measure in the last column of Table 4–1. This measure is the difference between the supportive and not supportive percentages. It represents an overall summary measure of the level of trust in each institution. A score of " + 100 percent" means everyone responded "agree"; a score of " − 100 percent" means everyone responded "disagree"; and a score of "0" means the proportion agreeing equals the proportion disagreeing. This point may be interpreted as a neutral support level. All the public institutions have a positive Net Diffuse Support score,

Table 4–1
Distributions of Diffuse Support for Public and Private Institutions

	Supportive*	Not Sure	Not Supportive	No Opinion	Net Diffuse Support**
Public Institutions					
The president	65%	8%	21%	6%	+44%
State governor	57	9	28	6	+29
The Supreme Court	50	10	33	7	+17
United States senators	54	9	32	5	+22
Local judges	54	10	27	9	+27
Private Institutions					
Business and industry	26	12	56	6	−30
Labor unions	27	11	53	9	−26

*% of sample giving an "agree" response to question "[Institution] can be trusted to do what is good for the people." Respondents classified "not supportive" gave a "disagree" response.
**Net Diffuse Support = % Supportive −% Not Supportive".

whereas the two private ones have negative scores. Thus, one can see the great degree to which the public differentiates among institutional support. The presidency leads the list among public institutions by a sizable margin. This finding simply demonstrates the special position of this institution in the eyes of most Americans. The four other public institutions are grouped next, still with relatively high levels of net diffuse support in the +17 to +29 percent range. Finally, the private institutions fall significantly below the neutral point.

If social theorists correctly assert that institutions need high levels of support to govern, then the level of support for private institutions suggests a reluctance on the part of most citizens to permit unregulated private initiative in the governmental sphere. This evidence does not indicate that two major actors in the private sphere—business and labor—are untrustworthy; rather, the comparisons show that Americans have not acquired as trusting an attitude toward important private institutions as they exhibit toward public ones. If the theory about the role of diffuse support is correct, these low levels of diffuse support would act as a potential constraint on business and labor to become an effective social and political force for long range political change. Those who desire private, as opposed to public, solutions to national problems will find little encouragement from these results. In sum, one learns from the comparisons presented in Table 4–1 of the broad, unqualified nature of mass feelings toward public institutions. To better understand the basis for these judgments, one must consider the citizens' perspective of the complex system of governments we know as the federal structure.

Citizen Attention to Levels of Government

In his presidential address to the annual meeting of the American Political Science Association, Professor Robert Dahl (1967) raised the question of how the ancient ideal of citizen involvement in democratic government could be achieved in a modern nation-state. In the time of the ancient Greeks, the dominant form of political organization was the city-state, small in comparison to the nation-state of today. Dahl observed that Iceland, the smallest democratic nation-state in the world, has over twice the number of adult citizens as ancient Athens; and India, the largest, has between 5,000 and 6,000 times more citizens than the ideal Greek city-state. Even contemporary subunits, such as the American states, are enormous by comparison. New York and California each have more citizens than 80 percent of the world's nation-states.

Dahl observes that the American state falls into a kind of limbo between the national (nation-state) government and local units. Americans are not as attentive to the affairs of their state governments as citizens in a comparably sized nation-state are to its activities. Dahl sees state governments as too big and remote from people's daily lives to evoke strong allegiances; yet they cannot command the public's attention as the federal government does. At the other extreme, local governments are sufficiently close to the daily business of the average citizen to fulfill a democratic ideal for citizen interaction.

The empirical question implied by Dahl's remarks, then, is how generally do citizens perceive and evaluate various levels of government, as one finds in the American federal structure? Jennings and Zeigler (1970) collected evidence in 1966 on how citizens view the federal structure and confirmed Dahl's argument that the state level was least likely to tap the awareness of citizens. Table 4–2 reports their findings, along with those collected three years later in the Southeast Regional Survey. Both studies show that national and local affairs compete for first attention; international events are third; and state affairs are last. The 1969 survey also demonstrated that 19 percent, about one-fifth of all citizens, could not differentiate the activities of the various levels. In summary, one finds the many levels of government competing for attention. National and local af-

Table 4–2
Citizen Attention to Levels of Government: A Comparison of Findings

	1966 National Survey*	1969 National Survey**	Adjusted 1969 Results
International	20%	14%	17%
National	32	29	36
State	17	10	12
Local	30	28	35
All the same	—	16	—
Not sure	—	3	—
	100%	100%	100%

*The data are from Jennings and Zeigler (1970) for the first choice responses to the question: "Which one of these kinds of public affairs do you follow most closely?" The authors did not report results for "all the same" and "not sure" responses.

**The question in the 1969 survey was "Which one do you follow most closely—international affairs, national affairs, state affairs, or local affairs?" The "adjusted 1969 results" are the percentages recomputed after excluding the last two categories.

fairs predominate in the public's attentiveness, but about one-fifth of all citizens cannot say which level they follow most. Such a response suggests either a broadly based interest or a degree of confusion resulting in the inability to differentiate the textbooklike terms of "national," "state," and "local" govern ments.

Since the foundation of a participatory political system rests partly on how well citizens orient themselves to multiple governments, the question of how well citizens relate to government needs some further clarification. In the 1969 survey, several open-ended questions about what citizens disliked and liked about the activities of various institutions were administered. These questions took the form: "Is there anything [Institution] has done lately that you (don't like) like? Would you please tell me about that?" Separate questions for dislikes and likes were used, and three institutions were measured: the president or his assistants, the governor of the respondent's state, and the Supreme Court in Washington. In addition, several questions were asked concerning United States senators, including an open-ended question about what the respondent knew about the senators he identified. In all, there were seven open-ended questions focused on the activities of four political institutions. The information from these questions provides a means for measuring how salient each respond-ent found political matters across a relatively wide and varied landscape of public affairs. Furthermore, the open-ended questions permitted some judg-ments about the overall coherence of a respondent's political information.

The responses to these questions were coded and summarized into an Institu-tional Saliency Index. This index provides a measure of awareness of individual citizens to institutional behavior. An index score of "0" was assigned to re-spondents who made no codeable open-ended remarks about any of the four institutions. A score of "4" was given to each citizen who made comments about all four institutions. Thus, the value of the Institutional Saliency Index assigned to each person is simply the number of institutions receiving codeable comments to the open-ended questions.

Since respondents tend to make meaningless comments if probed too much, several specific guidelines were applied in coding the data. First, responses con-taining policy-related comments were classified according to an elaborate code (see chapter 3). References to population group associations for president, state governors, and United States Supreme Court were excluded from the analysis. Second, all vague and unclarified responses were eliminated. Thus, the procedures for reducing the information found in the questionnaires to a manageable number of analytic categories served to filter out many low level and meaningless responses. These uncoded responses no doubt contain a high degree of nonattitudes—responses created merely because the question was asked and not because the comment was related to underlying attitudes or feelings. The coding scheme, then, can be characterized as conservative, in the sense that the written comments collected by the interviewers met standards of acceptability before being processed into data for analysis. This coding procedure is similar to that used by the authors of *The American Voter* (Campbell et al., 1960) and later replicated by Field and Anderson (1969).

Figure 4–1 presents the distribution of the sample for the Institutional Saliency Index. Almost one-quarter of the sample (22 percent) fall into the high saliency end of the distribution and only 8 percent are at the low saliency end. One also finds that the distribution is bunched to the right, indicating a tendency toward higher saliency among individuals.

Figure 4-1
The Distribution of the Number of Specific Mentions to Four Institutions

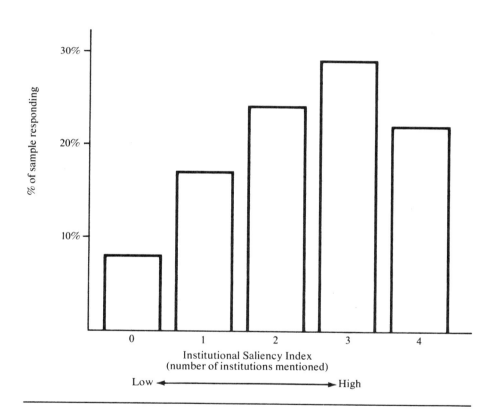

These findings give a more favorable picture of citizen participation than *The American Voter* classification, which reported a maximum of 12 percent of the population as ideologues (see chapter 1), and more nearly duplicate the findings of Field and Anderson (1969) for the 1964 election. Some differences may occur, however, simply because these results are based on responses to questions about a range of institutions, whereas *The American Voter* classification was based on open-ended questions about parties and candidates in presidential elections. Thus, the Institutional Saliency Index captures a broader range of information based on questions focused toward institutional policies rather than on campaign-oriented questions. The implications are clear nevertheless: citizens show a high degree of awareness to a wide range of political events associated with many diverse institutions.

The amount of political knowledge held by a respondent is inherently related to his level of classification on the Institutional Saliency Index. Other studies (Campbell et al., 1960; Converse, 1964a) have confirmed this relationship—that is, the ability to respond in a coherent manner to open-ended questions about public policy is related to the amount of political knowledge held by the respondent. In this context, political knowledge is another indicator of citizen responsibility. One need not expect all institutional information to be equally salient to each respondent. In fact, one would expect otherwise. To measure a range of political information, five knowledge questions about various levels of government were included in the survey instrument. Table 4–3 summarizes these five knowledge questions by the Institutional Saliency Index. In all cases, people with higher saliency are more likely to give correct answers, and respondents with the highest awareness have near complete information, as measured by these simple questions. Although the respondents at the low end show less knowledge, it would not be accurate to assert, as some authors have (cf. Glenn, 1972), that the low saliency group has insufficient political information. There is no absolute standard for measuring the threshold of minimally acceptable political information. No one would assert, for example, that the questions reported in Table 4–3 are an absolute test for the amount of political knowledge

Table 4–3
The Salience of Institutional Politics and the Level of Political Knowledge

*Institutional Saliency Index** *(Citizen Awareness of Institutional Activity)*	*Low* ⟵				⟶ *High*
	0	1	2	3	4
Indicators of Political Knowledge					
Correctly identifying one or more Supreme Court justices	6%	32%	49%	67%	84%
Correctly identifying one or more U.S. senators	0	66	86	95	100
Correctly naming the political party having a majority in Congress	28	54	69	81	90
Correctly naming the political party of the state governor	53	77	86	92	96
Correctly identifying the location of their state capital	89	93	95	97	98

*Number of coded responses for series of questions on institutional activities.

required to be a good citizen. Table 4–3 shows only that people with lower salience have a lesser, but not necessarily insufficient, degree of correct political knowledge than those with higher levels of salience.

Glenn (1972) suggests a distraction thesis for explaining variations in political information. This thesis suggests that other interests and needs competing for an individual's attention push political matters aside. The media have provided political information in abundance, but they also have provided, as Glenn notes, a "super-abundance of other stimuli to distract from political ones." This explanation is a compelling one, for most studies of media show that the majority of people watch television, listen to radio, and read the printed word. The problem is not so much the unavailability of political information as the lack of ability for dealing with a wide range of political and nonpolitical stimuli.

Formal education generally enhances an individual's capacity to organize and interpret a complex set of information. One would expect that citizens with less education would be more prone to distraction. A comparison of the levels of Institutional Saliency by amount of formal education confirms this expectation (Table 4–4). The "Some College" group have a large proportion (36 percent) of respondents with high institutional saliency whereas the "Less than High School" category has a higher proportion of low salience respondents. Respondents with lower education nonetheless followed institutional politics to a substantial degree. Almost two-thirds (64 percent) commented about two or more institutions. Thus, increased formal education enhances one's capacity for integrating wide-ranging political information into a useful form. Citizens with lower levels of education are not without a sufficiently broad range of information, though, to be compared favorably with the college-educated group.

Table 4–4
The Relationship of Education to the Saliency of Political Institutions

		Less than High School	High School Diploma	Some College
Institutional Saliency Index*				
Low	0	14%	6%	1%
↑	1	22	18	8
	2	26	28	18
↓	3	24	28	37
High	4	14	20	36
		100%	100%	100%

*Number of institutions mentioned

How citizens view politics in general greatly affects which level of government captures their attention. The Institutional Saliency Index represents an overall measure of citizen involvement in institutional affairs.[2] When this is compared to the question on which level of government is followed most closely, it becomes evident that where one falls along the Index dramatically affects one's focus of attention. Citizens with low institutional salience are predominantly interested in local government. As saliency increases, concern for national and international affairs increases and attention to local matters declines. State government shows only modest change, but the net effect is that state government is of relatively little interest to all citizens, regardless of their level of institutional saliency.

One by-product of increased institutional saliency is a decline in people unable to focus on specific levels of governmental activity. The "All the Same" and "Not Sure" categories show a modest decline as saliency increases, suggesting that the inability to distinguish levels is tied to lack of information and attentiveness. Lower saliency implies more localized attention and less differentiation whereas higher saliency implies an expanded view of government encompassing public affairs more remote from the lives of individual citizens and creates differentiation of governmental activities.

Institutional saliency also is related to how citizens formulate notions of diffuse support. In Table 4–1 approximately 5 to 9 percent of the national sample expressed no opinion to any given trust question. If one conceives of diffuse support as an attitude formed early in life and relatively central in a citizen's belief-structure, then the rate of no opinion response would be an approximate measure of the degree to which citizens had been socialized into forming supportive beliefs. In other words, one would expect near complete existence of supportive attitudes. The low rates of nonresponse are evidence confirming these expectations.

A related question pertains to how well citizens are socialized across a range of political institutions—federal, state, and local. To measure this aspect, one can construct an index based on the number of no opinion responses each respondent gave to the seven items listed in Table 4–1. A score of "0" means that the respondent has formed supportive attitudes—positive and negative—to all seven institutions. At the other extreme, a score of "7" means the respondent has not formed supportive attitudes about any of the institutions. This Support Saliency Index then provides an indication of how extensive are the respondent's supportive attitudes.

As one might expect, feelings about the trustworthiness of political institutions are much less common among citizens with low levels of institutional saliency. Less than half of the sample (47 percent) with low levels of saliency responded to all seven "trust" questions. Among respondents with high institutional saliency, 87 percent responded to the seven trust questions. Respondents with lower levels of involvement do not form supportive attitudes as readily. They have lesser degrees of participation in two senses: first, they do not form as many judgments about the general nature of political institutions (diffuse support), and second, they are not as likely to respond to specific policy events initiated by elites.

Specific Support for Public Institutions

Specific support is an attitude directed to day-to-day political events, individuals holding a position of public power, and the consequences of governmental actions. Specific support is tied to the authorities who hold positions of influence and power. Change them and one changes the basis for specific support. In contrast, diffuse support is directed toward institutions where history, tradition, and prestige provide continuity. The difference between diffuse and specific support is the difference between feeling that "State Governors are unresponsive to the people's needs," and that "Governor X will not pay any attention to my letter." Current events affect specific support more directly and rapidly than diffuse support. Because elites play some role in shaping these events, they have some ability to affect specific support. Most public opinion poll results reported in daily newspapers provide information about the public's levels of specific support. Thus, the Gallup question, "Do you approve or disapprove of the way [president's name] is handling his job as president?" provides information on how citizens evaluate a particular president's performance in office.

The open-ended questions about "the president and his assistants," "the governor" of the respondent's state, and "the Supreme Court in Washington" also permit the measurement of levels of specific support. Two questions about specific support will be raised: first, what is the relative level of response versus nonresponse (saliency); second, what is the distribution of favorable and unfavorable responses?

Table 4–5 shows the distributions of specific support for the three institutions.

Table 4–5
Distributions of Specific Support for Three Public Institutions

	President	*State Governors*	*Supreme Court*	*All Three Institutions*
Giving only favorable responses	36%	18%	6%	17%
Giving only unfavorable responses	10	29	27	19
Giving both favorable and unfavorable responses	12	14	6	46
No response	42	39	61	19
Net specific support*	+26%	−11%	−21%	−2%

*Net Specific Support = % Favorable Only − % Unfavorable Only

In contrast to diffuse support, a greater proportion of citizens had not formed any judgment regarding the desirability of various institutional activities. Somewhat over half of the sample made responses about presidential and gubernatorial activity, but only 39 percent commented about the Supreme Court's actions. These figures show the relative visibility of political institutions to the average citizen. One should expect the saliency of specific attitudes to be less than diffuse ones because of the differing foci. Current events change often; thus, the citizen must continually reorient himself to political events. Furthermore, different institutions are involved in selective kinds of political activities, some of which may not have much interest to a given citizen. In the case of diffuse attitudes, however, once one learns the political litany, there is little new content to acquire.

Even though the saliency levels of institutional activity will vary according to the behavior of the incumbents, Table 4–5 provides some estimate of the relative size of the attentive publics associated with each of these three institutions. They vary in size from a high of three-fifths (president and state governors) to a low of two-fifths (Supreme Court). Each public is distinct, yet some overlap still exists. Only one-fifth (19 percent) of all respondents were not attentive to the day-to-day activities of any one of these three institutions.

The relatively high level of awareness to governors' activities is in marked contrast to the attentiveness given state affairs. Most likely, state politics is equated with the activities of governors. Since the governor is the principal political actor in state affairs, the high attentiveness accorded this institution can be partially explained.

The important contrasts, however, center on the relative levels of positive and negative specific support. Of these three institutions, only the president has net favorable specific support (36 percent − 10 percent = +26 percent). State governors (18 percent − 29 percent = −11 percent) and especially the Supreme Court (6 percent − 27 percent = −21 percent) have negative specific support. Diffuse support is usually more favorable than specific support.

It is important to recognize that levels of specific support are more determined by incumbents and events than is diffuse support. Thus, the problem arises concerning the degree to which the evidence in Table 4–5 represents the normal state of affairs. Does the president always have favorable specific support? Is an incumbent president better able to create a favorable reaction to his policies than an incumbent state governor? In chapters 5, 6, and 7, I shall examine in some detail both the process by which specific attitudes are generated and some of the forces critical for creating uniformly favorable and unfavorable public judgments. These chapters will explore specific public reactions to the incumbents of the White House and the state mansions, America's highest tribunal, and Capitol Hill.

The Relationship of Diffuse and Specific Support

Three propositions about the relationship between specific and diffuse support are implied by support theory. The first proposition states that diffuse support is the more salient attitude. Specific support rarely exists in isolation from diffuse support but only in conjunction with it; however, diffuse support often does exist without specific support. Two percent of the sample at most had specific attitudes without also having diffuse ones, but a substantial part of the sample (between 36 and 58 percent) expressed diffuse attitudes only. It was also a common occurrence (38 to 59 percent) to find diffuse and specific attitudes expressed together, but it was a rare occurrence (3 to 6 percent) to find no attitudes of either kind. People are more likely to have diffuse attitudes alone or specific attitudes along with diffuse ones.

The one-third to one-half of all Americans who hold diffuse attitudes alone are individuals having only vaguely focused feelings toward a particular political institution. These individuals are not responsive to the day-to-day actions of public officials and in this sense are somewhat unresponsive to governmental activity. They fail to exercise any powers of judgment and decision about current governmental activity. This group of uninvolved citizens might represent a potential threat to the operation of government, particularly if their diffuse attitudes were unfavorable. This, however, is not the case, since among these uninvolved citizens, the ratio of favorable to unfavorable diffuse feelings is about 3:1 for the president, state governors, and Supreme Court. Far from posing a threat of revolution, these individuals are extremely favorable to government in an unfocused way. This lack of directed attitudes could pose a threat of unresponsiveness in the case that government became corrupt, dishonest, or incompetent. Should the time come that citizens would be required to act to remove these officials and seek political change, these individuals would be an unlikely source of political action.

The other large group of citizens are those who have both diffuse and specific attitudes. This group presents the opportunity to examine the second proposition derived from support theory: that the *direction* of specific support is shaped by the direction of diffuse support. Table 4–6 reports the level of net specific support by type of diffuse support. In every case, the existence of favorable diffuse attitudes significantly increases the favorableness of specific attitudes.

Table 4–6
The Effects of Diffuse Support on Net Specific Support for Three Public Institutions

	Supportive	*Not Sure*	*Not Supportive*
President	+35%*	+ 5%	+13%
State governors	+ 9	−26	−40
Supreme Court	−10	−17	−42

*The entry in the "Net Specific Support" defined as Net Specific Support % = % Favorable Only − % Unfavorable Only. A positive sign (+) means that a greater proportion of positive responses than negative ones were made. A negative sign (−) means the opposite.

The data for the Supreme Court also provide a confirmation of a third proposition about the relationship of specific to diffuse support: specific support can exist in contradiction to diffuse support. Citizens may have positive attitudes at the diffuse level and negative ones at the specific level. Table 4–6 shows that the citizens with positive diffuse support are much more favorable at the specific level than those with negative diffuse support, a confirmation of the second proposition above. But in the case of the Supreme Court, the absolute level of specific support is negative in all situations. In other words, the individuals with positive diffuse support were not as critical of the court as were those with negative diffuse support. Thus one has an average level of positive diffuse support existing with an average level of negative specific support.

Murphey and Tanenhaus (1968) have theorized this relationship to be a common one where the court is concerned. As an institution, its role is to examine and sometimes change long-standing rules in the society. The Warren Court is most noted for its profound impact on the rules affecting the civil rights of individuals. Although the civil rights decisions were not generally popular (negative specific support), Murphey and Tannenhaus argue that positive levels of diffuse support help the enforcement of these controversial decisions. The relationship is nicely illustrated by a reported comment of a white Southerner given in response to a question about civil rights decisions, "I don't like what the Court is doing with all this civil rights stuff, but if the Supreme Court says I gotta send my kids to school with colored people, I guess I gotta do it." At the specific level, the respondent opposed the decision, yet he accepted the decision because of his overriding positive feeling about the Court in general.

Across time, one can expect to see these relationships between diffuse and specific supportive attitudes. A decline in specific support will precede a decline in diffuse support. Changes in specific support will be greater and subject to more extreme reversals. This pattern is simply a reflection of current events affecting specific attitudes. Although diffuse attitudes will be more favorable, periods of unusually unfavorable specific support will diminish the degree of favorable diffuse support. It is extremely unlikely, however, to find diffuse attitudes as unfavorable as specific ones.

The Watergate period has provided some valuable data confirming the relationship between diffuse and specific support. During President Nixon's second term, the American Institute of Public Opinion (Gallup Poll) reported a number of questions at critical occasions that provide an overview of opinion trends. Among the many questions asked by the Gallup organization, two are especially relevant. One question of the form: "Do you approve or disapprove of the way Nixon is handling his job as president?" (Approve, Disapprove, No Opinion) has been asked since the Truman administration. It represents a reasonable measurement of specific support, since it elicits evaluations of the incumbent as president. The measurement of diffuse support is more difficult, since ideally the incumbent should not be tied to the office. Gallup used two questions about impeachment, which approximate the concept of diffuse support. For the period June, 1973, to February, 1974, the question: "Just from the way you feel now, do you think his (Nixon's) actions are serious enough to warrant his being removed from the presidency, or not? (Yes, No, No Opinion)" was used without explanation. Most polls of the period suggest that the public did not understand the technical term "impeachment" and equated this process with tampering with the presidency. Subsequently, Gallup began to give explanations of the term and to use the question: "Do you think President Nixon should be impeached and compelled to leave the presidency, or not? (Yes, No, No Opinion)." In any event, both forms of the question raised a more fundamental issue about altering long standing practice (a president serving out his elected term) and therefore "get at" more basic feelings about the institution. A "no" response would indicate that the respondent was cautious.

Figure 4–2 shows the trends in these three questions from June, 1973, to August, 1974, when Nixon resigned. We can see first that the impeachment questions always brought a more favorable response than the performance question. Responses to the job performance question not only were consistently more negative but also showed an almost precipitous drop during the summer, of 1973; they then leveled out to about 25 to 28 percent approval. If one interprets the impeachment question as principally a measure of diffuse support, Figure 4–2 suggests that diffuse support never declined at the rate of specific support nor reached the levels of specific evaluations. By the summer of 1974, one year after the performance question had stabilized, the impeachment question approached, but never reached, the levels of the performance question. As the media explained the meaning of the impeachment process during the 1973–74 period, the response of the public to the impeachment question approached the levels of critical evaluation demonstrated by the performance question. This is another way of saying that impeachment ceased to be interpreted as an attack on the system of government (diffuse referent) and was seen more as a response to an objectional incumbent president (specific referent).

It is important however to note that early in the Watergate controversy, the public's presumption was in favor of Nixon, the president, and especially the presidency as an institution of government. Soon after Ford replaced Nixon, the Gallup Poll asked the performance-in-office question about President Ford. The poll for August, 1974, showed that 71 percent approved of President Ford's handling of his job. There had hardly been time for the president to act, yet the American public's tendency to believe in the presidency had still given him the benefit of the doubt. In other words, had the Watergate period fundamentally tarnished the presidency—that is, significantly reduced favorable diffuse support—then this response would be unexplainable.

Is there a legacy resulting from the negative attitudes toward the presidency fostered by the Watergate affair? No one at the present time can say precisely, but some informed speculation is possible. Those who say "No" will note that the press played an important role in informing the American public about the Watergate evidence and the meaning of the constitutional processes such as the impeachment hearings. Gallup reported that by April, 1973, over 90 percent

Figure 4-2
Trends in Questions Asked by the Gallup Poll During the Watergate Affair

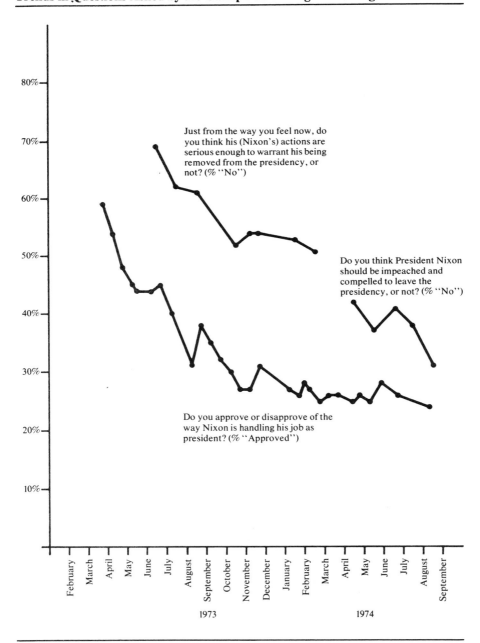

Just from the way you feel now, do you think his (Nixon's) actions are serious enough to warrant his being removed from the presidency, or not? (% "No")

Do you think President Nixon should be impeached and compelled to leave the presidency, or not? (% "No")

Do you approve or disapprove of the way Nixon is handling his job as president? (% "Approved")

Source: The Gallup Poll Index (selected monthly reports).

of all national samples were aware of Watergate. Thus, what Gallup's impeachment question measured changed, especially after the term was explained to the respondent (April, 1974, and afterward). In the beginning, the question tapped latent feelings about tampering but later, as the public came to understand the term, the question measured more specific issue content about Nixon's involvement. If this argument is correct, the decline in diffuse support was never as great as suggested by Figure 4–2. If diffuse support was as low as reported, then President Ford's popularity (71 percent approval) would be higher than diffuse support.

Those who say "Yes" will note that President Ford's approval rate entering office was the lowest of any president beginning his term. The highest levels of approval measured by Gallup for previous presidents were: Truman (87 percent), Roosevelt (84 percent), Kennedy (83 percent), Johnson (80 percent), Eisenhower (79 percent), and Nixon (68 percent). By October, Ford's approval rate had dropped to 52 percent, almost 20 percentage points. Thus, Ford's popularity, somewhat inflated because of the extremely low ratings of Nixon's administration, dropped precipitously.

There are many other implications of Watergate that we have not considered here. We only have examined the relationship of diffuse and specific support during the Watergate period and found our theoretical expectations confirmed. Specific support did plummet to a near-record low level, and there is some evidence that diffuse support declined more slowly. To judge the persistence of these effects, though, will require that we place some distance between this period and ourselves.

Citizens' Perceptions of Governmental Power

The relationship of a citizen to any government involves the potential exercise of power. Public institutions are distinguished from other institutions by the fact that they may legitimately exercise the ultimate sanctions against individuals who defy governmental policies. The political theorist David Easton defines government as institutions that "authoritatively allocate values" (1953). In other words, public institutions can make binding decisions about values (what people desire) and determine who gains and who loses. Governments can legally take or redistribute property or even life in ways that private institutions cannot.

The relationship of individual citizens to this exercise of public power is important. Power is not exercised without conditions or restrictions in this culture. In theory the people determine the legitimate exercise of public power. They delegate their authority through elected representatives and act as an overseer of the public sector. Such notions imply a behavioral role for individual citizens with respect to governmental actions. At a practical level, one can ask to what extent citizens perceive the exercise of public power over their day-to-day lives. Do they see important variations in the magnitude of public authority?

More importantly, do they believe the perceived exercise of power is desirable? The issue here is what people *believe* about the use of public power, not what the government actually does.

The subjective beliefs of citizens are as real as any actual consequences of public action. Many political scientists believe that feelings of powerlessness by individuals about what government does to and for them greatly affects levels of political support and degrees of active involvement (cf. Finifter, 1970; Aberbach and Walker, 1970). Theorists such as Almond and Verba (1963) believe that high levels of political alienation among the citizenry are incompatible with democratic government.

To measure how citizens perceived their relationship generally to the exercise of public power, four questions were administered to the national sample of the form: "[Institution] has the power to get almost anyone to do what he [it] wants them to." Perceptions of power exercised were measured for the president, the governor of the state, the Supreme Court in Washington, and a United States senator. One can expect a question in this extreme form to evoke a high rate of disagreement; thus, the percentage of the sample agreeing with the statement would indicate a pronounced feeling of powerlessness with respect to the exercise of governmental power.

A majority of respondents, in fact, disagreed with the statements in most cases, but two of the institutions—the Supreme Court and the president—are perceived as having substantially more power over individuals than either state governors or U.S. senators. Comparing the Supreme Court to the presidency, one finds that the Court is perceived as exercising slightly *more* power than even the president. The net percentage of perceived power (Net percent = percent Agree − percent Disagree) is the president (− 17 percent), state governors (− 43 percent), the Supreme Court (− 9 percent), and United States senators (− 49 percent). The perceptions of the public are in marked contrast to the views expressed in the writings of scholarly journals. For them, the presidency since the Roosevelt New Deal has grown in power and influence to the point that it overshadows the other two branches of government. One argument maintains that the executive power is the only means of responding forcefully and opportunely to public needs. The typical citizen, however, does perceive the president as powerful relative to others, but executives at the state level (governors) are thought to be as powerless as the senators. The Court has a special role in the public eye, which can better be understand by further investigation.

Perceptions of public power are strongly shaped by the degree to which citizens find governmental activity salient. As awareness of governmental activity increases, the level of perceived power decreases (see Figure 4–3). This pattern holds for all four institutions but is most pronounced for state governors and U.S. senators. The pattern in Figure 4–3 suggests that respondents with low levels of information and education, characteristics associated with low levels of institutional saliency, attribute greater amounts of power to public institutions, whereas citizens at the other end of the saliency index are much more likely to disagree with the assertions of the power questions. In part, this relationship

Figure 4-3
The Effects of Institutional Saliency on Perceptions of Governmental Power

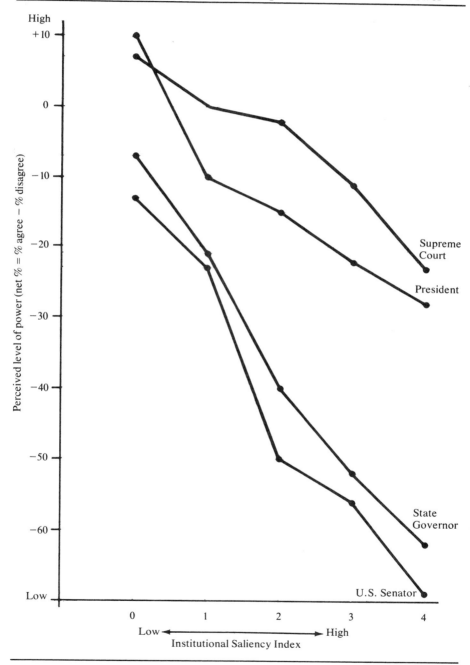

may simply reflect differing degrees of experience with government. People with high saliency may also know of ways to influence and direct governmental agencies toward their personal needs. One important finding of the Almond and Verba study (1963) was that middle- and upper-status people believed they could influence government if they chose to.

At this point, the concern is to determine how attitudes toward political power shape a citizen's evaluations of day-to-day governmental activity. Sigel (1966) and Sigel and Butler (1964) examined the attitudes of Americans toward the power of the presidency—especially as it related to the restrictions of a president seeking a third term in office. They found that most citizens were ambivalent in their evaluations of presidential power. Although a strong president was desirable, most Americans responded in a manner suggesting a fear of too much power.

Table 4–7 reflects some of these same themes. It summarizes the net level of favorable or unfavorable evaluations (specific support) to institutional activity based on perceived levels of power. A respondent who disagreed with the power statement may be seen as one who rejects the idea that the governmental institution has near unlimited power. In all cases, the individuals who rejected this notion were also more favorable in their evaluations of government than those respondents who accepted a view of unlimited power. In the case of the president, the respondents who agreed to the power question had a net evaluation score of +35 percent; the respondents who disagreed to the power question had a net score of +50 percent. Thus, Sigel's thesis that Americans prefer restricted power and feel uncomfortable with the idea of unlimited, even though benevolent, power is substantially confirmed here.

Popular Commitments to Grass-roots Democracy

The multiple levels of government common to the federal system pose interesting questions regarding the exercise of governmental power on individual

Table 4–7
The Effects of Perceived Power on Attitudes toward Specific Governmental Performance

[Institution] has the power to get almost anyone to do what he [it] wants them to.	*Agree*	*Not Sure*	*Disagree*
President	35%*	33%	50%
State governor	−27	0	−14
Supreme Court	−66	−58	−46
U.S. senator	88	91	87

*The percentage is the net level of specific evaluations of governmental actions. A positive score means a net favorable attitude; a negative score, a net unfavorable attitude. The format for the U.S. senator's question differs from the other three institutions. See chapters 5 through 7.

citizens: Which government do citizens perceive as affecting their lives most? What governmental actions are most readily perceived? To better understand how people understood the impact of governmental power on their day-to-day lives, each respondent was asked the question:

> Which level of government do you think has the *greatest* effect on your day-to-day life—the government in Washington, your state government in [name of respondent's state], or local government around here?

If the respondent answered the question, an open-ended queston was asked to determine how the respondent perceived governmental effect. The concept "effect" is an attempt to translate the idea of the consequences of governmental power into common terms. The responses to this series of questions provide some important insights about how citizens view public authorities.

Even though respondents reported that they followed local government as closely as national government, 41 percent perceived the government in Washington as having the most effect on their individual lives. An equal proportion (23 percent) of respondents viewed state or local governments as having the greatest effect, and 14 percent of the national sample could not decide or could not differentiate the effects of various levels of government.

The degree of institutional saliency greatly changes the world view of citizens toward government. One finds citizens being aware of the power of different governments, depending on their salience levels. As saliency of institutional activity increases, attention paid to the effects of the federal government increases and the rates of "don't know" and "all the same" responses decrease. Between 40 and 50 percent of the sample selected state and local government as having the greatest effect, regardless of the level of the respondent's degree of institutional saliency, but the perceived effectiveness of national government increases with higher saliency. One can describe the "high" salience respondents as having the same proportion of respondents perceiving state and local impacts on their lives, but a greater proportion of respondents oriented toward the effects of the federal government. Respondents at the "low" end have about an equal proportion of people oriented toward state and local effects, but a large proportion of respondents also are uncertain about how the public sector affects their lives. In sum, low salience implies perceptions of governmental effects from more localized government, whereas higher saliency implies a broader view of governmental impact with emphasis at the national level.

The specific comments made by the respondents to the open-ended questions further demonstrated how the choice of government having the most effect also implied a different awareness of what government is and does. The responses to the question about why a respondent selected a certain level of government covered a broad range, but three dominant themes reflecting answers to the implicit question "What does government do?" emerged. These three types of response content can be summarized as follows:

Emphasis on control: Respondents mentioned the power of government to control people and other governments through the application of the law, regulations, and force.

Policy-oriented: Respondents mentioned specific programs and activities of government having impact on their lives—for example, social security, taxes, and education.

Style of government: Respondents mentioned how government was close and accessible; familiar and understandable; and associated with them and their families in a personal way.

Comparing these three types of responses in many ways is equivalent to comparing apples, nuts, and peas. The responses emphasizing control are more abstract, suggesting a civics-book explanation of how government works. Statements such as "Governments made laws and can put people in jail" characterize the tone and emphasis of the individuals who are classified as giving "control" responses. These respondents used words such as "size" and "big" as synonyms for "power" and "force." One interesting variation occurred in references to the objects of governmental control. For many respondents, especially those who saw the national level as having the greatest impact, control was exercised over other governments as much as over individual citizens. Nevertheless, most respondents viewing government in this manner saw individual citizens as the objects of the exercise of governmental power.

One-half of the respondents who gave policy-oriented comments talked about taxes. Respondents who saw the state level as most effective were twice as likely to single out this aspect of governmental activity as those selecting other levels. In fact, respondents picking the national level mentioned other kinds of policy matters more often than tax matters by a ratio of 3 to 2.

The style-of-government responses, the third major category characterizing the impact of government, are interesting because they represent an articulation of a central part of the American ethos: the values characterized by grass-roots democracy. Grass-roots democracy is not a political or social philosophy. It is a set of values about what government is and how it should act in relation to its citizens. The people interviewed in the survey did not quote Andrew Jackson, Thomas Jefferson, or Abraham Lincoln directly, but they captured the sentiment of these Americans and others like them who have sought to characterize the American desire for government responsive to its citizens. For these respondents governmental effects were not in terms of "laws," "power," "size," "taxes," or "policy." They were "closeness," "familiarity," and "personableness." Respondents mentioned how they could call up their city councilmen or go down to the courthouse, if the need arose. They spoke of governmental impact on themselves in personal, almost emotional, terms and of effects on their families and other loved ones. No one interviewed spoke of the national government in such intimate terms; style-of-government responses were confined to local and state governments.

The selection of a specific level of government as "having the greatest effect" on one's day-to-day life implies a distinct view of governmental activity. Those choosing the "national" government were most oriented toward specific policies and programs or the power and influence of the federal government. These respondents were equally divided between policy-oriented (51 percent) and control (49 percent) responses. They did not see government in terms of its style or relationship to its citizens. Respondents selecting the state government as having the most effect were as policy-oriented (48 percent) as national respondents. State government was not perceived in such powerful terms, though (23 percent). About one-quarter (21 percent) spoke of the "closeness" and "style" associated with state government. The respondents oriented toward local government were most impressed by its closeness and accessibility (50 percent). For these respondents, specific policies and programs were of lesser importance (34 percent) and the power and control of local governments was almost irrelevant (9 percent). Thus, one finds that citizens ascribe different mixes of attributes to different levels of government. Government becomes important to people for different reasons, only partly because of its programs and services. How government operates and how it treats its citizens also is of substantial importance to them. The contrast may be characterized along a dimension bounded at one end by instrumental goals and the other by moral-philosophical ones. People who see government in instrumental terms evaluate governmental "effects" more in terms of specific policy consequences and the application of force. Those who take a moral-philosophical perspective are more oriented to how government acts, its assessability, and responsiveness to individual petition. Interestingly enough, these distinctions are associated with the two most salient levels of governmental organization—the federal (instrumental) and local (moral-philosophical). Such distinctions add a different perspective to arguments concerning the vitality of local government and the growing strength of the national government. From this instrumental-philosophical perspective, the argument becomes one of which set of political values (instrumental versus philosophical) will be maximized.

The Effects of Social Background on Some Aspects of Political Culture

In the previous sections we have examined several important aspects of political culture—diffuse and specific support, institutional saliency, perceptions of governmental power, beliefs about governmental effectiveness—and the relationship of these psychological states to each other. From this analysis of a representative cross section of citizens, we have gained some insights into the dominant relationships among these psychological predispositions. These predispositions represent conditions associated with the individual (micro-level) which are more or less subject to change, depending on a large and complex set of conditions. One important set of conditions shaping these opinions is the social background conditions of the individual.

Social background characteristics shape many characteristics that make up political culture. Because these background characteristics are relatively fixed, differences in political attitudes and behavior produced by such attributes as education, sex, and race define variations in the American political culture. When a social scientist speaks of background conditions, he is not simply referring to the physical attribute—say, the sex or color of a person. These physical attributes are simply convenient measuring points for a complex set of learned behaviors. For example, a female learns different social roles from a male. The sex of a person simply summarizes, albeit in an approximate sense, different patterns of learning. These variations in social learning are not absolute but relative to the political culture. In traditional societies, women have quite different political roles (social learning) from women in industrial societies. Language differences (French versus Flemish) are an important dimension for defining variation in political attitudes in Belgium, but it is of little importance in the United States (except possibly the Southwest). It is not the language that makes a difference. Certainly, Flemish does not cause a person to be radical or conservative, but people who speak Flemish in Belgium have different socialization experiences from French-speaking Belgians.

When these social characteristics produce large differences in the culture, this separate and distinct part of the general culture may be called a subculture. An important part of the study of political culture is to identify groups of people who share a socially meaningful characteristic that causes them to differ significantly in their political attitudes from other members of the dominant culture. In the United States, blacks are thought to have a distinct political subculture (cf. Matthews and Prothro, 1966). The common social characteristic distinguishing the subculture is a failure of members of the dominant political culture (white) to assimilate black political involvement. In the United States, three social background factors have had a consistently pronounced effect on various forms of political behavior. These factors are sex, race, and formal education. Sex and race effects in a social science context have already been discussed. Education effects can be viewed in a similar fashion. Again, it is not the fact that a person passed or failed a subject but the fact that he was exposed to different experiences that has ramifications for the political culture. Most studies of political culture in the United States show important differences in political attitudes among people who never finished high school, who did finish high school, and who entered a college or university. Other factors, such as religion, region, income, and place of residence also shape attitudes, but these factors appear to be of lesser importance. For this reason, I shall concentrate on how sex, race, and education shape political attitudes except where other conditions prove to be important. Since these three conditions are interrelated in reality, the analysis will show how sex and race each affect attitudes for each level of education. For example, I shall examine the differences between blacks and whites who all have less than a high school education. Thus, one can determine whether race makes a difference when people are alike with respect to education. To complete this analysis, I shall also look at high school graduates and those who went to college.

The reason for this more complex analysis is simple: in everyday life, people operate under combinations of conditions. A person may be male, white, and have never finished high school or may be female and black with a high school diploma. Only the limitations of complexity prevent me from examining all interesting characteristics and all their combinations. Instead, I shall focus on the most significant ones, recognizing as I do that other factors may play a lesser role in any given situation.

Social Background and Diffuse Support

The study of the levels of diffuse support has directed inquiry at related questions: is diffuse support distributed uniformly across various societal groupings or do certain social background conditions affect what kinds of supportive attitudes are formed and how they are maintained? The concern over the social causes of support has placed most emphasis on how people differ from each other under the assumption that support was distributed uniformly across all governmental institutions. Most comparisons have therefore concentrated on the effects of social conditions. The uniformity assumptions—that is, the treatment of diffuse support as consistent across all institution—has hidden some important variations in the levels of support for the different parts of the governmental structure.

Differences from sex and education.   One of the most persistent differences appearing among the findings about support concerns the effects of sex role (Greenstein, 1961; Easton and Dennis, 1965, 1967, 1969; Hess and Torney, 1967). Where diffuse support is concerned, females have much more supportive attitudes toward government than males do. There are two explanations of these differences: one suggests that even as early as the primary grades, girls learn values associated with home, family, and motherhood, whereas boys learn values directed at competition, success, and recognition outside the home. These differences in value learning make young females more trusting than young males. A second form of the explanation places less emphasis on the value-differences and more on their behavioral consequences. Boys, and supposedly men, have sex roles encouraging contact with the world beyond the home. These experiences are thought to temper the unrestrained support of childhood to more realistic levels. Whether or not the outside world does present more realistic experiences about government, it is obvious that it presents different experiences having consequences for feelings of diffuse support.

Research on children also suggests that as children advance through the primary grades, support decreases (Easton and Dennis, 1969; Hess and Torney,

1967). In the second grade, children have unqualified positive feelings toward many public institutions, but by the eighth grade they have moderated these judgments. Easton and Dennis suggest that this trend is normal, since by the eighth grade certain factual information combined with experience have provided a more reality-based notion of what government is and does. In other words, increasing education brings new information that diminishes unrestrained favorable feelings of diffuse support. Since formal education continues into adulthood, one might also infer that the process modifying these initial favorable feelings of diffuse support may continue.

If the overall influences are uniform, then females with lesser education will be the most supportive. These individuals have both background factors reinforcing favorable attitudes toward government. In contrast, college-educated males would be the least supportive, since both factors—sex and education—work to diminish favorable attitudes.

Table 4–8 presents some data to examine in light of these predictions. First, examining the effects of education alone, one finds a decline in favorable supportive attitudes for the private institutions as education increases. This pattern can be seen by comparing males at each level of education and then females. For business and industry, the percentages for males are −19 percent, −32 percent, and −53 percent, indicating an increasingly negative attitude as education increases. Similarly for females, the pattern is −7 percent, −26 percent, and −62 percent.

Table 4–8

The Effects of Sex on Diffuse Support for Selected Institutions, Controlling for Education

	Less than High School		High School		Some College	
	Male	Female	Male	Female	Male	Female
Public Institutions						
President	+42%*	+46%	+26%	+57%	+42%	+41%
State governors	+30	+35	+23	+34	+24	+20
Supreme Court	+15	+27	+ 7	+20	+16	+11
U.S. senators	+18	+33	+21	+22	+21	+12
Local judges	+28	+24	+26	+34	+26	+30
Private Institutions						
Business and industry	−19	− 7	−32	−26	−53	−62
Labor unions	− 4	+ 1	−40	−19	−61	−52

*% Net Diffuse Support = % Agree − % Disagree

For public institutions, the effects of education are not uniform across all institutions. Support for state governors shows only a slight decline as educational levels increase, and the decline in support for the Supreme Court and United States senators is only present for women. The president has a relatively constant level of support across educational categories.

The differences between the sexes are more pronounced though. Women view all institutions with more trust than men do. This generalization requires some qualification, however. The differences in sex diminish as education increases to the point that for respondents with some exposure to college, males are more trusting than females. Education appears to reverse the relationship between the sexes. This effect appears to result as follows. Women with less education are, in fact, more favorably inclined toward government. Increased education appears to modify the views in conformity with the attitudes of males. The data on U.S. senators is one good example of this process. Male respondents are relatively constant across education (18 percent, 21 percent, 21 percent), whereas females show a marked decline to the point where their attitudes are little distinguished from male ones (33 percent, 22 percent, 12 percent). Attitudes toward local judges do not show any of the patterns described above and thus are the exception to the rule.

In summarizing the results, it should be clear that neither sex nor education has the uniform effect predicted. For public institutions, education has little effect, although for private ones it is large. Since income and occupation are also closely related to education, this limited education effect is no doubt influenced by these other underlying conditions. Sex is the more important source of difference in diffuse support. There is much here to support the conclusion that men and women view government in the abstract differently.

Differences from race and education.   The color of one's skin is an expedient means for classifying the differences in life experiences encountered by two classes of people. Generally speaking, race differences are the effects resulting from a two-class society where opportunity, recognition, and privilege are awarded by color. One dominant thesis in the social science literature suggests that a class denied the benefits the other receives will be less supportive of political institutions (cf. Aberbach and Walker, 1970, 1973). In a comparison of institutional support by race one would expect whites to be more supportive than blacks in all cases. This hypothesis is simply a variation of the uniformity notion discussed earlier—namely, that differences in support between blacks and whites are uniform across institutions. Education plays the same role as described earlier. One can predict, then, that whites without a high school education will be most supportive and blacks with some college exposure will be least supportive.

Table 4–9 is similar in structure to Table 4–8. It summarizes the effects of race on diffuse support when educational levels are controlled. The same general education effects reported earlier are present again in Table 4–9—namely, private institutions show a marked decline in support with increased education and state governors show a similar but lesser trend.

Table 4–9 also reveals that among black respondents, support for the president, Supreme Court, U.S. senators, and local judges declines with increased education. White perceptions of these four institutions remain relatively constant across education levels.

Table 4-9
The Effects of Race on Diffuse Support for Selected Institutions, Controlling for Education

	Less than High School		High School		Some College	
	White	Black	White	Black	White	Black
Public Institutions						
President	+45%*	+41%	+46%	+21%	+42%	+25%
State governors	+32	+32	+29	+29	+24	−11
Supreme Court	+14	+50	+13	+35	+15	+10
U.S. senators	+23	+36	+22	+15	+19	−12
Local judges	+29	+10	+32	+ 3	+29	− 3
Private Institutions						
Business and industry	−18	+ 8	−29	−28	−57	−34
Labor unions	− 4	+12	−30	− 3	−58	−36

*% Net Diffuse Support = % Agree − % Disagree.

There are no uniform differences in how the blacks and whites view public institutions, but they are present for private ones. In this case, the differences are precisely opposite the predictions. Blacks view both business and labor more favorably than whites do, and these differences are present regardless of educational level.

The public sector presents a more complex pattern. The president and state governors produce one distinct pattern. There is little difference between the races in evaluation of these two institutions among respondents without a high school diploma. As education increases, however, blacks express many more unfavorable attitudes than whites do. Thus, college-educated respondents show important differences and black respondents are most negative about their feelings toward the president and state governors. To a lesser extent this pattern is also evident for U.S. senators.

The Supreme Court presents a marked and interesting contrast. Blacks are much more favorable toward the Court, especially those with lesser educations. Differences in the races diminish, though, as education increases. Interestingly enough, local judges are not viewed similarly. At all levels of education, whites are more positive about these officials than blacks. Undoubtedly, the pattern for the Supreme Court is a result of its role in civil rights activism. Chapter 6 will explore some of these effects in detail.

The effects of other social characteristics. Several other characteristics important to political behavior were examined for their effects on diffuse support. The income of a household was expected to show a relationship of increasing support with increasing income. In this instance, "household income" may be thought of as a measure of the extent to which the respondent shares in the benefits and success of society. No consistent pattern of relationship exists, however, between level of household income and diffuse support. Low income respondents were most supportive in some cases and least so in others.

The religious affiliation of a respondent had some effect on support. Catholics were more supportive of public institutions than either Protestants or Jews, but Protestants were more supportive of private institutions than either Catholics or Jews. Finally, certain characteristics of the respondents' childhood background were examined, since the family is one of the major socializing agents for political learning. Respondents were asked about the degree of political interest among their parents. It was hypothesized that respondents from families with two politically interested parents would be less supportive than those coming from less politically involved families. This hypothesis is a variation of the "education" hypothesis reported earlier: increased exposure from politically interested parents causes a decline in support. No such family effect was found. This finding was not completely unexpected, since the respondents were adults reporting about a familial situation that has ceased to affect their lives directly. One might expect such family-related effects to occur among children still residing with their parents.

Two dominant themes emerge from this analysis of social background characteristics. First, the hypothesis that diffuse support is a response to government dependent on the benefits received of society has not been borne out by the data. If one measures the degree of group benefits by either race or income, one finds that neither social characteristic consistently divides Americans into supportive (the "haves") and unsupportive ("have nots") factions. In fact, the data on race-related differences suggest the opposite effect. Blacks are more supportive of the system than whites in certain cases (cf. Lehnen and Koch, 1974). Second, the "exposure" hypothesis that support declines with increased political awareness is generally confirmed. The findings on sex and education both suggest that the group with more political experience is less supportive.

Recent comments by two English political scientists suggest that declining diffuse support is not necessarily an alarming situation. In response to an article by Jack Dennis and others on support for government by English schoolchildren (1971), A. H. Birch (1971) and Ian Budge (1971) each comment that these lower levels of support can be seen as reflecting realistic expectations about government. They note that American public education contains strong, ideologically based learning designed to instill feelings of strong allegiance, a situation not frequently encountered in the English school system. Yet English democracy has not suffered from internal political chaos.

From these comments it is clear that differences in diffuse support among social groupings may not necessarily lead to political upheaval. Although such variations in support may not always affect the stability of the political system, these differences in support can affect the range and mode of more conventional political participation. The kinds of demands and supports made on the system will be shaped by these underlying attitudes. Though less dramatic, the process by which citizens routinely interact with their government is critical to the overall political process. It would be a mistake to minimize the importance of these effects simply because political violence was not likely to occur or governments were not toppled.

Social Background and Perceptions of Power and Effectiveness

The education, sex, and race of the respondent also had an important influence in how a citizen perceived the power of an institution over his day-to-day life. In an earlier research study Finifter (1970) found that perceptions of governmental control were greatly affected by education. As education increased, the feeling of powerlessness decreased. This pattern suggests a political reality—people with more education have more resources to confront government and obtain goods and services from it. If obtaining goods and services is seen as a measure of power, then more highly educated people are, in fact, more powerful in a relative sense, and their perceptions simply conform with their experiences. Using this same line of argument, one can infer that men will perceive government as having less control over their lives than women will. Similarly, whites will feel more powerful than blacks.

In an analysis of the combined effects of sex and education on perceptions of power, females with less than high school educations will be most likely to acknowledge great power over their lives. At the other extreme, males with some college education will perceive the least power. Table 4–10 confirms these expectations. It reports a Perceived Power Index for seven institutions. A score of "+100 percent" means that every respondent disagreed to the power question; "−100 percent" means that every respondent disagreed to that power question; and "0 percent" means that an equal proportion of respondents "agreed" and "disagreed."

Table 4–10
The Effects of Sex on Perceptions of Power in Seven Institutions, Controlling for Education

	Less than High School		High School		Some College	
	Male	*Female*	*Male*	*Female*	*Male*	*Female*
Public Institutions						
President	− 2%*	+ 1%	−33%	−18%	−28%	−27%
State governors	−22	−13	−60	−38	−66	−58
Supreme Court	0	+11	−14	0	−39	−20
U.S. senators	−39	−17	−59	−44	−58	−67
Local judges	−25	−35	−59	−47	−67	−59
Private Institutions						
Business and industry	−11	−10	−30	−18	−38	−26
Labor unions	−26	− 4	−33	−16	−40	−14

*The perceived power in the body of the table represents net percentage levels of agreement or disagreement to the question, "[Institution] has the power to get almost anyone to do what he [it] wants them to." A negative score means more disagreement than agreement.

Table 4–10 contains mostly negative scores because the general tendency for any respondent was to "disagree" to the power questions. There are important variations, however, in the level of disagreement—that is, the degree to which the notion of all encompassing institutional power is rejected. The effects of education are in the direction hypothesized: as education increases, the degree of negative response to the question—"[Institution] has the power to get almost anyone to do what he [it] wants them to"—increases also, indicating a rejection of the "all powerful" assumption contained in the question. Both males and females show this overall effect of education, but distinct differences exist between them. In nearly every case, males show a greater rejection (negative score) than females. Again, the different political roles associated with sex produce different perceptions of institutional power.

The race of the respondent also produced some effects on how public power is perceived. Blacks feel significantly more powerless than whites for any level of education (Table 4–11). In fact, blacks without high school diplomas agree more often than disagree to the assertion that government can get them to do almost anything. The fact that such differences appear for race, even after educational levels have been accounted for, is somewhat at odds with Finifter's findings (1970). She found that race effects on perceptions of powerlessness were relatively small once educational differences were controlled. Table 4–11 supports the argument that race has substantial influence on perceptions, regardless of education, and blacks have a greater sense of powerlessness than whites.

Table 4–11
The Effects of Race on Perceptions of Power in Seven Institutions, Controlling for Education

	Less than High School		High School		Some College	
	White	*Black*	*White*	*Black*	*White*	*Black*
Public Institutions						
President	$-$ 6%*	$+22\%$	-26%	$-$ 9%	-28%	-16%
State governors	-24	$+12$	-49	-31	-64	-45
Supreme Court	$+$ 3	$+18$	$-$ 7	$+$ 4	-32	-13
U.S. senators	-31	-16	-51	-40	-64	-19
Local judges	-34	-16	-53	-45	-65	-39
Private Institutions						
Business and industry	-14	$-$ 7	-24	$-$ 1	-36	$+46$
Labor unions	-19	$+$ 3	-23	-23	-30	-23

*See the note to Table 4–10 for an explanation of the perceived power score.

In an analysis of education, sex and race on how respondents perceived the impact of various levels of government on their day-to-day lives,[3] these three background conditions played an important role in shaping perceptions. More males than females are likely to believe the national government has the greatest effect, and this difference increases as education increases. Women are more likely to see state and especially local governments as most effective, and their perceptions are not substantially changed by educational differences. These differences are the consequence of the tendency for women to be closer to the home and concerned about many locally produced services such as education, sanitation, and law enforcement. Race more than education also influences how people judge government. For each level of education, whites are more nationally oriented than blacks, whereas blacks focus more on local government. Education does not increase or decrease feelings about which level of government has the greatest impact in any systematic way, and thus does not play as important a role in shaping these perceptions as either sex or race.

Some Summary Observations

Chapter 4 has explored how Americans view their governmental structure in an abstract and generalized sense. It has provided a general mapping of some key components of the American political culture that shape how the public perceives and interacts with its public officials. One important contribution that Americans give their public institutions is relatively favorable levels of diffuse support. Few citizens are without well-developed notions of support, and between one-third and one-half of all citizens have favorable levels of diffuse support that are almost immune from the day-to-day events of governmental officials. These citizens are relatively inattentive to daily governmental activities. Many other citizens have both well-developed and favorable specific ideas about institutions and reasonably well-grounded ideas about what public officials do. This latter group is an example of the attentive public who monitors the actions of government. The Watergate period showed how quickly a public reacted to the specific actions of a potentially malevolent president. During the Watergate period, many more people, who normally paid little attention to politics, became aware of governmental activity. Yet such events apparently did not influence the overall faith that people held in the system. No doubt this faith was partially unshaken because of large numbers of inattentive citizens.

Favorable levels of diffuse support have both good and bad implications. When political leaders are responsive and work in a democratic way, such levels of diffuse support can help shape specific evaluations toward their actions in a favorable direction and thus make governing and consensus building easier. But there is no guarantee that leaders will always be benevolent and adhere to democratic values. Then favorable diffuse support will slow the public's response.

The president, state governors, Supreme Court, and Congress all have sizable attentive publics who monitor the actions of these officials. Although their amount of political information varies, even the least attentive citizen possesses a wide range of knowledge about his government. Education increases attentiveness and knowledge. It is also evident that different people respond to different institutions and therefore the attentive publics are overlapping. Taken individually, no one public constitutes a majority of citizens, but taken together, the attentive publics compose about four-fifths of all citizens.

Americans have ambivalent views about the exercise of public power on their lives. They perceive the president and Supreme Court as relatively powerful institutions, but as the saliency of governmental activities increases, their belief in the existence of a powerful government declines. It is the uninvolved citizen who most thinks that government is powerful. The national and state governments are thought to have the most effect on people's lives, but if "effect" is conceived of as "force" and "law," then it is clearly the federal government that holds the pre-eminent position.

The ambivalence toward the exercise of governmental power is present not only in regard to which institutions or which levels exercise it but also in how such action is evaluated. Citizens are more likely to give higher levels of favorable diffuse support to institutions that they perceive to have less power over their lives. Furthermore, Americans express a great degree of interest in local government, not so much because it is forceful but because it meets their expectations about how government ought to be. Local government seems to symbolize the best of classical democracy in practice—what might be called grass roots democracy. Certainly respondents articulated no well-developed philosophy, but the themes of classical democracy are evident in the interview responses.

Americans are reasonably homogeneous regarding these aspects of political culture; nevertheless, important variations determined by sex, race, and education appear. Americans do not seem to be divided uniformly along lines of "haves" versus "have nots" (whites versus blacks and high income versus low income), yet blacks differ from whites in the way they support the system. Blacks are especially supportive of the Supreme Court. Sex differences also play a role: women are somewhat more supportive than men. Overall, the effects of education, sex, and race are not as uniform across institutions as predicted, and therefore require an institution-by-institution review.

Notes

[1]Responses were classified as "agree" (supportive), "disagree" (not supportive), "not sure" (ambivalent), and "no opinion" (not salient).

[2]One caution should be observed. The Institutional Saliency Index constructed here has a national bias, since three of the institutions on which it is based are federal. Nevertheless, conclusions in this paragraph are substantiated by Jennings and Ziegler (1970).

[3]The question is: Which level of government do you think has the *greatest* effect on your day-to-day life—the government in Washington, your state government in (name of state), or local government around here?

Public Views of Chief Executives: Comparisons at the National and State Levels

The concept of specific support was introduced in Chapter 4 to characterize political opinions pertaining to specific actions of authorities—individuals who hold positions in an institutional structure. Specific support is a barometer of public expectations and reactions to continuing policies. It is based on perceptions and misperceptions of the activities of political incumbents. A presidential news conference, a speech at a minister's breakfast, a ceremonial dedication, and an analysis in the local newspaper provide grist for the mill. From these communications and many more—private conversations, rumor, hearsay—citizens form attitudes comprising specific support for political authorities. In Chapter 4 only the presence or absence of this type of attitude was examined. Specific support was found not to be as generalized as diffuse support. In other words, many citizens do not have salient specific attitudes. They do not possess well-formed judgments regarding the political activity of elites.

The next sections will examine the content of the opinions expressed toward chief executives in the national and state governments. The president and state governors will be the basis for comparison. The chapter is organized around three basic themes. First, what is the content of the judgments formed about chief executives? Does it vary from level to level? Second, what are the basic psychological reasons motivating the evaluations of these political leaders? Finally, what influence does social background have on how people evaluate perceived policy actions of executives?

Public Opinion and Chief Executives: An Overview

There is a certain irony in writing about both state and national chief executives. The presidency is undoubtedly the most visible of American political institutions, at least as far as media coverage is concerned. Yet our knowledge of how the American public relates to it is confined to a few rather well-defined topics. The most heavily researched topic is that of electoral behavior—how and why a candidate becomes president. Over thirty years of systematic polling of the electorate has provided some understanding of the complex reasons shaping the individual choices of millions of voters. Yet our knowledge of how Americans view their president after Inauguration Day and during his tenure is sorely limited. For example, how do presidential activities shape the perceptions of individuals going about their day-to-day business, free from the bustle and clamor of a presidential campaign? How well do presidential activities compete for attention with television, movies, baseball scores, children, and household affairs? What are the sources of positive and negative evaluations made about incumbent presidents arising from their behavior in office? Do people like the president because he proposes legislation or because he has charisma? What is more salient to the average citizen—pocket-book issues, foreign policy decisions, or what?

Recent analyses of Gallup Poll information, compiled for the administrations of Harry Truman through Lyndon Johnson, provide a broad picture of the trends shaping the public's evaluation of presidents (Mueller, 1970, 1971, 1973). According to these findings, every president, with the exception of Dwight Eisenhower, has suffered a general decline in popularity from Inauguration Day onward. The general loss of support is caused by a coalition of minorities, each of which becomes increasingly opposed to the incumbent president as he takes actions against its interests. The expectations generated by the election campaign are not fulfilled, giving rise to increasing disaffection among various groups of citizens with special interests. This downward trend is accelerated in times of increased unemployment or prolonged war. Full employment and a healthy economy do not usually improve a president's rating. The one kind of event giving a president momentary upsurges in popularity is a sudden crisis, international in nature, which involves the United States and the president directly. Otherwise, it is downhill after Inauguration Day. A president wanting to leave office a popular man must do one of two things: be Dwight Eisenhower or resign the day after his inauguration.

This long-term analysis, though providing a valuable perspective, tells us little about the content of specific policy actions perceived by the public or about the relative evaluations attached to these actions. We know that presidents lose popularity but we do not know why. Clearly, unemployment lowers ratings and crises help increase them temporarily. Although we know minorities become disaffected and coalesce against an incumbent, our present state of research tells us nothing about the specific sources of dissatisfaction or which minorities are most affected. On what basis is a minority formed—race, status, education, region, or ideology?

Part of the difficulty in interpreting trends in public attitudes arises from the different types of policy events associated with the presidency. The first kind, called *cumulative* (Deutsch and Merritt, 1965), are continuing, interconnected actions occurring over a relatively long time—say, four years or more. Individual actions of a cumulative policy are generally indistinguishable. For example, the debate over a program of national health care has continued for well over twenty years. Legislative bills and presidential proposals are but episodes in the persisting health drama. Continuity and "historical baggage" are the key characteristics of cumulative policy events.

A second kind of policy event is the *spectacular* one. It is, as the name implies, a set of occurrences that is dramatic and well defined. In contrast to cumulative events, the duration of spectacular events is short. The Vietnam War represented a cumulative event for Lyndon Johnson. His day-to-day actions were episodes in the continuing sequence. But news that the North Vietnamese had attacked United States naval vessels in the Gulf of Tonkin represented a spectacular event, for it was a well-defined, sudden, and dramatic international occurrence directly involving the president as commander-in-chief. It stood as an issue in itself, presenting new, clearly focused questions about American foreign and military policy.

Political leaders are known for their ability to shape events, but in practice, they rarely have much power over the course of cumulative policy events. Their efforts can, at best, redirect the course of policy or shift the emphasis, but they cannot reverse the course. Executives can, however, shape spectacular events, especially in the international sphere. In this area, the president has great powers and few constraints. President Nixon's trip to China and the subsequent flood of news about the Chinese is an excellent example of a spectacular policy event.

Spectacular events are occurrences whereby presidents may enhance their popularity. Cumulative events, in contrast, usually detract from a president's popularity. By their very nature, sides have been formed and new proposals are treated in the context of the ongoing dispute. Thus, a president "takes sides" even if he does not intend to, and consequently, he causes increasing disaffection among opponents. Even the decision to do nothing is doing something that favors one side and not another.

Since governors do not have foreign policy issues and international crises to stimulate favorable public reactions, the essential conditions characterizing public attitudes at the state level are those associated with cumulative policy issues. The basic themes characterizing how citizens evaluate the role of governors in state and national politics can be summarized by three words: visibility, vulnerability, and taxes. State governors hold a highly visible position in the American political structure. As chief executives of populous and politically diverse constituencies, state governors can play prominent roles in national as well as state affairs (Beyle and Williams, 1972). A decisive victory at the ballot box or an imaginative approach to a major policy problem often brings national attention to a governor. Speculation about his possible presidential aspirations, usually from unidentified sources, appears in the press, and supporters organize favorite son movements and raise contributions.

Although governors may command a national reputation, several observers of state politics believe that they are becoming more vulnerable. Clotfelter and Hamilton (1972) suggest that governors face many of the same problems as the president in maintaining high specific support—in particular, they too face the coalition of minorities problem. Because of the diversity of state constituencies, the visibility of the office of governor, and the complexity of policy disputes, an incumbent governor is likely to alienate majority support on any single issue (Clotfelter and Hamilton, 1972; Harris, 1959). In this situation, it is easier to elect a relatively unknown and untried challenger than to re-elect an incumbent. Schlesinger (1960, 1970) has analyzed gubernatorial career patterns since the turn of the century, and he concludes that governors now find it increasingly difficult to become presidential candidates. The increasing complexity of state politics and the competition for office have limited these potential presidential candidates to careers at the state level. Turett (1971), however, argues that governors are not notedly more hampered in attaining electoral success today than they were around 1900, if one looks at the size of electoral victories. He finds that winning margins at the ballot box are not significantly narrower today than during an earlier period; hence, gubernatorial contests are not more competitive.

One key issue cited by most analysts of statehouse politics as contributing to the vulnerability of the governor is the problem of escalating demands for public services coupled with mounting pressures for reduced taxes (Beyle and Williams, 1972). Most writers, indeed, stress the importance of a governor's tax policy as a key determinant of his success, though they do so with suprisingly little systematic evidence to prove or disprove the tax hypothesis. One exception is Epstein's (1964) study of the 1962 Wisconsin gubernatorial election. He reports that one quarter of the Wisconsin voters identified the state sales tax issue (namely, whether or not to adopt one) as the most important reason for their vote decision. But Epstein also finds considerable misperception by voters as regards which political party supported what tax policy. General confusion concerning which party was responsible for various taxing policies, combined with party voting, reduced the overall impact of this important issue; nevertheless, the tax issue proved to be a substantial contributing factor in the close election.

Pomper (1968), using data on the aggregate level of tax increases from several states, finds a weak relationship between the nature and magnitude of tax and spending decisions and subsequent electoral success of incumbents. He concludes that single issues, even one as important as taxes, do not decide electoral contests, but that tax policy can play a decisive role in electoral results.

In summary, state governors enjoy a highly visible political life, but this visibility makes them vulnerable to competing and conflicting political demands. As decisions are made, individual factions are alienated, making the possibility of re-election or movement to higher political office more difficult. The major issue governors face in common is the problem of taxes: demands for lower taxes and less government spending without a corresponding reduction in the expectations for public services.

The Salience of Executive Activities

It is common knowledge that the president is the most perceived political figure in America. Studies devoted to explaining what and how children learn political values reveal that the president is one of the first political leaders perceived by children (Easton and Dennis, 1965). Adults show similar augmented awareness of the actions of the president. Presidents are regularly nominated as the Gallup Poll's "most respected person," and almost anything a president does, trivial or profound, makes news—whether it is pulling his dog's ears (Lyndon Johnson) or signing major legislation. Governors do not receive the attentions of press and public accorded the president, yet their activities are as visible to the average citizen as are the president's. A comparison of response rates to the questions about perceptions of presidential activity

> Is there anything the president or his assistants have done lately that you (don't like) like? What is that?

and the questions about gubernatorial activity

> Is there anything the governor of (name of respondent's state) has done lately that you (don't like) like? Would you please tell me about that?

presented somewhat of a surprise. Fifty-eight percent of the sample commented on presidential actions, while a slightly greater proportion, 62 percent, had things to say about their state governors. This finding is in marked contrast to the prevailing assumptions about the relative salience of state and national political affairs. This simple fact suggests the pre-eminent position held by the governor in state affairs.

The content of these perceptions is a revealing picture of the differing impact of national and state affairs on the lives of citizens. Tables 5-1 and 5-2 summarize the content, the likes and dislikes expressed by the sample to these open-

Table 5–1

Favorable and Unfavorable Responses to the Policies of the President

	Favorable	Unfavorable	Total	Relative Difference*
Trip to Europe	54%	11%	41%	+43%
	(432)	(39)	(471)	
ABM	13	27	18	−14
	(107)	(97)	(204)	
Vietnam	8	17	11	− 9
	(65)	(61)	(126)	
Taxes and spending	1	17	6	−16
	(5)	(61)	(66)	
Management of office	11	12	11	− 1
	(87)	(44)	(131)	
Other policies	13	17	14	− 4
	(102)	(61)	(163)	
Total	100%	100%	100%	0
	(798)	(363)	(1161)	

*Relative % Difference = % Favorable − % Unfavorable (based on 798 favorable and 363 unfavorable responses).

Table 5–2
Favorable and Unfavorable Responses to the Policies of State Governors

	Favorable	Unfavorable	Total	Relative Difference*
Taxes and spending	15%	59%	40%	−44%
	(79)	(394)	(473)	
Education	13	11	12	+ 2
	(66)	(73)	(139)	
Law and order	25	0	11	+25
	(126)	(0)	(126)	
Welfare and poverty	3	2	3	+ 1
	(15)	(15)	(30)	
Management of office	7	11	9	− 4
	(38)	(71)	(109)	
Other policies	36	17	26	+19
	(186)	(116)	(302)	
Total	100%	100%	100%	0
	(510)	(669)	(1179)	

*See the note to Table 5–1.

ended questions about presidential and gubernatorial activities. Given the format of the questions, these responses represent unprompted responses unsolicited by closed alternatives. The responses show how distinct the degrees of public awareness are to different levels of government.

One cannot avoid noticing the importance of foreign affairs as a focus of public concern pertaining to the presidency and the almost total lack of concern about domestic issues. Only the taxes and spending issue was mentioned with sufficient frequency to warrant listing as a separate category (Table 5–1). At the state level, however, taxes and spending dominate the political picture for most Americans, but other fundamental service issues—education, law and order, and welfare—are mentioned with considerable frequency.

There are particular and well-defined reasons why foreign affairs are so salient to Americans. A spectacular event occurred during the period of the survey which provided an important opportunity to assess the relative visibility of such presidential activity in contrast to cumulative events. Nixon made the first of his many trips abroad to meet and discuss political affairs with foreign leaders. During his first trip abroad, which received considerable attention in the press, the president went to France and had a cordial meeting with Charles de Gaulle, then president of the Fifth Republic. Forty-one percent of the total responses were devoted to comments about this trip. Two other policies—the war in Vietnam and the question of an antiballistic missile (ABM) defense—provoked a surprisingly high rate of comment also. These three policies accounted for about 70 percent of all policy responses. Response to domestic policy, with the exception of taxes and spending comments, was focused on everything from social security to the environment. Finally, the management of office category was a relatively broad group of responses that referred to how the president was conducting the affairs of the White House. It included comments pertaining to such matters as appointments to the Cabinet, his handling of an oil spill off Santa Barbara, and his experience and honesty as an administrator.

Table 5–1 demonstrates the ability of a president to focus public attention to some degree. The trip to Europe clearly is a spectacular event accounting for one-third of all recorded responses. To a much lesser extent the ABM issue has certain characteristics of a spectacular event, since the emphasis of the congressional debate focused on the desirability of building a defense against missile attack. In this sense, the debate took on a spectacular nature, despite the fact that appropriations for aircraft carriers, missiles, and long-range supersonic bombers had been discussed periodically throughout the 1960s. Two other policies—the war in Vietnam and the question of taxes and spending—are more correctly classified as cumulative events. The data from the first Nixon administration show the ability of presidents to center public attention on certain areas—namely, on foreign and defense policy—and away from the myriad of domestic policy issues.

In an absolute sense, the actions of the president are seen in favorable terms by a ratio of two to one (798:363). The favorable/unfavorable response rate is especially high for the presidential trip. Over half of all favorable comment (54 percent) was focused on this one event. A cumulative policy such as taxes and spending, in contrast, showed more negative than positive responses (5:61). Since the number of positive responses is momentarily inflated by the presidential trip, a more stable comparison can be obtained from the relative rates of positive and negative commentary. The relative rates of favorable and unfavorable reaction show that the main source of favorable comment regarding the presidency centered around Nixon's trip to Europe. This single issue had a net favorable difference of 43 percent (see Table 5–1). All other issues, however, show a net unfavorable difference. The areas in which the president received the most critical remarks were taxes and spending (− 16 percent), ABM (− 14 percent), and Vietnam (− 9 percent).

The general thesis concerning the erosion of presidential popularity is not contradicted by the results of Table 5–1. The president gained support as the result of a well-defined, short-term (spectacular) event, whereas he either barely maintained or lost support on the day-to-day (cumulative) policies. One could say that the president was viewed in favorable terms in an absolute sense, but this positive effect was primarily the result of a ceremonial trip to Europe, and not the consequence of ongoing substantive policy decisions, either foreign or domestic. Since it would be difficult for a president to repeatedly orchestrate spectacular events, we can expect the public's attention to return to cumulative policy events. In the face of persistent cumulative events—say a declining economy—spectacular events can have effects of only limited duration. Figure 5–1 shows the trends in President Nixon's popularity from 1969 to 1974. Clearly, spectacular events—many within the control of the president—caused momentary interruptions in his declining popularity. His Vietnam speech and

**Figure 5-1
The Effects of Events on the Public's Evaluation of the Nixon Presidency**

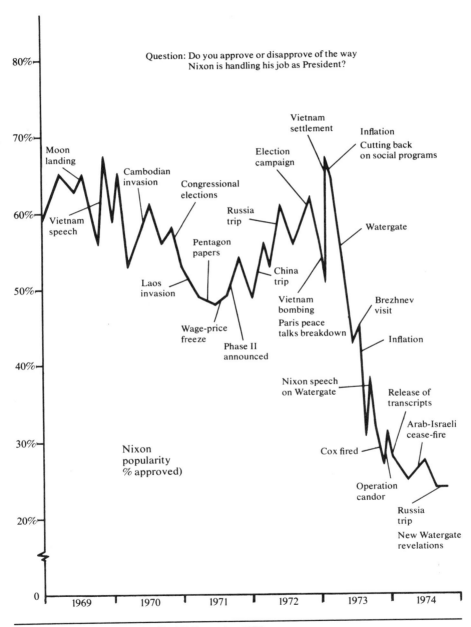

Question: Do you approve or disapprove of the way
Nixon is handling his job as President?

Source: The Gallup Opinion Index No. 111 (September, 1974)

final settlement and the trips to China and Russia boosted popularity. The re-election period of 1972 also caused a turnabout in popularity; but Nixon's first term popularity declined nevertheless as had past presidents', and Watergate prompted a cataclysmic drop during his second term. The period in which data in Table 5–1 were collected (spring, 1969) represents a high point in Nixon's presidential career. It is obvious that his foreign policy was one principal reason for his favorable image.

The responses to the questions about gubernatorial activities (Table 5–2) illustrate some of the reasons why governors are politically vulnerable. Unlike their evaluations of the president, people had more unfavorable comments to make about their governors (favorable/unfavorable: 510/669). Three policies—taxes and spending, education, and law and order—received the most comment. Two-fifths of all responses concerned the tax issue, and most of it was unfavorable. The relative difference on this issue was −44 percent. Education, and especially law and order, tended to enhance the image of governors. The relative differences for these issues were +2 percent and +25 percent respectively. The response to the law and order issue arises from the governor's role as chief law enforcement officer of the state. He has the power to call up the National Guard or assign other authority to maintain the public peace. It is apparent that across the fifty states law and order policies received general public endorsement. Welfare and poverty policies were hardly salient and neither added nor subtracted significantly from gubernatorial popularity. The miscellaneous category "other policies" covered a broad scope of issues ranging from highways, civil rights, and health to issues unique to individual states. In this miscellaneous area state governors fared well (+19 percent) in the eyes of their publics.

In sum, two well-defined policies dominated state politics of this period, one contributing to decline in specific support (taxes and spending), and one producing an increase (law and order). The tax hypothesis—the assertion that the dominant cause of gubernatorial unpopularity is the tax issue—is confirmed in its essential form. But our findings also reveal the potential of alternate issues to offset the depressing influences of tax controversy. In the late 1960s this alternate issue was law and order.

Political Knowledge and Perception of Executives

The general level of political information available to the respondent usually influences his ability to respond to survey questions. Political knowledge can be measured by an index which provides a measure of political information, in the same sense that tests given in elementary schools measure selected verbal and quantitative achievement. There is no more reason to expect any citizen to have basic knowledge or skills pertaining to the political aspects of life than to expect eighth graders to master algebra. The average person has many responsibilities associated with home, work, and leisure time that compete for his attention. What he knows about politics is learned much as everything else is. Thus, a political knowledge index—actually a test of political information—is a useful device for classifying respondents according to their level of accumulated political information or political learning.

Levels of political information[1] are related to the rates of response on spectacular events, but not on cumulative ones. Cumulative events have been around the public scene for a sufficiently long period that variations in political information are not important for determining the rate of response. They have also receded from the public's attention and have been replaced by nonpolitical considerations. Thus cumulative events show low response rates, regardless of the level of the respondent's political knowledge.

Spectacular events, by definition, are new to the political scene. In these circumstances the amount of political information possessed by a citizen determines how quickly and thoroughly the individual will perceive and assimilate a new political occurrence. Spectacular events, therefore, show relatively high rates of response among the informed public and low response rates among the uninformed.

Figure 5–2 provides a pictorial display of the effects of political knowledge on the perception of presidential and gubernatorial activity. The two spectacular events—the European trip and ABM—show a dramatic increase in response rates as the level of political information increases. Although 28 percent of the national sample mentioned something favorable about the trip to Europe, the rate of response varied significantly according to the level of knowledge. Only 16 percent of those with low levels of political knowledge commented favorably about the trip; for those with higher levels, the response rate reached 42 percent. The same pattern—one of increasing response rates in proportion to increasing political knowledge—is present for the other spectacular policy: the ABM defense. Response rates concerning ABM, both favorable and unfavorable, exhibited a decided increase directly attributable to high levels of political information.

The cumulative policies affecting the president—Vietnam and taxes and spending—do not show the marked increase in response rates with increased knowledge that the two spectacular policies exhibit. Both policies have little variance from the sample mean of 4 percent. This lack of relationship between political information and response concerning cumulative events is demonstrated by the nearly horizontal lines in Figure 5–2.

At the state level politics is free from such sudden, emotion-laden crises as those prompted by the international events encountered at the national level. Yet there are policy events at the state level which can be distinguished from ongoing issues. These dramatic events receive more than the usual attention accorded by the press and electorate, and tend to provoke sharp divisions among various decision makers—private and public—regarding the correct course of action. The tax issue, though a recurring one, often falls into this category.

Epstein (1964) found that approximately one-quarter of the voters in the 1962 Wisconsin gubernatorial election identified the tax issue as the single most important incentive for voting. Almost any proposed restructuring of tax policy

Figure 5-2
Political Knowledge and Response to the Policies of Chief Executives

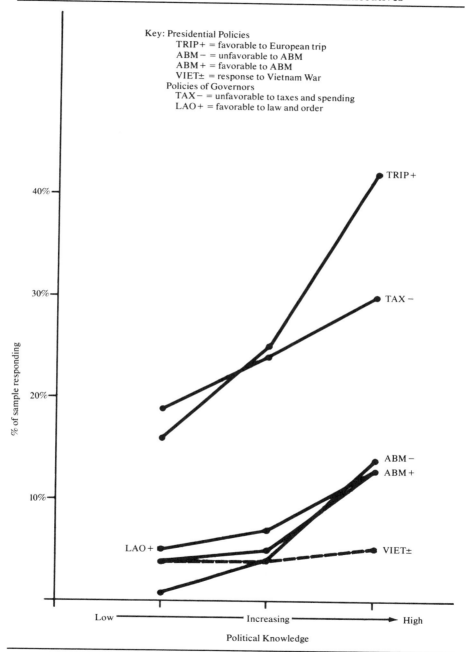

creates immediate public reaction. During the late 1960s another set of events, urban disorders, sensitized many state electorates to the problem of law and order. In many areas, state executives were forced to call up their national guards and take other extreme measures in order to maintain the public peace. These events had a truly dramatic impact on state publics. Even though dramatic state issues can be singled out for analysis, however, cumulative policies are more common at the state level. Education and social services, in particular, present challenges to state administrations that continue beyond the boundaries of any particular administration (cf. Rockefeller, 1973).

Figure 5–2 also illustrates the general effects of increased political knowledge on the rate of response to cumulative and dramatic state events. Individual policies show marked variation. The dramatic nature of the tax issue and, to a lesser extent, the law and order issue, caused a decided increase in unfavorable response about tax information and favorable comment about law and order as political knowledge increased. Education, a less sensational issue, did not vary much with the degree of political information. In addition, Figure 5–2 demonstrates the need to distinguish dramatic policies at the gubernatorial level from spectacular ones at the presidential level. Spectacular events at the presidential level are usually rooted in international affairs and often pose a threat or challenge to the United States or enhance the prestige of the nation. In either case, the public's reaction is generally favorable. At the state level, the international aspect is absent. Dramatic events rooted in domestic issues may produce either positive (law and order) or negative (taxes) effects on public attitudes.

Figure 5–2 also illustrates that regardless of whether a respondent is favorably or unfavorably inclined toward an issue, his level of political information is not a factor determining the direction of his evaluation. For example, the lines for the Vietnam and ABM responses, both positive and negative, are essentially parallel, indicating that the effect of political information is the same, regardless of whether the opinion is favorable or unfavorable.

One cautionary note is in order pertaining to these comments on the ABM issue. Although the ABM topic is the second most discussed policy in the survey, it is not significantly higher than the third (Vietnam), and is mentioned less frequently than the trip to Europe. Yet response patterns to ABM resemble more closely the trip responses, indicating that it is a spectacular event.

Bernard Cohen (1966) has suggested an alternative explanation for these findings, based on a sample of adults in Wisconsin. In his study, he contrasted the knowledge levels of the general public attentive to foreign policy matters with those attentive to the more limited topic of military affairs. The military public tended to have more specific information and more formal education than the general foreign policy public, itself a rather select subset of the general public. Cohen's research suggests that the rate of ABM response may be increased by the characteristics of an attentive military affairs public, as well as by the characteristics of the event (spectacular).

To summarize some important observations, public policy events that involve chief executives differ significantly in scope, duration, and impact. Cumulative events have low salience generally and cost incumbents popularity. Spectacular events are highly salient, especially among the politically knowledgeable, and contribute to presidential popularity, particularly where international affairs are concerned. Conditions partially under the control of a political actor—a spectacular event—and characteristics of the audience (level of political information) both combine to determine the opinion response. If the event is spectacular and the respondent has at least a moderate degree of political information, the saliency of the policy will be much higher. Under all other combinations of these two conditions, the public's level of saliency will be less. There are some practical limitations on the ability of political leaders to create a desired response.

Partisanship and Policy Evaluations

An incumbent president plays important partisan roles, separate from the nonpartisan tradition and ritual prescribed for him. An incumbent president is the head of his party and one of its most influential members. He leads the election campaigns for many state and local candidates. Public evaluations of him, therefore, must be affected both by the prestige of his office and by his role as partisan leader.

Since individual citizens cannot ignore the partisan nature of the president, specific support of presidential activity must be shaped by a citizen's partisan commitments. Supporters of the incumbent will react differently to his administration than will his opponents. One would expect the incumbent's supporters to be more in favor of or less critical of his actions.

Figure 5–3 demonstrates this general pattern. Citizens reporting a vote for Nixon (1968) liked his policies most, followed next by Wallace voters, and lastly by Humphrey voters. This pattern is revealed by the higher rates of favorable response and lower rates of unfavorable response toward all items by Nixon voters. The trip to Europe (Figure 5–3) illustrates the general pattern for individual policy responses. Forty-one percent of the reported Nixon voters expressed favorable comments on this subject, whereas 22 percent of the Wallace voters and 20 percent of the Humphrey voters had favorable comments. The taxes and spending issue exhibits this same pattern with respect to unfavorable response: Nixon voters were the least critical, followed next by Wallace and then by Humphrey voters.

Gains in presidential popularity came mostly from the incumbent's supporters. Nixon voters, compared to Wallace and Humphrey voters, favored the trip to Europe by a ratio of 2:1. Thus it would be misleading to characterize the favorable comments arising from spectacular events as a "gain" in popularity,

Figure 5-3
The Effects of Partisanship on Response to the President's Activities

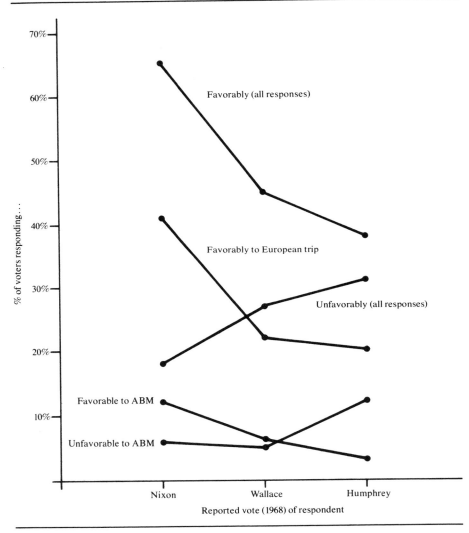

since a large proportion of the responses came from people most likely to vote for Nixon again. It is more correct to label such popularity as "reinforcement" of existing supporters. These patterns of partisan evaluation help explain why presidential popularity is usually downhill. Spectacular events have relatively little impact on the opposing coalition groups.

After the 1968 election the Republican party not only had gained the presidency but it also had made significant advances in contests for state-house positions. Thirty Republicans occupied governor's chairs, many of which were in the largest and most powerful states: New York (Rockefeller), California (Reagan), Illinois (Ogilvie), Michigan (Millikin), Ohio (Rhodes), and Pennsylvania (Shafer). Democrats held twenty governorships, including those in New Jersey (Hughes) and Texas (Smith). At the time of these Republican victories, many in states long controlled by Democrats, the resurgence of Republicanism at the grass-roots was a highly publicized theme. Republican governors would provide evidence to traditionally Democratic voters that there was nothing to fear from a Republican administration. These Republican governors would also supply the impetus for local party organization. The successful application of this theory, however, was dependent on two important factors: how the particular governors were evaluated by partisan voters and the inherent advantage incumbents have over challengers.

Cowart (1973) has analyzed the impact of such partisan evaluations and incumbency advantages in gubernatorial contests. He reports that party identification is an important factor shaping voter choices in these elections. During the period 1964–70, voters with strong Democratic preferences were likely to vote for Democratic gubernatorial candidates over 80 percent of the time. Strong Republican identifiers preferred their party's candidate over 95 percent of the time. Yet split-ticket voting—voting for one party in presidential races and another in other contests—is commonplace in American elections. Clearly, partisan voters do not systematically vote for all of their party's candidates, but the likelihood of this pattern increases as partisan loyalty increases.

For most voters in gubernatorial races, the evaluation of the incumbent is an important force in addition to traditional party loyalties in shaping electoral choice. When a voter likes an incumbent governor of another party as well as his party's presidential candidate, he is most likely to vote against his party's candidate at the state level and for the incumbent. When the voter faces the opposite situation—an attractive presidential candidate of the other party and an incumbent governor from his own party—he will vote for his party at the state level, yet split his ballot at the national level by voting for an opposition candidate. The critical factor is whether the voter views the incumbent governor favorably. If he does, even an appealing opposition presidential candidate will not significantly alter his choice at the state level. Eisenhower's victory in 1956 provides an insightful historical example. Even though his victory margin was one of the most impressive ever, he was not able to "carry the ticket." Eisenhower served his second term with a Democratic congressional majority and many Democratic governors.

The important question, then, centers on why people identifying with political parties like and dislike their governors. To analyze the relationship of voter preferences to partisanship, the governor's party in each state was matched with the respondents' party preferences,[2] thus producing four combinations:

(1) Democratic identifiers in Republican states; (2) Republican identifiers in Republican states; (3) Democratic identifiers in Democratic states; and (4) Republican identifiers in Democratic states. Based on the analysis of partisan evaluations of the president, one would guess that partisans would criticize a governor of the opposition more than one of the same party.

Table 5–3 summarizes the evaluations of state governors on selected policy dimensions by the four partisan combinations. With the tax issue first, the basic pattern anticipated becomes obvious: partisans of the opposition party are more critical than supporters of the party in office. For Republican governors, Democrats are more negative about taxes than Republicans, and for Democratic governors Republicans are more critical. Education policy also produces the same pattern of evaluation.

Table 5–3
The Effects of State Party Identification on Perceptions of Governors' Policies

The respondent is a: The governor is a:	Democrat Republican	Republican Republican	Republican Democrat	Democrat Democrat
Taxes				
% Difference*	−27	−21	−14	−12
Law and Order				
% Favorable	8	16	4	3
Education				
%Difference*	− 3	0	+ 2	+ 4

*" % Difference" is the percentage responding favorably minus the percentage responding unfavorably. A negative score means that more unfavorable comments were expressed than favorable ones.

Another prominent pattern is present in Table 5–3 that demonstrates the difficulties the new Republican governors face: Republican governors are criticized much more heavily on the tax issue than Democrats are, even by members of their own party. Republicans in the study were more unfavorable toward taxing policies of Republican governors than of Democratic ones. Although education policy did not produce quite as dramatic an effect, the same pattern holds. Thus, incumbent Republican governors seeking re-election faced a situation almost certain to produce defeat at the polls.

Why then were so many Republicans elected to chief executive positions in the states? Table 5–3 suggests a possible answer: the law and order issue. In 1968 the effects of this single issue were devastating to Democratic candidates in general and to Hubert Humphrey in particular (Converse et al., 1969). At the state level, Republican governors benefited from their law and order positions more than did Democratic ones. Even Democrats in Republican states were more positive about their governors' policies than were Democrats in Democratic states. Also, Republican voters were more concerned generally about law and order than were Democrats. In sum, the law and order issue was the single most important reason for Republican governors experiencing favorable public reactions. The Republicans "captured" this issue and received short-run benefits from it, yet even this volatile issue could not entirely offset the long-range effects of education and tax problems at the local levels.

Law and order and "crime in the streets" continued to be important issues to Americans as late as 1973, when concerns about the economy and Watergate began to displace them. Harris (1973) reports that only 8 percent mentioned crime and violence as a major problem in 1964. By late 1968, 65 percent mentioned the issue. Similarly, Gallup (Index No. 91) found the following problems reported to the question, "What do you regard as your community's (your city's) worst problem?": crime (13 percent), transportation (11 percent), drugs (8 percent), juvenile delinquency (5 percent), taxes (5 percent), sanitation (5 percent), and unemployment (5 percent). Other problems—education, pollution, race, slums and housing, and welfare—received comment by less than 5 percent of the sample. Crime, drugs, and delinquency are clearly components of the law and order issue (cf. Harris, 1973), suggesting the high salience of this issue in 1969 relative to other issues, such as inflation and unemployment.

By 1972 the Republicans had lost the advantage associated with law and order. Early in the 1972 campaign, pollster Louis Harris asked who could better control crime and law and order. The responses were divided as follows (Harris, 1973):

Democratic Congress	24%
Nixon administration	21
Neither	24
Both equally	18

The respondents were also asked which party could "control crime and law and order" best. The results were Democrats, 26 percent; Republicans, 20 percent; neither, 14 percent; and both equally, 26 percent. As Harris (1973) observes, "The obvious truth was that there simply was not a Republican or Democratic way to enforce the law. . . . Charges such as 'soft on crime' or easy promises 'to get tough' simply did not solve the crime problem. By the early 1970s, such old rallying cries had lost almost all political credibility."

The Role of Long-term Psychological Attitudes on Perceptions of Executives

Reaction to presidential policies is greatly influenced by long-term psychological predispositions. The essential task of any analysis of the role of long-term attitudes in shaping perceptions is to identify the attitudes relevant to these perceptions. These attitudes may or may not be inherently political in nature, but they nevertheless may have an important effect on political perceptions. If a respondent mentioned a need for a guaranteed annual income, one would expect that his views on the proper role of government in providing aid and assistance to its citizens would be a relevant dimension explaining his policy views. Those citizens who feared the increasing role of the federal government most likely would be opposed to government programs supplying a minimum income. From Table 5–2 we find that four topics produced policy-related responses about presidential activity of sufficient focus for analysis: the president's trip to Europe, Vietnam, the ABM issue, and taxes. The first three of these policy areas are related to foreign affairs, and as such, the common roots shaping these three areas of response will be analyzed in the next section. The meaning of the taxes and spending responses, however, will be considered separately in the next section on gubernatorial policies.

Some Long-term Foreign Policy Attitudes

Since the end of World War II, the American public's generalized view toward foreign affairs has tended to be shaped by the Cold War debate. (See Stouffer, 1954; Hero, 1969.) This debate has centered on evaluations of Communist countries and consideration of the proper role of the United States toward them. To a lesser extent, the role of the United States toward other, particularly underdeveloped, countries has also been an issue. Three attitudinal dimensions characterize how Americans are predisposed toward Cold War issues: (1) the nature and degree of perceived Communist threat to the United States and other nations; (2) the desirability of international cooperation in the form of trade and arms agreements, especially with the Communist countries; and (3) the question of whether the United States should provide foreign aid assistance. These three foreign affairs dimensions are significant determinants molding the public's reaction to the president's foreign policies.

Each individual in the sample was measured by means of an index of opinion for the three foreign affairs dimensions: Communist threat, international cooperation, and foreign aid. As described in Appendix B each of the three indices is based on two questions measuring some aspect of the psychological dimension. By combining the respondent's answers to two questions into an index, one gains a more reliable estimate of his feelings toward that dimension. Each respondent was classified according to whether he had a "strong," "mixed," or "weak" attitude toward a given dimension. On the Communist threat dimension, for example, a respondent classified as "strong" had well-defined beliefs that the United States and other countries faced a danger from Communist activity. A person classified as having a "weak" attitude tended to discount the likelihood of such a threat. Similar classifications of all respondents were made concerning support for international cooperation (strongly supportive versus weakly supportive) and belief in the need for foreign aid (strongly favor versus weakly favor). In the following sections we shall examine how these three dimensions shape the public's attitudes toward presidential foreign policies.

Trip to Europe.   Table 5–4 reports the impact of three foreign affairs attitudinal dimensions as they affected the public's judgment of the presidential trip to

Table 5–4

Strength of Attitudes toward Foreign Affairs and Perceptions of Presidential Foreign Policy Activities

	Strong	*Mixed*	*Weak*
Trip to Europe			
The effects of a—			
belief in a Communist threat	$+25\%$ [a]	$+32\%$	$+30\%$
need for international cooperation	$+27$	$+26$	$+17$
desire to aid foreign countries	$+29$	$+24$	$+25$
The Vietnam War			
The effects of a—			
belief in a Communist threat	$+1$ [b]	0	-1
need for international cooperation	-1	-1	$+2$
desire to aid foreign countries	0	-2	-1
Antiballistic Missile Defense (ABM)			
The effects of a—			
belief in a Communist threat	$+1$ [c]	-2	-8
need for international cooperation	-2	$+4$	$+17$
desire to aid foreign countries	-1	0	-1

[a]The percentage represents a net difference between the percent favoring the trip to Europe and the percent opposing it. A positive score ($+$) means that a greater proportion favored the trip than opposed it.

[b]The percentage represents a net difference between the percent giving a "dove" response and the percent giving a "hawk" response. A positive score means a greater proportion gave a response opposing military action in Vietnam; a negative score means that a greater proportion supported military action in Vietman.

[c]The percentage represents a net difference between the percent favorable to the ABM defense and the percent unfavorable. A positive score means that a greater proportion supported the ABM defense than opposed it.

Europe. The most distinct effect resulted from attitudes related to the need for international cooperation. In Table 5–4 one finds that those respondents having "strong" attitudes concerning the need for cooperation were also most favorable toward the trip. The net percentage difference is $+27$, indicating that 27 percent *more* of the national sample favored the trip than opposed it. As the degree of support for international cooperation weakened, however, the net percentage declined, resulting in $+26$ percent for those with "mixed" attitudes and $+17$ percent for those with "weak" attitudes. Those respondents with "weak" attitudes were less likely to support the president's trip.

Attitudes toward a Communist threat did not have as clear an effect on evaluation of the European trip as did attitudes toward international cooperation. Those with a "strong" belief that a Communist threat existed were least supportive of the presidential trip ($+25$ percent), but support for the trip did not systematically increase as the fear of Communism decreased. Similarly, for the foreign aid dimension, those most supportive of foreign aid were also more favorable toward the trip than the less supportive ($+29$ percent versus $+25$ percent). Approval of the trip was only slightly less for those having weak support for foreign aid. In sum, the data reported in Table 5–4 gives us a mixed pattern of the relationship between prior attitudes toward foreign affairs and the public's present evaluation of the president's current foreign affairs activities. The most obvious effect on evaluations of presidential excursions abroad is linked to the values citizens placed on the need for international cooperation; and in this particular case, judgments about the trip were influenced most by this specific set of values.

Vietnam.   Because of the complexity of the issues associated with the war in Vietnam, several attempts to clarify the dimensions of the conflict among American citizens have produced somewhat contradictory results (Verba et al., 1967; Verba and Brody, 1970). Background characteristics such as income and education have not had strong predictive power in characterizing who supported and who opposed the war. The exceptions have been the race and sex dimensions. Generally, blacks and women were more supportive of de-escalation than whites and men.

Previous analyses have found it necessary to determine not only who opposed and supported the war but also why. Because of the complex nature of the policy, the war has made strange bedfellows. Among opponents it has been necessary to distinguish those people opposed because the war had not been fought with more intensity from those opposed because they felt the war was ill advised or unwise. Most studies on the war have not considered the importance of general psychological commitment to foreign policy dimensions as a significant determinant of Vietnam-related attitudes. Although no specific mention of the war was made in the questionnaire, 8 percent of the national sample nonetheless mentioned this issue in reply to the questions regarding presidential activity.[3] In analyzing these respondents, it was necessary to make further distinctions concerning the reasons for support or opposition to the president's Vietnam policy. A respondent who supported escalation or opposed de-escalation of the fighting was classified as a "hawk"; one who supported de-escalation or opposed escalation was classified as a "dove." Of the 8 percent of the sample mentioning Vietnam, 1 percent were hawks, 2 percent were doves, and the remaining 5 percent were either contradictory or ambiguous in their responses. This failure to explicitly classify respondents into opposing positions is a reflection of more than the interview technique. The Verba study (1967) encountered similar difficulty even though it used specific questions about escalation and de-escalation. The authors of that study noted that in spite of many years of intense discussion and argument regarding the war, the American people were still relatively uninformed or ambivalent on this issue.

Using the 3 percent of the sample who were clearly hawks or doves, one can examine the effects of the three foreign affairs attitudinal dimensions on perceptions of Vietnam policy. Table 5–4 reveals that the Communist threat dimension had a decided effect on response to Vietnam: the percentage of hawks exceeded the percentage of doves for those individuals having strong beliefs in a Communist threat, whereas the percentage of doves exceeded the percentage of hawks among the group discounting the existence of a threat. The international cooperation dimension also showed a definite pattern: those *supporting* cooperation were more "dovish"; those *opposing* cooperation were more "hawkish." The foreign aid dimension, however, did not follow the anticipated pattern, suggesting that opinions on this dimension were not influential in shaping Vietnam-related attitudes. Undoubtedly, this lack of a relationship may be explained by the lack of a Communist aspect to the dimension, as is the case with the other two foreign affairs dimensions. Thus, one finds that for a small, informed public, presidential actions concerning Vietnam are clearly related to a long-standing consideration—Cold War attitudes—but the effects appear limited and confined to a relatively small group of citizens.

ABM defense. During the first debate on an antiballistic missile defense the arguments "for" and "against" centered around both domestic and foreign considerations. As a domestic issue, ABM was seen as a spending decision competing with other domestic programs. As a foreign affairs issue, ABM was debated in terms of national defense against a foreign attack. The foreign affairs considerations tended to displace domestic ones: if the case could be made that ABM was needed to protect the country from ultimate destruction, then it would be difficult to oppose the policy because of its cost.

Table 5–4 clearly suggests that the American public responded to the debate as a foreign affairs issue. Attitudes toward the Communist threat strongly influenced feelings about ABM. Those citizens fearing Communism supported the ABM (+1 percent), while those with lesser fears of Communism were, on the whole, opposed to ABM (−2 percent and −8 percent). Attitudes toward international cooperation and support for ABM followed similar patterns: those with "strong" feelings about cooperation were opposed to the program; those with "weak" desires for cooperation were strongly supportive of ABM (+17 percent). In the case of the foreign aid dimension, the pattern, though not as well-defined as for the other two dimensions, was also consistent.

The size of the differences in Table 5–4 indicates that among Cold War issues, belief in a Communist threat and support for international cooperation were most influential in molding foreign policy attitudes. Although much of the congressional debate on ABM centered on the technical feasibility of the project, it is safe to assume that such considerations were not as relevant to the general public as more long-standing considerations. In fact, the data demonstrate this one fact clearly: Communism and cooperation were much more salient than the question of foreign aid for all aspects of foreign affairs.

The Meaning of Tax and Spending Responses

That Americans complain about taxes should come as a surprise to no one. What may be judged as a bit unusual is the fact that the tax issue is more salient at the state and not the national level. Approximately one-third of all respondents (32 percent) raised the tax issue during the survey. Of this group, 90 percent mentioned taxes in relation to the governor; only 16 percent mentioned them in relation to the president.[4] Such data amply demonstrate that taxes are primarily a state problem. Certainly, the role President Nixon played in foreign relations served to displace the attention of citizens away from this issue, and the president was not facing serious economic problems at home. Yet it is still significant that taxes and spending were not commented on with more frequency at the national level.

Given the overwhelming negative response to the tax issue, one's first advice to a public authority might be to spend less. Is not the public's unfavorable reaction to taxes a demand to retain more money in their own pockets? Although this advice may appear obvious, there is considerable evidence suggesting a need to spend more (in the right places, at least). As Eva Mueller (1963) illustrated in an early survey on public attitudes toward taxing and spending, there is considerable ambivalence toward the entire subject of taxes and spending. Although Americans want to retain more of their earnings, they also demand more public services, and in some cases are willing to pay for them. This ambivalence is very much a part of the responses given in our survey.

In response to the statement, "The government in Washington wastes a lot of money we pay in taxes", 81 percent of the national sample exhibited acceptance of the traditional American presumption that the public sector wastes their hard-earned tax dollars. But respondents were also asked, if given a choice, what they would do with public monies. Each respondent was asked to explicitly order seven alternatives, from what he would prefer most to what he would prefer least. The seven alternatives ranked by the respondents were:

—build schools and help education
—end water pollution
—cut taxes
—increase antipoverty programs
—help other countries through foreign aid
—provide people with enough money to live on
—provide people with better health care

The significance of this question lies in the fact that it presents a forced choice for a specified set of alternatives: if a respondent selected the health care item first, then any one of the other six alternatives could be ranked no higher than second. Respondents could not answer that all alternatives were equally desirable. Thus the format of the question is reasonable, in the sense that it reflects how most decisions about taxes and spending are made: the selection of one alternative tends to preclude the attainment of others.

By examining the average rank assigned for each of the seven alternatives, one can determine the average preference ordering. An average choice of "1" would mean that everyone in the sample picked that alternative first; the higher the number, the less popular was that alternative. An average of "7" means that everyone placed the alternative last.

Table 5-5 reports the average ranking of the alternatives by critics and non-critics to tax policies. Reducing the level of taxation obviously is a popular option, but it is also clear that spending for some programs—particularly education and health—has considerable public appeal. In contrast, foreign aid has virtually no support whatsoever, and guaranteed income and poverty programs are only slightly more desirable. Many political commentators have stressed the fact that programs to help the poor, both at home and abroad, have little political support. Table 5-5 suggests nothing that would contradict that assertion. Among the critics of the president's tax policies, the "cut taxes" alternative was most preferred, but the educational spending option was almost as popular. Spending for health care and pollution control were also highly favored. The three remaining alternatives—guaranteed income, poverty programs, and foreign aid—fell far behind

The individuals who did not mention taxes as an important issue pertaining to the president had different preference orderings. Spending for education exceeded even the "cut taxes" alternative, and the health care provision was tied with it. Pollution control, guaranteed income, poverty programs, and foreign aid made up the remainder of the list.

At the state level, spending for education has a strong base of support among critics and noncritics alike. Critics of state tax policies prefer reducing taxes second, but programs for improved health care and pollution abatement are also quite popular. Noncritics prefer the same policies, but in slightly different order. Again, welfare and poverty programs and guaranteed jobs and income policies have significantly less support among both groups.[5]

What is true for the chief executive is all the more true for state executives: critics of taxing policies prefer some reduced taxes but not at the expense of preferred programs such as education and health. Thus governors face demands to maintain, improve, and increase certain services and programs but come under heavy criticism for the policies that collect revenue. What may come as a surprise is the high popularity of some programs. Decisions as to whether tax money is well spent are grounded on a rather extensive order of priorities, some of which require the government to spend more, not less, and moreover to spend on the "correct" programs.

Law and Order

Many diverse events that were focused in the 1968 presidential campaign became known as the law and order issue (Converse et al., 1969; Robinson, 1970). The issue materialized in dramatic fashion in consequence of the behavior of student demonstrators and the Chicago police outside the Democratic National

Table 5–5
The Relationship of Criticism of Executive Tax and Spending Policies to the Ordering of Spending Preferences

Criticized President's Tax Policies	Average Choice*	Did Not Criticize President's Tax Policies	Average Choice	Criticized Governor's Tax Policies**	Average Choice	Did Not Criticize Governor's Tax Policies	Average Choice
Cut taxes	2.6	Build schools and help education	2.3	Build schools and help education	2.4	Build schools and help education	2.3
Build schools and help education	2.7	Cut taxes	3.3	Cut taxes	3.0	Provide better health care	3.3
Provide better health care	3.5	Provide better health care	3.3	Provide better health care	3.3	Cut taxes	3.4
End water and air pollution	3.8	End water and air pollution	3.8	End water and air pollution	3.6	End water and air pollution	3.9
Provide people with enough money to live on	4.5	Provide people with enough money to live on	4.3	Provide people with enough money to live on	4.4	Provide people with enough money to live on	4.2
Increase antipoverty programs	4.6	Increase antipoverty programs	4.7	Increase antipoverty programs	4.9	Increase antipoverty programs	4.7
Help other countries through foreign aid	6.2	Help other countries through foreign aid	6.2				

Question: "Here is a list of things that might be done with your tax money. I'd like you to tell me which one of these things you think should be done first with your tax money." Respondents ranked the seven items from "1" to "7." The fifty-three respondents who did not give complete orderings of the seven choices have been excluded from the table.

*The lower the mean score, the more favorable the preference.

**The foreign aid alternative has been eliminated from the data on gubernatorial perceptions.

Convention. This single event magnified the underlying tensions resulting from urban disorders, increasing crime rates, antiwar protests, and court decisions. Most analysts acknowledge the fatal effects of the convention on Hubert Humphrey's presidential aspirations. Evaluations of the behavior of the Chicago police toward demonstrators at the convention divided the electorate into three distinct camps. Those voters approving the amount of force used by the Chicago police against the demonstrators tended to vote for George Wallace; those who were ambivalent on the issue voted for Nixon; and individuals disapproving of the use of force voted mainly for Humphrey (Converse et al., 1969; Robinson, 1970). In sum, subjective evaluations of police behavior decisively shaped the political choices voters made in 1968.

Perceptions of police behavior were an important element in citizens' evaluations of public policy in subsequent years. Table 5–6 summarizes responses to six law and order questions covering three dimensions of the issue: police behavior, the administration of the law, and the causes of disorder. With respect to perceptions of police behavior, most citizens saw policemen as having restricted power and as playing a protective role in society (see Table 5–6). On the

Table 5–6
Some Indicators of the Dimensions of the Law and Order Issue

A. *Attitudes toward the Behavior of Police* (POLICE)

    1. A policeman has the power to get almost anyone to do what he wants them to.

Agree	21%
Disagree	70
Not sure—no opinion	9

    2. Policemen usually try to bother me instead of protecting me.

Agree	8%
Disagree	85
Not sure—no opinion	7

B. *Attitudes toward the Administration of the Law* (LAW)

    1. Criminals have too many advantages in this country right now.

Agree	74%
Disagree	16
Not sure—no opinion	10

    2. Are there any laws which you object to strongly?

Yes	42%
No	58

C. *Attitudes toward the Causes of Disorder* (CAUSES)

    1. Poverty, poor health, and low education are the main causes of disorder in the United States today.

Agree	62%
Disagree	29
Not sure—no opinion	9

    2. A man who has been denied the chance for a good job and education still has no excuse to riot and cause disorder.

Agree	78%
Disagree	15
Not sure—no opinion	7

question of how the law was administered, most Americans felt that "criminals" were given too much freedom, yet almost half of the Americans objected strongly to some laws. Considering the causes for crime and disorder, a majority of respondents believed that social conditions—poverty, poor health, and low education—contributed to crime. But a clear majority believed that such conditions did *not* justify breaking the law.

A national study conducted in 1971 by Louis Harris further confirmed the general trends illustrated in Table 5–6 (Erskine, 1974a). Respondents were asked the question, "Now I want to read you a list of things some people think are causes of an increase in crime. For each, tell me if you feel it is a major cause, a minor cause, or hardly a cause at all for an increase in crime." Of the many alternatives presented, the responses to three are relevant to the discussion. Sixty percent of the respondents indicated a general sympathy for police by rating a "lack of support for local police" as a "major cause" of increased crime. These same respondents also saw "too lenient sentences" and "poverty conditions which breed crime" as major causes (65 percent and 59 percent respectively). Most Americans are generally supportive of their police, believe that criminals have too many advantages, but recognize the social causes of much criminal behavior. In this latter regard, 61 percent of a Gallup Poll sample questioned in 1972 believed that "cleaning up social and economic conditions in our slums and ghettos that tend to breed drug addicts and criminals" would be a good way to reduce crime (Erskine, 1974b).

Because of the many complexities associated with the law and order issue, the six questions in Table 5–6 were used to create summary indices of law and order attitudes along three dimensions: police behavior (POLICE); how the law is administered (LAW); and what causes and justifies breaking the law (CAUSES). The creation of these summary measures is described in Appendix C. Each respondent was classified according to his overall attitudinal position on each of the three dimensions. A citizen who viewed police as exercising restrained power for benevolent reasons was classified as maintaining "strong" attitudes with regard to police behavior. This position was judged as being most favorable toward policemen. Individuals with less supportive attitudes were classified as having either "mixed" or "weak" attitudes.

On the second dimension, which characterized attitudes toward the role of the law in society, respondents were classified on their views respecting court activity and the fairness of existing laws. Three-quarters of the sample believed that criminals "had too many advantages" and 42 percent found at least one law highly objectionable (Table 5–6). Those respondents who believed the courts were too lenient on criminals and objected to existing laws had the most pronounced negative feelings toward the administration of justice. They were classified as "strong" on the LAW dimension; others with less clearly defined negative feelings were placed in the "mixed" or "weak" category, according to the strength of their attitudes.

The final law and order dimension emphasized the need to explain, and in particular to justify, the behavior of those engaged in crime and disorder. Respondents were classified according to their support for the "environmental" hypothesis—that is, whether social environment caused criminal activity and justified the resultant behavior. Although most Americans (62 percent) accepted this hypothesis concerning the causes of crime, 78 percent rejected the environmental explanation as a justification. If a citizen rejected both the environmental hypothesis and the justification for breaking the law, he was categorized as having "strong" attitudes.

In sum, there are three dimensions of attitudes pertaining to response to law and order policy—attitudes toward the causes of disorder. Each respondent was classified according to whether his attitudes were strong, mixed, or weak. These three categories are summarized as follows:

Strong: attitudes on the dimension that provokes the most negative response toward permissive law and order decisions and the positive response toward aggressive ones.

Mixed: attitudes on the dimension that provokes the next greatest level of negative response toward permissive law and order decisions and the next most positive response toward aggressive ones.

Weak :   attitudes on the dimension that provokes the least negative responses and the greatest positive ones.

The president was not the focus of much concern for crime and disorder, but governors received only favorable comments concerning their law and order policies. Most comments made in the interviews were in response to "aggressive" enforcement decisions made by governors. These governors were praised primarily for supporting police activity; use of the National Guard; "cracking down" on criminals; and restricting riots, violence, and student protests. One can expect, therefore, that citizens with strong feelings on the three dimensions of law and order would be most supportive of the governors' policies.

Table 5–7 summarizes the relationships between these underlying attitudes of the law and order issue and evaluation of state policy. The police behavior dimension (POLICE) produced the most definite results. Citizens with strong

Table 5–7
The Effects of Attitudes toward Law and Order on Response to Governors' Policies on Law and Order

	Strength of Attitude		
	Strong	Mixed	Weak
Dimensions of the Law and Order Issue*			
1. Attitudes toward behavior of police (POLICE)	10%**	7%	3%
2. Attitudes toward the administration of the law (LAW)	9	8	6
3. Attitudes toward the causes of disorder (CAUSES)	9	8	9

*See Appendix C for definitions of the dimensions of the law and order issue.
**Percent giving a favorable response to governors' law and order policies.

feelings were most supportive and those with weak feelings were less so. The general trend showing an increase in support for the enforcement policies of governors as support for police increases is a manifestation of the public's belief in the ability of law enforcement agencies to handle "crime and lawlessness." Gallup reported that 83 percent of a 1972 survey favored agencies being "tougher than they are now" (Erskine, 1974a).

These attitudes obviously carried over to the question of how the law was administered. Governors received more favorable comments from those people who believed that society was too lenient. In general, the courts and not the governor were seen as one principal source of leniency. A California poll conducted in 1972 comparing various institutions on the "job" they were doing in "dealing with the causes of social unrest and violence in the country today" found that the governor of California received a "good job" rating from 49 percent of the sample, whereas "the courts of law" received only a rating of 32 percent (Erskine, 1974b).

Finally, the attitudes toward the causes of disorder did not show a systematic relationship to the enforcement policies of governors. Some hint as to the reason is reflected in the ambivalent position most Americans have toward the law and order issue. Although they strongly support policemen and policies of stricter enforcement, they also believe the fundamental causes of crime should be corrected. When asked to decide between these alternatives, the choices are mixed and somewhat contradictory. In a 1968 survey by the National Opinion Research Center,[6] the question asked was: "Thinking about the next five to ten years, what do you think would be the best thing to do about the problem of riots—build up tighter police control in Negro areas, or try harder to improve the conditions of Negroes?" The sample divided 16 percent for tighter police controls and 54 percent for improving social conditions.

But a Gallup survey in the next year (1969) asked whether the new Congress should "try to improve the lot of poor people and try to get at the cause of social problems" or "give more support to the police and get tough with law breakers." Fifty-nine percent of the sample supported more enforcement and 38 percent preferred correcting social conditions. Finally, two University of Michigan surveys in 1968 and 1970 posed identical questions about whether people preferred to "stress doing more about the problems of poverty and unemployment" on one hand or to "stress the use of force." Responses were as follows:

	Attack Problems	*Neutral*	*Use Force*	*Don't Know*
1968	39%	28%	29%	4%
1970	40	26	31	3

From these poll results, we see a country of citizens evenly divided between wanting to protect themselves from perceived threats yet desiring to correct the social conditions underlying criminal behavior.

The Role of Social Background on Perceptions of Executives

As we have seen in the case of diffuse support, socioeconomic status, sex, and race shape the formation of general attitudes toward political authorities. These factors also play an important role in determining how policies of executives are evaluated. This is true in part because each public defined by socioeconomic characteristics has different interests or needs. Furthermore, policies affect these publics differently. Welfare programs service low status individuals more often than high status ones. Tax policies—such as the selection of a sales tax in place of a graduated income tax—benefit upper status individuals more often. Thus, socioeconomic status again can be treated as an important condition to consider when examining how policies are evaluated. In keeping with the pattern established previously, I shall also examine the effects of sex and race on perceptions, controlling for socioeconomic status.

Differences Resulting from Sex and Status

Table 5–8 summarizes the differences resulting from sexual role in the evaluations of executives, with socioeconomic status controlled. The entries in the table are net figures representing the differences between positive and negative responses for each combination of sex and status. Social status plays an especially important role with regard to the direction of response to the president's activities. As status increases, the net level of favorable response also increases, regardless of the respondent's sex. For example, males demonstrate an increase from +17 percent, to +25 percent, to +39 percent. Similarly, females show

Table 5–8

The Effects of Sex on Policy Perceptions of Chief Executives, Controlling for Socioeconomic Status*

	Low Status		Medium Status		High Status	
	Male	Female	Male	Female	Male	Female
President						
Total response	+17%	+20%	+25%	+23%	+39%	+31%
Trip to Europe	+15	+16	+28	+26	+40	+30
ABM defense	+ 2	0	+ 3	+ 2	0	− 2
Vietnam	+ 1	0	− 3	0	0	+ 2
Taxes and spending	− 4	− 3	− 6	− 4	− 5	− 2
State Governors						
Total response	−13	− 7	−15	−10	− 9	− 8
Taxes and spending	−19	−22	−24	−15	−21	−18
Education	+ 1	0	− 1	+ 1	− 1	− 3
Law and order	+ 6	+ 5	+ 8	+ 7	+12	+10

*See Appendix E for a description of the socioeconomic status index.

+20 percent, to +23 percent, to +31 percent for each increase in status level. This pattern is not found at the gubernatorial level, suggesting that status-related differences in evaluations are tied to specific issues and personalities.

A closer examination of specific policies reveals that systematic status-related differences exist only for the trip to Europe affair. Other presidential issues do not appear to be so greatly influenced by this condition. Since we have already learned that the trip was viewed favorably by Republicans, and Republicans tend to concentrate in the high status levels, it is a reasonable conclusion that most of the status-related differences in presidential perceptions observed here result from this underlying partisan influence.

To some extent, the same argument holds for the law and order issues at the state level. This policy is the only issue where systematic differences in perceptions based on status appear. A Gallup survey conducted in December, 1972, suggests that socioeconomic background also plays an important role in shaping perceptions of crime (Index No. 91). Education and income were important factors influencing responses to the question "Is there more crime in this area than there was a year ago, or less?" As education and income increased, the respondent was much more prone to respond "more" to the question. Although Republicans were also more likely to say "more," it is clear that upper class people believe that crime is an increasing problem and are, therefore, more likely to view the enforcement policies of governors with favor.

Even after socioeconomic considerations are controlled, sex role has an important effect on evaluations. Men are more favorably oriented toward the trip abroad and the ABM policies of the president, and they tend to be more negative than women are about the tax issue. The other issues—Vietnam at the national level and education and law and order at the state level—show only small systematic differences, if at all. The law and order issue presents somewhat of a surprise here. Most surveys presenting closed-questions pertaining to the threat of crime show women to be more concerned than men (cf. Gallup Index No. 91). In sum, social status and sex each have pronounced effects on perceptions of executives on limited issues. There is, however, no tendency for systematic differences to appear at all levels and on each issue.

Differences from Status and Race

Table 5–9 presents a similar comparison for the effects of race when socioeconomic status is controlled. Since I have already discussed how status has a limited effect on evaluations, I shall concentrate on the race-induced differences after status factors are allowed for. Looking at the general picture, one finds that whites are much more favorable to the president's policies than blacks are, but they are more unfavorable to governors' activities, especially at the lower levels of status. The individual issues at the national level show rather systematic differences among the races. Whites are more favorable to the trip, regardless of

Table 5–9

The Effects of Race on Policy Perceptions of Chief Executives, Controlling for Socioeconomic Status

	Low Status		Medium Status		High Status	
	White	Black	White	Black	White	Black
President						
Total response	+20%	+14%	+27%	− 2%	+36%	+ 5%
Trip to Europe	+18	+ 7	+29	+ 1	+36	+16
ABM defense	+ 1	− 1	+ 2	0	− 1	− 4
Vietnam	+ 1	+ 3	− 1	− 4	+ 1	+ 4
Taxes and spending	− 3	− 1	− 5	− 4	− 3	0
State Governors						
Total response	−12	− 1	−13	− 4	− 9	−15
Taxes and spending	−23	−13	−20	−12	−19	−15
Education	0	+ 3	0	0	+ 2	+ 2
Law and order	+ 6	+ 3	+ 8	+ 7	+11	+ 8

status, and also support the ABM policies more. Only Vietnam does not show a systematic difference between the races.

Whites are also more negative toward the tax and spending issue, especially at the state level, and are somewhat more supportive of law and order policies. Race is an influence which produces rather distinct evaluations of executive policies. Even though socioeconomic variations are controlled for, whites and blacks come to distinctly different conclusions about their political leaders.

Before concluding this chapter on specific evaluations of presidential performance, I should make explicit the impact of long-term attitudes on the different kinds of presidential policy. Long-term attitudes had their greatest shaping effect on evaluations of cumulative events. Spectacular issues—particularly the trip to Europe—were less affected by long-range foreign affairs attitudes than were cumulative events. Although the foreign affairs dimensions had some relevance to the European trip, they had the most distinct influences on public evaluations in the case of cumulative issues. This pattern is predictable: by definition, spectacular issues—those new and dramatic to the public scene—are not encumbered by the previous judgments and existing attitudes that become associated with cumulative events. Spectacular events, depending on their nature, should either evolve into cumulative ones over time or disappear from public attentiveness altogether. The full implications of cumulative events on assessments of an incumbent president are clear. These policy events evoke long-term attitudes which shape public evaluations. Thus the president who is responsive to public opinion is faced with severe restrictions on his ability to gain a public response that is not, at least in part, predetermined. At the state level, the constraints are even greater. Governors cannot manipulate events as easily, yet the long-range attitudes must be confronted if policy is to be implemented.

Moving one step farther from the actual policy attitudes, a chief executive must also consider the impact of his policies on various publics. I have examined only those publics defined by status, sex, and race. These social conditions must be seen as "fixed" for a political leader; these constituencies must be dealt with as they are. Since it is unlikely that he can change them, he must find issues and programs favorable to them and de-emphasize those policies viewed negatively by them. In sum, pre-existing attitudinal conditions and social characteristics provide a varied landscape in which the political actor must travel.

Notes

[1] The respondents were administered five questions which asked for information pertaining to their state capital and state governor, the political party controlling Congress, and identification of United States senators and Supreme Court justices. See Appendix A for a complete description of the five knowledge items and the methods used to construct the Political Knowledge Index (KNOW).

[2] State party identification was measured by the question "Regardless of how you vote, do you think of yourself in *state politics* as a Republican, Democrat, Independent, or what?"

[3] Unlike the data presented in Table 5–4, this percentage is the proportion of total respondents and not of total response.

[4] A small number of respondents (6 percent) mentioned taxes at both levels.

[5] The foreign aid alternative, which scored last for critics and noncritics, is excluded from Table 5–5.

[6] The results summarized in this section are from Erskine (1974b).

Chapter Six

The Supreme Court and Political Opinion

The United States Supreme Court holds a special place in America's pantheon. Through its powers to decide which cases shall be heard and to declare legislation unconstitutional, the Court exercises a distinctly political function, namely to resolve constitutional conflicts, often of the most profound nature. Such conflicts, when left unsettled, have threatened the political integrity of the United States. In the nineteenth century, one such conflict—slavery—was ultimately settled by extra-constitutional means: a civil war. In the twentieth century, the Court has often been in the forefront of movements changing the fundamental character of the American system. It was the Surpeme Court's decisions, not those of state legislatures, that initiated the principle of one-man, one-vote. Prior to the 1960s, state legislatures regularly disenfranchised urban voters to the advantage of rural citizens. On the subject of civil rights, the Supreme Court has initiated profound social and political change. Except for President Truman's desegregation of the armed forces, the Supreme Court guided both Congress and the Executive on the matter of civil rights.

Yet for the average person, the Court's proceedings are shrouded in secrecy, ceremony, and symbolism. Most citizens probably take the Court for granted, never once fully considering the ramifications of its actions. Students of judicial behavior, however, have scrutinized the Court more critically. They have questioned, in fact, the capability of nine men to resolve the profound conflicts arising from interpretation of the Constitution. They have sought to compare the myths of judicial sacredness and supremacy with the realities of the exercise of political power.

In this context, the role of political perceptions is of fundamental importance. The Court deals with broad values and goals of the society—the rights of the citizen regarding the state; the power of the state over individual lives; the relationships of public entities to each other. Instituting the correct course in these decisions is as much a matter of persuasion as of fact-guiding-decision. The Court does not merely decide questions of fact; it decides which political values shall prevail and which ones shall not. The Constitution, laws of Congress, and past decisions of the Court greatly influence the direction of a decision, but the latitude exercised in specific judgments pertaining to particular cases is still very wide.

Because of the discretionary nature of Court decision making, it must convince its various publics, elite and mass, of both the soundness of its arguments and the wisdom of its decisions. Thus its power is constrained both by the expectations of these publics and by the threat of resistance to decisions they can exercise.

There have been several important occasions in the 180-year history of the Court when elite reaction to Court decisions was virulent. During Franklin Roosevelt's first term the Court declared many pieces of New Deal legislation unconstitutional. Roosevelt launched a major public campaign against the "old men" on the Court and proposed to expand its membership from nine to fifteen justices.[1] Through campaign speeches, he sought public support designed to elect Congressmen favorable to his position. The court-packing plan ultimately failed, Roosevelt meeting public resistance in his attempts to tamper with the institution.

This example illustrates the important role of public opinion in the functioning of the Supreme Court. Because of its rather isolated position, the Court finds it necessary to play the role of educator and persuader. Since the public is relatively uninformed about the Court, the Court needs to inform the public not only of its decisions, but also of the legal context in which the decisions were made, the correctness of its approach, and the justice of its decisions.

From the citizen's standpoint the Court, though operating in relative isolation, makes decisions that affect his day-to-day life: what schools his children shall attend and with whom; the methods by which the police and lower courts shall maintain public order; and generally the way in which he shall exercise his cherished individual rights of speech, religion, press, assembly, and property. The broad constitutional guidelines and precedent-setting cases are rarely understood by the average citizen. Given that the citizen is aware of the Court, he may or may not approve of the consequences of its decisions. In fact, he could conceivably evaluate the consequences without understanding on what grounds the Court acted. The questions, of course, are just how well the citizen understands, and in what terms he reacts to, the activities of the Court.

In this chapter I shall examine the Court through the eyes of the average citizen. What aspects of the Supreme Court's many activities are salient? How do citizens judge the Court's decisions? To use a concept introduced earlier, our concern will be with the nature of specific support accorded the High Court. Beyond this mapping of public attitudes toward the Court, I shall also consider the causes for these attitudes. Knowledge and awareness of politics and partisan biases will be examined, and the role of long-term psychological influences will be explored. Finally, I shall consider how social background can create distinct publics with divergent political values.

The Salience and Perception of Court Activity

Several past studies show that the Supreme Court's activities have not been particularly salient to the general public. The most extensive of these studies, a national sample conducted during 1964–66 by Murphey and Tanenhaus (1968, 1972), found that over half of the respondents surveyed did not mention anything they particularly liked or disliked about what the Supreme Court was doing. Another study, based on Gallup Poll data from the 1940s and 1950s, also concluded that the Supreme Court's attentive public was not large (Dolbeare and Hammond, 1968). The situation was not dramatically different by 1969; only 40 percent of the national sample expressed either a favorable or unfavorable comment in response to questions about Court activity:

> Now thinking of the Supreme Court in Washington, is there anything the Supreme Court has done lately that you (don't like) like? What is that?

The salience of the Court's activities was significantly lower than either the president's or state governors.'

Although the degree of precise knowledge was lower, the American public nonetheless formed judgments about the High Court. In response to the 1969 SERS survey question mentioned above, the ratio of negative to positive comments exceeded 3 to 1.

A series of Gallup surveys provides a historical perspective for this negative evaluation of the Court's activities (Index No. 98). During the early 1960s, the Court's rating was higher than in 1969, when it reached its nadir. By 1973, the Court had begun to re-establish its position with the American public. Gallup recorded this trend with the question, "In general, what kind of rating would you give the Supreme Court—excellent, good, fair, or poor?" The results for the years 1963 to 1973 were as follows:

Year	*Responding* *"Excellent" or "Good"*
1963	43%
1967	45
1968	36
1969	33
1973	37

Thus, the end of the Johnson years and beginning of the Nixon administration represented a low point in the Court's popularity.

Specific decisions of the Court have had immediate impact on public attitudes, even though the Court's general activities are relatively isolated from attention. In their study done in the middle 1960s, Murphey and Tanenhaus reported that civil rights, prayers in the public schools, and criminal justice cases had received the most comment.[2] In 1964, civil rights was the most salient area of Court activity, but the level of salience declined by 1966. The Court's decisions restricting prayer in the public schools was the next most frequently mentioned issue in 1964, but it also showed a marked decline in salience over the two-year period. Decisions affecting the rights of the accused were the third most discussed area of decision, and this area, in contrast, increased in saliency. Several other, more limited, studies tend to support these general conclusions about the content of perceptions of the Court. Dolbeare and Hammond (1968) mention the importance of civil rights and school prayer in a study done in Wisconsin. Kessell (1966) also confirmed these results in a study of Seattle, Washington, during 1965.

By 1969 the content of response to the Court's activities had changed markedly. Criminal justice cases, which are now labeled as the problem of law and order, were the single most salient issue in the public's mind, followed next by civil rights decisions. School prayer cases were the third most discussed area of Court activity. Table 6–1 summarizes the total number of specifically favorable (168) and unfavorable (611) responses expressed by 40 percent of the sample. Law and order accounted for 44 percent of all comment; civil rights, for 21 percent; and school prayer, for 15 percent. The remaining 20 percent of comments directed at the Court's activities were evenly divided between discussion of other Court policies and how the Court conducted its business. This latter category included responses pertaining to such matters as the characteristics of the justices—for instance, their age, integrity, and wisdom; the expansion of the Constitution; and the public activities of the justices (for example, Douglas's speeches and Warren's role in the investigation of the death of John Kennedy).

Table 6–1
Favorable and Unfavorable Responses to the Policies of the United States Supreme Court

	Favorable	*Unfavorable*	*Total*	*Relative Difference**
Law and order	23%	49%	44%	−26%
	(39)**	(301)	(340)	
Civil rights	53	12	21	+41
	(89)	(75)	(164)	
School prayer	4	18	15	−14
	(6)	(113)	(119)	
Management of office	5	12	10	− 7
	(9)	(71)	(80)	
Other policies	15	8	10	− 7
	(25)	(51)	(76)	
Total	100%	100%	100%	0
	(168)	(611)	(779)	

*Relative Difference = % Favorable − % Unfavorable (based on 168 Favorable and 611 Unfavorable Responses respectively).
**Numbers in parentheses are the number of responses coded.

Table 6–1 shows the responsiveness of the attentive public to the Court's activities. In spite of the relatively low salience of the Court, changing patterns of Court output are reflected in changing patterns of topics that attract public awareness. Law and order issues tended to displace the civil rights movement as the principal topic of national discussion after the emergence of student activism on the campuses, the assassination of public leaders, increased urban violence, and the televising of the confrontations during the 1968 Democratic National

Convention. In this contex, the decisions of the Court pertaining to pretrial rights of the accused and to the introduction of evidence in courts had clearly struck a responsive note in the public's awareness. One interesting continuity, however, is the school prayer issue: even though the Court had not made a major decision concerning this area since the middle 1960s, the issue still retained public attention (cf. Carroll, 1967).

Gallup (Index No. 98) has measured the impact of specific rulings on law and order, civil rights, and prayer in the public schools. He reports that the 1966 decision restricting the admissibility of confessions as evidence in trials, unless the accused had been properly informed of his right to remain silent and have a lawyer, was opposed by the ratio of 2 to 1. This decision contributed to a feeling among the American people, which is well documented by various polling results, that the courts in general and the Supreme Court in particular were responsible for the breakdown in law and order. A Harris survey done in 1969 found that 77 percent agreed that the Supreme Court was "too soft on criminals." Similarly, a CBS news survey in late 1970 revealed that 63 percent of a national sample believed that the Court gave "too much consideration to the rights of people suspected of crimes." As late as 1973, a Gallup Poll measuring reasons why people believed there was more crime than a year before reported "increased use of drugs" (13 percent) and "courts too lenient" (11 percent) as the principal reasons (Erskine, 1974a). The law and order issue was a volatile issue which contributed substantially to the decline in the Court's support. By 1973 however, inflation, the economy, and the problem of governmental integrity, which grew out of the Watergate affair, had replaced crime and law and order as the major foci of public attention. Thus, the displacement of the issue by more current problems not specifically related to the Supreme Court accounts for some of the improvement in the Court's rating (cf. U.S. Senate, 1973).

Other cases also produced strong public reactions. The 1963 decision on prayer in the schools was opposed by a rate of 3 to 1, but the civil rights decisions have produced generally favorable reaction. The 1954 decision to integrate the public schools was favored by 52 percent of a 1954 sample and by 62 percent of a 1961 sample (Gallup Index No. 98). It should be noted, however, that bussing to achieve integrated schools has been opposed consistently by a majority of Americans.

The data reported in Table 6–1 confirm the reasons for the marked decline in Court popularity in 1969. The area of activity eliciting the greatest number of positive comments was civil rights, whereas the Court's law and order policies accounted for the greatest number of negative comments. The comparison of the relative rates (percentages) of favorable and unfavorable comment is revealing. Although the absolute number of negative responses widely exceeds the number of positive reasponses, one area of Court activity—civil rights— had a net favorable response of 41 percent (see Table 6–1). Law and order and school prayer had negative relative differences (−26 percent and −14 percent). These relative rates of response have not changed significantly since the middle

1960s (cf. Murphey and Tanenhaus, 1968, 1972). At that time, civil rights cases evoked a net positive difference of 35 percent; school prayer and law and order cases evoked a negative difference of 29 and 5 percent, respectively. By 1969 the difference of relative positive response for civil rights had increased; the negative differences for law and order had increased also, but the negative difference on school prayer had lessened. Thus the size of the difference had varied, but the emphasis on what the people liked and disliked about the Court had not changed dramatically.

We have seen the reasons for the marked decline in the Court's rating but have little evidence to explain why the Gallup Poll reported an increase in favorable comment by 1973. Gallup notes that 58 percent agreed with the 1973 ruling that "each community can set its own standards [for deciding what is obscene or indecent with regard to movies, books, and plays] regardlesss of what standards are set elsewhere," but in general there were no decisions having the dramatic effect or impact of the law and order cases. One must look elsewhere for an explanation of the resurgence of favorable attitudes toward the Court. The displacement of the law and order issue by concern about Watergate, the economy, and popular rulings do not explain the change in perspective toward the High Bench. The answer is found, in part, in how the public views the personnel of the Court and how partisan and ideological considerations shape perceptions of the Court.

Political Knowledge and Perceptions of the Justices

One can measure the attentiveness to the activities of the Court by determining the amount of factual information about the Court possessed by each respondent. Attentiveness is a matter of degree. Citizens can be ordered according to increasing degrees of attentiveness, from unawareness to high salience. Attentiveness toward the Court was measured by asking each respondent to identify as many of the justices sitting on the Supreme Court as possible. Thus each person received a score from 0 to 9, depending on the number of correct identifications. Forty-four percent of the respondents could not name anyone on the Court. In comparison, the Murphey and Tanenhaus study (1972) of the middle 1960s reported 51 percent unable to name one or more justices. Only 3 percent of a national sample could identify five or more justices.

The identification of the justices by the representative sample of respondents, however, showed an interesting pattern. In 1969 the Supreme Court was very much identified with one man: Earl Warren, its chief justice. Of the 56 percent identifying at least one justice, 48 percent mentioned the chief justice (Table 6–2). Justices Black and Douglas, two other pillars of the Warren Court, were also mentioned frequently, but in spite of the controversy surrounding Justice Fortas, only 11 percent of the sample identified his name.[3] In the more than fifteen years of the Warren tenure, the attentive public had come to identify the man with the institution.

Table 6–2

Supreme Court Justices Identified by National Sample (1969)

	Sample Identifying
Warren	48%
Black	23
Douglas	17
Fortas	11
White	9
Marshall	4
Brennan	1
Harlan	1
Stewart	1

One can hypothesize that the degree of attentiveness to the Court would also be related to the tendency to make evaluations about the activities of the institution. As the degree of attentiveness increased, the tendency to express judgments, whether favorable or unfavorable, would increase. This increased tendency to respond about an institution should not be related to the direction of response. In other words, as attentiveness increases, the level of nonresponse should decrease, and the level of both favorable and unfavorable response should increase. Thus attentiveness is an indicator of involvement with Court affairs, but it is not directly related to the judgments citizens make based on this awareness. An examination of the data shows that the nonresponse rate for people unable to identify the names of any sitting justices is in excess of 80 percent, but nonresponse drops below 20 percent when five or more justices are correctly identified. The percentage of respondents giving favorable and unfavorable comments increases at about the same rate as awareness of the Court's personnel grows, indicating that knowledge of the Court's business does not explain the negative evaluations of the Court. The reason for these unfavorable comments lies with the combining of awareness of the Court's personnel and decisions with the influence of party and ideological values of the respondents.

Partisanship, Ideology, and Evaluations of the Court

The Supreme Court is not a partisan body in the traditional sense. Supreme Court justices do not run for election but are appointed and tenured for life. They are not publicly aligned with political figures, such as the president, senators, and congressmen, and they avoid public statements about current political controversies. When they do make public comments, the primary vehicle is a written opinion released by the Court pertaining to a legal case before it. These written opinions are rarely attributed to individual justices; they represent instead a consensus of opinion among the majority who sign the opinion. Individually authored concurring or dissenting opinions are much rarer, and only then can one gain an unambiguous insight into the thinking of a particular justice. Nor are these decisions identified, as in congressional committee reports, as Republican and Democratic positions on the issue in question. The Supreme Court, therefore, is well insulated from the usual partisan associations common to other political decision makers.

Yet the Court does make decisions affecting political interests, and even though decisions are not presented in partisan terms, these decisions affect partisan political goals. Without the traditional partisan cues associated with the Court, the question of whether the Court should be evaluated in partisan terms is problematical. If Senator Kennedy speaks on some major bill before the Senate, Republicans will tend to view it as a bid to become president, and Democrats will see a great senator speaking on an important topic. When Justice Burger writes an opinion for the Court, will the public respond in such partisan terms? Should Republicans think the opinion is good (because Nixon appointed Burger) or bad (because Burger is reportedly a Democrat)? Probably, neither reaction is likely, since both facts about Burger's partisan commitments are not likely to be salient. In sum, one might expect people to respond to decisions, but not because they are Republicans or Democrats.

In spite of the fact that direct partisan labels are absent, the public nevertheless forms rather distinct judgments about the ideological content of rulings and the men who make them. Gallup found that the public consistently applies ideological notions, such as liberal and conservative, to the Court. In 1973, he administered the question, "In general, do you think the U.S. Supreme Court is too liberal or too conservative in its decisions?" Thirty-five percent of the national sample said too liberal and 26 percent answered too conservative. In all, over 60 percent of the sample made an ideological judgment about the Court's rulings. Significantly, the public linked the ideologically based evaluation to the Court's personnel as well. When asked the question, "When new appointments are made by the president to the Supreme Court, would you like these to be people who are liberal or conservative in their political views?" the following results were obtained (Gallup Index No. 98):

	Conservative	*Liberal*	*No Opinion*
June, 1968	51%	30%	19%
June, 1969	52	25	23
April, 1973	49	27	24
July, 1973	46	30	24

It is clear that the desire for a conservative appointment was at its peak in 1968–69. Since the term "liberal" was associated with permissiveness on law and order matters, Nixon's appointment of conservative justices contributed to the increase in the Court's popularity.

Partisan alignments played a decisive role in determining how the Court was evaluated. Gallup (Index No. 98) reports that Republicans showed an increase of 12 percent in favorable rating of the Court's performance from 1969 to 1973.

Democrats and Independents showed little or no increase (0 percent and +2 percent, respectively) during the same period. Furthermore, the demand for a conservative appointment came mostly from Republicans (54 percent) and Independents (48 percent) rather than Democrats (41 percent). Thus, the increase in Court popularity from 1969 to 1973 was primarily associated with Republicans and to a lesser extent Independents. The improved image results from the appointment of conservative justices as much as from the decisions they have made.

Although the partisan bases for changes in net specific support have been well documented, we have gained no insight into how particular decisions were evaluated. Table 6–3 suggests that in 1969 traditional party identification produced significant differences in how decisions were evaluated. Republicans were much more negative about the Court's activity than either Independents or Democrats. Responses to law and order and civil rights policies were especially structured along partisan lines. In contrast, responses to the school prayer decisions were not—all groups disliked the decisions about equally. One finds that in spite of the insulation of the justices from overt partisan alignments, the decisions of the Court are perceived in partisan terms. This partisan-oriented judgment was not confined to 1969. Murphey and Tanenhaus (1968) reported the influence of partisanship in a 1966 study of evaluations of the Court. As in 1969, the Democrats were more favorable to the Court than Republicans. By 1973, Gallup reports some evidence showing that the tables had turned. Republicans and Independents were more approving of the Court's obscenity decision than Democrats. In sum, partisan and ideological considerations play an important role in shaping perceptions. The complex interaction of the content of rulings with the perceived ideology of the justices and the political alignments of the citizens help determine whether the Court will find a hostile or responsive citizenry.

Long-term Attitudes and Evaluations of the Court

Three policies of the Court—law and order, school prayer, and civil rights—received the most public attention. As has been demonstrated in the preceding

Table 6–3

The Effects of National Party Identification on Response to Supreme Court Policies

	Republican	*Independent*	*Democrat*
Law and order	−23%*	−16%	−12%
Civil rights	−17	0	+ 3
School prayer	− 7	− 8	− 6
Total response	−30	−23	−18

*Percentages are the "% difference." A negative sign means that the "% negative" was greater than the "% positive."

chapters, evaluations of policy are not formed in isolation. Rather, they are shaped by underlying public attitudes. In this section, the principal focus will be on the role of selected long-term attitudes in shaping the perceptions of the Court on these three issues.

Law and Order

The public's reactions to the Court's activities in the area of law and order, in contrast to its reactions to state governors' policies, was overwhelmingly unfavorable. Most of the respondents who expressed negative opinions thought that Court decisions were permissive and too lenient. Respondents objected most to the restrictions placed on police enforcement activity (when police collect evidence and interrogate suspects) and the Court's lenient attitude toward criminals, riots, violence, and student demonstrators. Many people had the general impression that the Court's decision contributed (in some unspecified way) to laxity and permissiveness in society. Although the public's indictment was at times vague, the intensity of its reactions was nonetheless definable.

The three dimensions of law and order were highly relevant for explaining the full meaning of the unfavorable reactions. The POLICE dimension—attitudes toward police behavior—was most important for characterizing differences in attitudes toward state governors, but the administration of the law (LAW) dimension was more important for shaping evaluations of the Court. Table 6–4 shows a difference of 24 percent between the citizens with strong attitudes on the LAW dimension and those with weak ones. The strong category was heavily negative (−26 percent) regarding the law and order decision, whereas the weak group was only slightly so (−2 percent). A similar pattern holds for the POLICE and CAUSES dimensions: the respondents classified as strong were most adamant against the Court, while those classified as weak were least adamant.

Table 6–4
The Effects of Attitudes toward Law and Order on Response to Supreme Court's Decisions on Law and Order

	Strength of Attitudes		
	Strong	*Mixed*	*Weak*
Dimensions of the Law and Order Issue*			
1. Attitudes toward behavior of police (POLICE)	−19%**	−12%	−5%
2. Attitudes toward the administration of the law (LAW)	−26	−16	−2
3. Attitudes toward the causes of disorder (CAUSES)	−18	−16	−9

*See Appendix C for definitions of the dimensions of the law and order issue.
**This percent is the difference % Favorable − % Unfavorable. A negative sign means that the % Unfavorable exceeded the % Favorable.

The strong relationship between these three dimensions and perceptions of the Court provides some information on the underlying (and unarticulated) reasons for the public's reaction. Reactions to specific laws and feelings of too much leniency toward criminals were most important reasons for this reaction. Combined with the view that police used restrained power to work for the benefit of each citizen, these underlying attitudes caused the Court to have the most negative rating of all institutions studied. Although poverty, poor education, and other social conditions might explain why people committed crimes, the average American remained unsympathetic to such explanations as justifications for criminal behavior.

School Prayer

In spite of the constitutional provision for the institutional separation of church and state, individual religious experiences nevertheless have shaped the nature of conflict in political institutions. An important example of the connection between individual religious beliefs and institutionalized politics occurred in the 1960 presidential election. At that time, attitudes toward Kennedy's Catholicism became one of the dominant forces determining electoral choice (Converse, 1966; Converse et al., 1961). This election revealed that both denominational affiliation and the degree of religious commitment shaped perceptions of Kennedy's candidacy. This latter characteristic—religious commitment—was a measure of the intensity of religious belief; it was measured by the frequency of church attendance.

The full implications of religious affiliation and religious practice for the shaping and maintenance of political attitudes can be understood better by examining how related religious values are associated with these characteristics. Table 6–5 presents the sample divided into the three dominant religious groups—Protestant, Catholic, and Jewish—as well as by reported frequency of attendance.[5] These five categories of respondents were then compared on their response to the question, "Society will be saved only by faith in God." The figures

Table 6–5
The Effects of Religion and Religious Practice on Religious Belief and Attitudes toward School Prayer Decisions

Religion	Church Attendance	Religious Belief*	Percent Unfavorable**
Protestant	Regularly or often	59%	10%
Catholic	Regularly or often	47	11
Protestant	Seldom or never	42	5
Catholic	Seldom or never	32	6
Jewish		7	0

*% agreeing to question: Society will be saved only by faith in God.
**% giving an unfavorable response to the Supreme Court's decisions limiting prayer in the public schools.

in the body of Table 6–5 represent the percentage of each group agreeing with the question. Since an agree response would represent a more literal or fundamental belief in the role of a deity in the temporal order, the more each group agrees, the more it may be judged to be fundamentalist. By this standard, both religious affiliation and religious practice are important indicators of religious belief. Regular church attendance, regardless of religion, is associated with stronger agreement with this statement. Within levels of attendance, Protestants were more fundamentalist than Catholics. Ordering the five groups according to intensity of religious fundamentalism, one would find the following:

	Affiliation	*Attendance*
Most fundamentalist:	Protestant	Regular
	Catholic	Regular
	Protestant	Infrequent
	Catholic	Infrequent
Least fundamentalist:	Jewish	————

One may guess that if fundamentalism, as defined here, is related to unfavorable comment toward the school prayer decisions, then a similar ordering should occur with respect to the rate of negative response.

Table 6–5 also reports the percentage of each group giving unfavorable comments toward the school prayer decisions. It reveals that the important contrasts in public attitudes is between Christians and Jews, and between regular and infrequent church attenders. Although there is a slight tendency for Catholics to respond more negatively than Protestants, the ordering of the five groups may be simplified as follows:

	Affiliation	*Attendance*
Strongest unfavorable school prayer response:	Christian	Regular
Weakest unfavorable school prayer response:	Christian	Infrequent
	Jewish	————

Thus, we have important evidence that response to the Supreme Court's decisions on prayer in the public schools is strongly grounded in religious attitudes, and the response is more related to religious practice than to religious affiliation. One will find both Protestants and Catholics strongly opposing this decision and showing less active concern for the policy. The lines of conflict are between the "church-goers" and the "stay-at-homes." In one sense, this is a reasonable distinction, since the Court's rulings have been directed at a matter of religious practice: whether children shall exercise a form of religious devotion in a government-supported institution or whether they shall pray only in other circumstances free of government involvement.

A Comparison of Law and Order and School Prayer Response

People who criticize the Court, both on its law and order and school prayer decisions, apparently do so because of a common set of beliefs about a decline in the quality of society. Both issues have a moralistic tone to them. The belief that criminals are "getting away with something" is grounded more on a moral judgment that this is wrong than on a personal interest violated by a criminal act. Most respondents were not victimized by criminal actions: rather, the wrong they feel is based more on a notion of rightness and wrongness, that society must punish wrongdoers much as parents discipline their children. The law and order issue and the school prayer debate are symbolic controversies about standards of correct behavior. Even the most avid supporter of prayer probably would not argue that children would be improved substantially by a single, isolated act of devotion starting the school day. The debate is more about abstract standards of behavior and conduct than material political outcomes.

With these thoughts in mind, the comparisons presented in Table 6–6 relating attitudes toward the law and order dimensions to negative response to the school prayer decisions have some significance. Some dimensions of the law and order issue were very much tied to response on school prayer—specifically, the police behavior and administration of the law dimensions. Significantly, the dimension relating to the role of social environment as causing disorder did not show any particular relationship to school prayer response. On the police behavior dimension, those respondents expressing strong supportive attitudes were most critical of the prayer decisions (9 percent). Respondents who were most critical of leniency in administering the law also were most unfavorable to these rulings (13 percent). Thus matters such as whether the police were fair, whether criminals have too many advantages, and whether the law was objectionable were more relevant to attitudes toward prayer in the public schools than attitudes toward social conditions.

Table 6–6

Effects of Attitudes toward Law and Order on Response to Supreme Court's Decision on School Prayer

	Strength of Attitude		
Dimensions of the Law and Order Issue*	*Strong*	*Mixed*	*Weak*
Attitudes toward behavior of police	9%**	7%	3%
Attitudes toward the administration of the law	13	7	5
Attitudes toward the causes of disorder	8	7	9

*See Appendix C for the definition of the dimensions of law and order issue.
**Percent giving an unfavorable response to the decisions of the Supreme Court on prayer in the public schools.

Table 6–7 shows the relationship of religious affiliation and practice to unfavorable response toward law and order issues. Although the table demonstrates the importance of both affiliation and practice in response to law and order, the differences are quite distinct from those pertaining to school prayer (Table 6–6). In Table 6–6 we find that Catholics were the most dissatisfied with the law and order issue, followed next by Protestants, and lastly by Jews. The degree of attendance was also important. In general, regular attendance was

Table 6–7
Effects of Religion and Religious Practice on Attitudes toward Law and Order Decisions

	Protestant	Catholic	Jewish
Frequency of Church Attendance*			
Regularly or often	18%	25%	20%
Seldom or never	15	20	

*Percent giving unfavorable response to Supreme Court decisions on law and order issues.

more associated with negative law and order responses. An ordering of the five groups produces the following:

	Affiliation	*Attendance*
Strongest unfavorable response:	Catholic	Regular
	Catholic	Infrequent
	Protestant	Regular
	Protestant	Infrequent
Weakest unfavorable response:	Jewish	————

This ordering is markedly different from the one for fundamentalist religious beliefs.

The pattern relating unfavorable law and order and school prayer response essentially is as follows: although law and order and school prayer have some common dimensions accounting for the responses, the differences in the dimensions—particularly relating to the environmental hypothesis—are substantial. Even though the basis for response is shared, most respondents expressed negative attitudes either to one or to the other policy, but they usually did not mention both. Religious affiliation and religious attendance each affected response to these policy areas, but the effects differed in important ways. In the case of school prayer responses, the ordering of the various kinds of religious experience parallels that produced by the fundamentalism question; in the case of the law and order responses, the ordering of the groups is in no way similar to the fundamentalism question. These contrasting results indicate that religion has an important effect on response to Court policy, but many varied aspects of religious experience influence attitudes toward the Supreme Court in differing ways.

Civil Rights

Since 1954 the Supreme Court has made decisions affecting the rights of black people to attend public schools, use public accommodations, and exercise other fundamental legal rights. Among the salient areas of Court activity the civil rights area is the oldest and most sustained area of decision. It would take little imagination to expect that reaction to the Civil Rights decision, both favorable and unfavorable, should be based on the respondent's race. Although one might expect blacks generally to give more favorable response to the Court, does it necessarily follow that whites give more negative response? An examination of the rates of negative and positive response, compared by race, revealed an important pattern: although whites gave more negative response to the civil rights cases than blacks, they also gave more negative response on all other areas of Court activity. In sum, whites, much more than blacks, generally disliked the Court in all areas.

A second dimension having relevance for the response to civil rights is the respondent's degree of stereotyped racial beliefs. Essentially, stereotypical thinking is the tendency to treat a class of people—say, blacks, females, the elderly—as all having the same social characteristics. These characteristics are qualities that are difficult, if not impossible, to verify for a class of people. For example, respondents were asked to compare whites and "Negroes" and make a judgment according to whether one group was intelligent, dependable, industrious, and better behaved than the other. Although it is theoretically possible to compare two individuals with respect to these four qualities, to judge two groups of people with respect to these qualities is a much more tenuous task. A stereotyped response was one attributing better or worse qualities to a race of people. A nonstereotyped response was one refusing to make a choice or attributing no difference between the races. Each respondent was scored according to the number of times he selected a stereotyped response to four comparisons of whites and "Negroes."[6] The assigned score reflected whether a respondent tended to: (1) view blacks in the aggregate more favorably than whites, (2) have either mixed responses or no stereotyped attitudes, and (3) view whites more favorably than blacks. Each race stereotyped the other in both favorable and unfavorable ways, although members of each group tended to view their race in a somewhat more favorable light.

Table 6–8 shows the effects of both the race of the respondent and the degree of stereotyped thinking on his comments about civil rights. The percentages in the body of Table 6–8 show the difference between the percent of favorable and unfavorable remarks on civil rights. A positive score means that the group had a net favorable difference—that is, a generally accepting outlook on

Table 6–8

Effects of Race and Stereotyped Racial Attitudes on Response toward Civil Rights Decisions

	White	Nonwhite
*Degree of Stereotyped Racial Attitudes**		
Stereotyped favoring Negroes over whites	+ 7%**	+12%
Mixed or not stereotyped	+ 4	+ 7
Stereotyped favoring whites over Negroes	− 7	+ 7

*See Appendix D for a description of the stereotype index.
** Relative Difference = % Favorable to civil rights decisions − % Unfavorable to civil rights decisions. A positive sign means a net favorable response by the group for civil rights decisions.

the civil rights decisions. As anticipated, blacks are more favorably inclined toward the Court's civil rights activities than whites are. The most favorable group was blacks with stereotypes favoring "Negroes" over whites. The relative level of positive response toward civil rights declines for both blacks and whites, however, as the degree of stereotyped thinking shifts toward a pro-white viewpoint.

Table 6-8 presents one important finding: only one group of whites, those with stereotypes favoring whites over blacks, have a relative level of unfavorable response. The remainder of whites are nearly as supportive of civil rights as many blacks. Although all negative comment toward civil rights came from whites, only those whites with pro-white stereotypes responded more unfavorably than favorably. Thus the opposition to civil rights decisions, though centered in the white community, is most concentrated among a minority of white citizens—approximately 30 percent of all citizens. For this group, the assumption of racial superiority plays an important role in shaping their perceptions.

The Role of Social Background on Perceptions of the Court

The education, occupation, income, sex, and race of a respondent were important influences on the judgments people made in 1969 about the rulings of the Supreme Court. These factors have repeatedly played an important role in public reaction to Court affairs, both past (cf. Murphey and Tanenhaus, 1968) and present. A 1973 Gallup study (Index No. 98) showed that education, occupation, and income—the three major components of social status—produced significant variation in the favorable rating given the Court. In general, people of higher status—that is, having higher education, professional and white collar occupations, and incomes in excess of $10,000—were more likely to give favorable comments about the Court. There were much less important differences associated with race and sex.

Such relationships between background and attitude have not always been the case. As late as 1969, socioeconomic status was strongly related to increased negative ratings of the Court. Table 6-9 shows how status and sex shaped opinions about the Court. Examining the "total response" levels in Table 6-9 one

Table 6-9
The Effects of Sex on Policy Perceptions of the Supreme Court, Controlling for Socioeconomic Status

	Low Status		Medium Status		High Status	
	Male	Female	Male	Female	Male	Female
Total response	−14%*	−14%	−34%	−20%	−31%	−15%
Law and order	− 9	− 8	−23	−12	−26	−16
Civil rights	0	− 2	− 1	− 1	+ 3	+ 7
School prayer	− 5	− 7	− 9	− 9	− 8	− 6

*The percentages are net specific support. A negative sign means a net unfavorable response; a positive sign means a net favorable response.

finds that as status levels increase, net unfavorable response becomes greater, regardless of the sex of the respondent. Thus, one finds a distinctly different pattern occurring in 1969 than existed in 1973.

What can explain the differences in 1969? The reasons are found by looking at responses to individual Court rulings. Response to law and order was strongly related to status. Males of higher status became increasingly critical of the Court's decisions (−9 percent, −23 percent, −26 percent), as did females (−8 percent, −12 percent, −16 percent). The civil rights and school prayer decisions did not generate this type of response. In fact, high status respondents were more favorable to the civil rights rulings than other citizens.

Although Gallup found no effects on the overall rating of the Court resulting from sex, Table 6–9 indicates that in 1969 the sex of the respondent was a contributing factor influencing opinions. Males, especially higher status ones, were more critical of the Court than females, but this overall difference is primarily the result of the law and order issue. There was little or no difference between the sexes on the other issues.

The race of the respondent was an especially significant force in shaping opinion about the Court. In 1969 blacks were much more favorable to the Court than whites (See Table 6–10). The differences are worth noting: for low status

Table 6–10
The Effects of Race on Policy Perceptions of the Supreme Court, Controlling for Socioeconomic Status

	Low Status		Medium Status		High Status	
	White	Black	White	Black	White	Black
Total response	−20%	− 7%	−29%	+ 4%	−24%	+11%
Law and order	−10	0	−18	− 6	−22	0
Civil rights	− 3	+ 7	− 2	+10	+ 5	+11
School prayer	− 7	− 1	− 9	− 1	− 8	0

individuals, blacks were 27 percent more favorable (+ 7 percent − (−20 percent) = +27 percent); for middle status respondents, the difference was 33 percent; and for high status persons, it was 35 percent. On every issue, whites judged the Court differently from blacks. The negative responses to law and order came mostly from white respondents, whereas blacks were at best only slightly unfavorable toward the Court on this issue. As we have seen elsewhere, blacks were more supportive of civil rights than whites, and the school prayer rulings also created unfavorable responses among whites, whereas blacks were only marginally opposed to these decisions.

We have observed a marked change in attitudes toward the Court from the late 1960s to the early 1970s. The supporters of the Court now are those of higher status, and race and sex have lesser influences. Earlier a single issue, law and order, divided the nation on lines of status and race. This issue is now dormant, displaced by concerns for inflation, recession, and corruption (U.S. Senate, 1973). Contributing to a muting of these differences of opinion are the conservative appointments to the Court. The groups most critical of the Court in 1969 are precisely the ones supporting the appointment of conservative judges —males, whites, the highly educated, the professionally employed, and the wealthy (Gallup Index No. 98). In addition to the decline of the law and order issue and to the conservative appointments, recent decisions of the Court have also appeased those groups critical to the Court in 1969. The 1973 ruling on community standards for deciding what is obscene has contributed also to the Court's enhanced position. Citizens of higher status and whites were most favorable to this important decision.

In summary, we have found that opinions toward the Supreme Court, a relatively isolated governmental body, are affected by the same forces shaping opinion toward other more political institutions. The Court can affect opinion by avoiding some decisions and making others, but many situations beyond its control also determine the response to the Court. The actions of other political actors, particularly the president, are important; and events not totally under the control of any political actor—the state of the economy, the social and ethnic composition of the citizenry, and certain long-term psychological states—also determine opinion toward the Court. The impact of Court decisions—in other words, the levels of specific support—can be understood only by considering these many contributing causes.

Notes

[1]The size of the Court is determined by Congress.

[2]Comparisons of the rate of response among past studies are somewhat tenuous, since the earlier studies asked questions in somewhat different form.

[3]Justice Fortas subsequently resigned from the Court under increasing pressure, particularly from the White House, Senate, and press.

[4]See chapter 5 and Appendix C for a full description of the three law and order dimensions.

[5]Jews were not classified by frequency of church attendance, since the more appropriate question to apply here would measure adherence to orthodox religious practice.

[6]See Appendix D for a further description of the Racial Stereotype Index.

The Congress and Public Opinion

The United States Congress has set the pattern for organization of legislative power throughout the nation. In the eighteenth century the framers of the Constitution compromised on a bicameral, or two chamber, legislature at the federal level. The lower chamber, the House of Representatives, had popularly elected representatives with two-year terms. The upper chamber, or Senate, had two senators from each state, appointed by their respective state legislatures for a six-year term. This organizational principle, which allowed a balancing of power between the large, populous states and the smaller ones, has provided the model for the establishment of the legislative power in all but one (Nebraska) of the fifty states. During the first part of this century, the Seventeenth Amendment to the Constitution provided for the direct election of United States senators. Today all 435 House members and one-third of the 100 member Senate must stand for election every two years.

Each chamber has a different role with regard to public opinion and the exercise of legislative power. Two conditions more than anything else distinguish the House of Representatives from the Senate: the length of the elected term (two versus six years) and the size of the chamber (435 versus 100 members). The House is a body tied closely to local interests in each member's district. Smaller constituencies and two-year terms facilitate the "back home" emphasis of a congressman's role. The size of the House also submerges most individual congressmen's identities under the organizational structure of committees, subcommittees, and party leadership. In order to acquire information, influence legislation, or initiate action, the congressman is much more dependent upon his committee assignments and the caucuses of his party and state delegations than a senator is. In sum, the House is a highly institutionalized legislative body that absorbs the identities of its individual members.

In contrast to the House, the Senate is a much smaller body, with members elected for six-year terms. Even though a committee system is necessary for the Senate to conduct its business, this organizational structure does not diminish the individual identities of senators as much as that of the House. Unlike most congressmen, senators represent large, heterogeneous states and often enjoy national reputations before entering the Senate. The Senate frequently serves as a platform for national debates and, in the past, has produced many presidential aspirants. Thus, the role of a United States senator is much more individualized and is less tied to local or state interests. These institutional arrangements affect how legislators from each chamber can and do relate to their constituencies, and even the choice of what constituency is relevant. Because of these differences, the nature of public attitudes toward these institutions differs.

In the ensuing sections of this chapter, I will examine the public's view of the Congress. The emphasis of this chapter will be on two themes. First, how do attributes of individual legislators interact with the organizational characteristics of his legislative chamber to influence the public perceptions of Congress? Second, what variations exist concerning public attitudes toward the individual representative and the collective body of which he is a member?

The Responsible Party Model and Public Opinion

One of the most popular intellectual arguments for relating public opinion and congressional decision making is that associated with the notion of "responsible party government." According to this theory, the frequent election of legislators will create representatives responsive to the interests of their constituencies. These interests will be represented in Washington by means of an organizational structure centered on the member's political party. The party-in-Congress—a system of majority and minority leaders, whips, caucus spokesmen, and committee and subcommittee chairmen—will organize and promote a legislative program in each session of Congress in pursuance of generally stated party principles. At election time, each party will have a record for the constituency to judge, and each incumbent seeking re-election will have taken positions on legislative issues, either consistent with or in opposition to his party's position. As one writer has put it, the election is "the period of accounting: either the representative is instructed further, or he is defeated for malrepresentation, or he is warned, or he is encouraged" (Jones, 1966).

At first glance, the theory of responsible party government has some support. In a study of the 1958 congressional elections, Stokes and Miller (1962) found that among those who voted, 95 percent were party identifiers and 84 percent selected the candidate of their own party. Only 5 percent of the voters were Independents.[1] Thus, the *prima facie* evidence supports the conclusion that party voting based on legislative performance shapes the attitudes of voters for congressional candidates.

The 1958 congressional elections represented an important test of the responsible party model, since at that time the Democratic party controlled the Congress and the Republicans occupied the White House. It was a time of economic recession and related domestic problems. The interesting question posed by this situation was which party would bear the burden of public judgment. Would the Democratic Congress or the Republican president be held responsible for the nation's problems?

Stokes and Miller (1962) measured public opinion during these elections and probed the public's knowledge and interests in key issues associated with the 1958 campaign. They found that only 47 percent of the sample were aware that the Democrats controlled Congress. Allowing for the fact that some guessing also occurred, they concluded that no more than half knew which party had a majority in Congress. This was hardly the type of evidence to build an argument for the existence of responsible party government. If the political party controlling Congress was not a highly salient fact for most voters, neither were the candidates running for office. Only 25 percent of voters had heard of both candidates; another 29 percent had heard of only one of the two candidates; and 46 percent of all voters had not heard of either candidate. An examination of the kind of information most respondents possessed about congressional candidates showed a "popular image of the Congressman . . . almost barren of policy content . . ." (Stokes and Miller, 1962). References to legislative issues of the day accounted for less than one-thirtieth (1/30) of all comments about congressmen. Most responses were unfocused, evaluative judgments about the candidate, his experience, his knowledge of problems, and his overall performance.

Stokes and Miller's research is important because it lays to rest any belief that the responsible party model is a meaningful explanation of how public opinion relates to congressional behavior. At the constituency level, people are virtually uninformed about legislative issues and have only minimal knowledge even of who the candidates are. Furthermore, the party organization in Congress is perceived, at most, by only half of the electorate.

Criticism limited to the electorate's failure to behave in a manner consistent with this theoretical model does not tell the entire story. If the voters in congressional constituencies do not conform to the model, neither do congressmen or senators. It is a well-documented fact that party control in Congress is weak (cf. Jewell and Patterson, 1973). As a result, congressmen do not develop strong identifications with the congressional party structure; nor do they consistently support a party program in the legislature. When election time comes, congressmen do not view their support of a party program or the articulation of critical legislative issues as a critical part of their campaign re-election strategy. As Jones (1966) observes:

> The campaign period is a regularly scheduled event in the life of a representative, in which he makes an intensive effort to advertise himself—to project a generalized image of himself as a capable representative—so that he will win. It is not an issue-oriented event . . . and campaign-electoral conditions are such that the representative need not be bound by the election in his policy-making behavior.

Stokes and Miller (1962) confirm Jones's observations, for they report that 57 percent of incumbent congressional candidates in 1958 thought personal record and standing were "very important" factors in their re-election, but only 26 percent felt that national issues were "very important" and 25 percent that traditional party loyalties were "very important." In sum, neither the conditions in Congress nor the expectations of congressional candidates conform to the predictions of the responsible party model. For the model to work, both the Congress and the voters in the constituencies must change their behavior.

One apparent by-product of the failure of responsible party government in Congress is the failure of the attitudes of a congressman to conform strongly on important legislative issues to the average attitudes in the constituency he represents. According to Miller and Stokes (1963), American legislative politics is a mixture of two distinct models of representation. On some issues the behavior of the representative conforms more closely to an instructed delegate role, where the congressman's actions agree more closely with constituency opinion. In the area of civil rights policy, this model is most common. In the area of social welfare policy, political party provides an organizing principle akin to the notion of the responsible party model. Miller and Stokes observe that social welfare policy distinguishes party identifiers most clearly, and therefore, congressmen provide a force for representation of these attitudes. Finally, the area of foreign affairs presents a situation where the representative votes his conscience with little conformity to constituency opinion.

Supportive findings come from a related study of the relationship of constituency opinions and state legislators in Iowa. The greatest agreement in opinion occurred between the legislator and attentive constituents residing in the district and not between the legislator and his district (Boynton, Patterson, and Hedlund, 1969). These attentive constituents were not typical of the legislative district in which they lived; rather, they were a small group of people whom the legislator depended on for information about affairs "back home." The implication is clear: the people selected by the legislator to provide information about the district were not representative of public opinion in the district.

To summarize findings to this point, neither congressional candidates nor the party organization in Congress are highly salient political facts for most citizens. Nevertheless, party label is an important factor shaping the vote in congressional elections.

Citizens' Perceptions of Congress between Elections

The patterns of public awareness of the affairs of Congress and the activities of its members during elections are repeated with some interesting variations during nonelectoral periods. Studies of children in primary school show that knowledge about and salience of legislative bodies is slower to develop and never reaches the level of awareness associated with the executive branch (cf. Easton and Dennis, 1969). Adult awareness of the organization and activities of Congress is somewhat limited also. In a 1973 study conducted for the Senate Subcommittee on Intergovernmental Relations, the question, "What do you think of, when you think of 'the Congress'?" produced the following responses (U.S. Senate, 1973, Part II):

Both House and Senate	62%
House only	6
Senate only	4
House, Senate, and U.S. Supreme Court	20
Not sure	8
	100%

Nearly 40 percent of the national sample had incomplete or incorrect information about the basic composition of the nation's legislative body.

If there is some confusion about the organization of Congress, the names and party affiliations of the respondent's congressmen and senators were somewhat more salient facts. Fifty-nine percent of the sample correctly gave the name of at least one senator, 46 percent named their local congressman, and a similar proportion could identify the party of the legislator.

The public's knowledge of name and party labels has one well-documented implication for the legislator. Name identification, party affiliation, and issue-free campaigns produce an overwhelming advantage for the incumbent seeking re-election. A study of four congressional elections covering the years 1954 to 1960 reported that among those election contests where an incumbent congressman faced a challenger, the success rate of incumbents varied from a low of 70 percent to high of 85 percent (Jones, 1966). Other researchers have documented the incumbent's advantage both for the House of Representatives (Erickson, 1971, 1972) and Senate (Hinckley, 1970; Kostroski, 1973). Thus, the parameters of public opinion described above limit the competitiveness of legislative elections and thus restrict the possibility of significant change in the composition of the Congress.

The Salience of U.S. Senators

Because of the size and organization of the House of Representatives, few congressmen are known beyond their districts. In contrast to the House members, many United States senators establish reputations beyond their home states. Three explanations account for the differing public awareness accorded some senators and not others. The first and perhaps best known explanation is the "presidential ambitions" thesis (Matthews, 1960). Historically, the Senate and fifty state houses have produced the largest number of presidential candidates, and in recent years, more senators have become presidential timber.

To become a candidate for the presidency, most senators must violate a set of unwritten rules of behavior, called "folkways" and "norms," which, if followed, limit a member's exposure to public view (cf. Jewell and Patterson, 1973). These unwritten rules encourage individual members to submerge their identities within the workings of the Senate's organizational structure of leadership and committees (Matthews, 1959; Lehnen, 1967). Newer senators defer to older, more experienced members and "do their homework" until they rise to positions of expertise in some area of public policy. This process may take many years, and even though a new member may be fifty years old and have had a distinguished career elsewhere, he is still expected to serve his apprenticeship. Senators who play by these rules become associated with a group known as the Senate Club (cf. White, 1956). The club has no membership cards, formal roster, or fixed meeting place. It is a group of senators who have developed strong personal ties based on mutual recognition, respect, and acceptance. The principal characteristics that distinguish these men are their loyalty to the Senate, deference to more senior members, and reputation for expertise in some policy area.

A few senators do not fit comfortably into this mold. They do not always defer to the establishment, do not limit themselves to public statements within their area of expertise, and often have ambitions for higher office. These senators assume a role labeled as "outsider" or "maverick" (Huitt, 1961). The "outsiders" frequently ignore group pressures to conform to Senate expectations, partially because they hope for careers beyond the Senate.

Several distinguished senators have played the outsider role in the past. The late Senator Wayne Morse of Oregon entered the Senate as a Republican, became an Independent, and later a Democrat, and always maintained a reputation for speaking out. Senators Proxmire (D-Wisc.) and Humphrey (D-Minn.) had maverick reputations during their early careers. Senator Saxbe (R-Ohio) had a maverick image before resigning to become Nixon's attorney general. However, most senators conform to expectations about senatorial behavior within the Senate's organizational structure (Lehnen, 1967). These men usually do not build national reputations until late in their careers, if at all. In contrast, the outsider does not conform to the expectations of the club. He does not always specialize in his committee subject area or remain silent about legislative matters not before his assigned committee. Many times such behavior can only be explained by personality differences, but often such mavericks have chosen this mode of behavior to achieve recognition beyond the halls of the Senate.

The presidential ambitions thesis provides a reasonable explanation of why some Senate mavericks might have high public salience, but it does not explain why many other senators gain the public's attention. Two other factors associated with senators' roles help account for their saliency: their position within the Senate leadership and their expertise on specialized policy matters. Senate leadership positions such as majority leader, minority leader, and some committee chairmanships enhance public prominence. Because the Senate role encourages a senator to develop expertise in a specialized policy area, his committee assignments usually determine what areas he is most qualified to speak on publicly. As a result, committee chairmanships combine both leadership and expertise characteristics. These factors explain why some club members achieve national reputations.

In examining the Senate's roster for 1969, five senators might be expected to appear in any list of "most mentioned" because of their past, present, or future efforts to become president. Barry Goldwater had run in 1964; Eugene McCarthy had opposed Lyndon Johnson in the 1968 primaries; Edward Kennedy, George McGovern, and Edwin Muskie had been seriously considered as future candidates. The two major Senate leadership positions were held by Mike Mansfield (majority leader) and the late Everett Dirksen (minority leader). Among the most prominent of committee chairmen was J. William Fulbright of the Foreign Relations Committee. He had taken the role as critic of White House foreign policy-making, under both Johnson and Nixon, especially as it pertained to the Vietnam War. In a broader context, he sought to reassert the Senate's role in foreign affairs. One could expect these eight men to be mentioned more often than their ninety-two other Senate colleagues.

Table 7–1 presents a list of thirteen senators who were identified by at least 5 percent of the national sample. Over one-half of the senators received no mention at all and most others fell well below the 5 percent identification level. Two senators stand apart in the amount of public awareness from the others: Kennedy (45 percent) and Dirksen (39 percent). Among "presidential" senators only Goldwater and McCarthy received identifications from 10 percent of the

Table 7–1

Proportion of National Sample Identifying Selected Members* of the United States Senate

	% of Sample Identifying Senator	% of Sample Selecting Senator as "Best Known"	Frequency per Week Mentioned in AP Wire in 1964**
Edward Kennedy (D-Mass.)	45	22	16
Everett Dirksen (R-Ill.)	39	14	41
Jacob Javits (R-N.Y.)	14	4	13
J. William Fulbright (D-Ark.)	10	1	(a)
Barry Goldwater (R-Ariz.)	10	< 2	223
Eugene McCarthy (D-Minn.)	10	2	(a)
Charles Percy (R-Ill.)	9	< 1	(b)
Strom Thurmond (R-S.C.)	7	1	20
Mike Mansfield (D-Mont.)	7	< 1	31
Russell Long (D-La.)	6	< 2	(a)
George Murphy (R-Cal.)	6	< 1	(b)
Edmund Muskie (D-Me.)	6	< 1	(a)
Edward Brooke (R-Mass.)	6	< 1	(b)

*Senators listed either have at least 5% of the sample identifying them or have received at least 1% of "best known" selections.

**Wilhoit and Sherrill (1968).

(a) Not in the top 10% in 1964 analysis of AP wire dispatches.

(b) Not a member of the Senate in 1964.

sample. Muskie was mentioned by only 6 percent in spite of his vice-presidential candidacy only one year earlier. Senator McGovern received slightly less than 5 percent and therefore does not appear in Table 7–1. Among the Senate leadership positions Dirksen, Mansfield, and Long were mentioned. Fulbright was the most important committee chairman in the list.

One factor contributing to public awareness of certain senators is the exposure given certain members by the national press. Wilhoit and Sherrill (1968) demonstrated that all senators are not equally newsworthy. An analysis of Associated Press "A" wire dispatches to over 1,700 daily newspapers revealed that only a few senators received frequent mentions during a sampled week of dispatches. Six of the senators listed in Table 7–1 were among the most frequently discussed senators (top 10 percent) in AP wire dispatches in 1964; four others did not receive wide press coverage; and the remaining three individuals were not members of the Senate in 1964. The correspondence between the lists, even with five years intervening, suggests the critical role the media play in developing and sustaining name identification among the public. Yet it is clear that other factors discussed previously also contribute to the public's identification of individual members. Wilhoit and Sherrill found that length of service of a senator, the prestige of his committee assignments, and the size of the state he represented were factors affecting press coverage. High seniority, membership on a more prestigious committee, and representation of a populous state enhanced a senator's visibility to newsmen. Wilhoit and Sherrill also reported that the senator's ideology (liberal or conservative) and the competition for his seat (whether he faced a difficult re-election fight) did not affect the frequency of press reporting.

The Content of Senatorial Perceptions

Senators become known for their interest in the presidency, their positions of leadership in the Senate, or their stands on public policy questions. To determine how well these theoretical explanations accounted for public awareness, respondents were asked to identify the senator among those mentioned whom they knew the most about. The reasons why citizens mentioned particular senators are summarized in Table 7–2. The eight categories of response used are as follows:

Presidential Activity: comments about the senator's past, present, or future possibilities as a presidential candidate.

Senate Leadership Role: references to positions of leadership, past or present, in the Senate.

Other Office Holding: comments regarding an individual's experiences in other offices, such as state governor or representative.

Represents "Home" State: senator is known because he represents the interests of respondent's state.

Ideology or Party Label: senator is identified as being "conservative" or "liberal" or a leading member of a political party.

Table 7-2
The Salient Characteristics of Selected U.S. Senators*

	Kennedy	Dirksen	Javits	Fulbright	Goldwater	McCarthy	Other Republicans	Other Democrats
Presidential activity	10%	1%	2%	0%	29%	17%	2%	4%
Senate leadership role	7	10	2	19	0	0	1	5
Other office holding	0	0	0	3	6	0	9	6
Represents "home" state	1	2	25	9	0	11	21	19
Ideology or party label	4	10	24	6	23	11	12	5
Policy positions	7	10	6	34	21	33	8	11
Population group identification	9	3	7	0	0	6	8	6
Personal characteristics	61	64	34	3	21	22	39	45
Total	99%**	100%	100%	100%	100%	100%	100%	100%
	(512)	(328)	(103)	(32)	(48)	(36)	(229)	(455)

*Senators identified by at least 10% of sample (see Table 5–1).
**The percentage may not equal 100 because of rounding error. Numbers in parentheses are the total number of responses for each senator.

Policy Positions: comments regarding a specific policy position of senator (for example, foreign affairs or civil rights).

Population Group Identification: senator is identified with the interests of a major population group such as "the working man," "Negroes," or "the poor."

Personal Characteristics: references made to a senator's personal attributes or qualities.

Senators Kennedy and Dirksen received the most "best known" identifications, and four other senators were singled out sufficiently to permit inquiry concerning the causes for their popularity.[2] All other senators mentioned less frequently were grouped into the Other Republicans and Other Democrats categories. These two composite categories permit examination of why the less well-known senators are mentioned.

The composite categories permit several preliminary conclusions. First, the less well-known senator gains most of his public identity from two situations: his role as representative of the respondent's home state and his past political experience in other public office. A good example of this pattern was Senator Harold Hughes (D-Iowa). Since Senator Hughes did not have 5 percent of the national sample identifying him, he would not be classified as a national senator. Of the small number of people who identified him, 46 percent did so because of his experience as former governor of Iowa. The association of personal characteristics also was an important component of all identification. Thus, many senators were characterized as hard-working, honest, and likable.

The characteristic not readily associated with less prominent senators was either an ideological or party commitment or stands on policy. These two categories accounted for about one-fifth of all responses. With a few exceptions to be noted below, United States senators are not seen in partisan, ideological, or policy-oriented terms. This composite picture is similar to the one provided by Stokes and Miller (1962) and Jones (1966) in regard to perceptions of congressional candidates—namely, an emphasis on personal characteristics, identification with the constituency, and a lack of issue content.

The six senators singled out for closer examination are viewed in ways distinctly different from the composite given above. Three senators—Kennedy, Goldwater, and McCarthy—appear on the list because of their association with presidential aspirations. Senate leadership explains the appearance of Dirksen, Fulbright, and Kennedy, who in 1969 was the majority whip of the Senate. Three senators—Fulbright, Goldwater, and McCarthy—have gained public attention because of ideological or policy identifications. Thirty-four percent of Fulbright's responses pertained to his positions on policy—principally foreign affairs. Goldwater was labeled as a "conservative" and a "Republican" by many people, while McCarthy evoked comments of "liberal" and "antiwar." Jacob Javits appears on the list for two reasons: he represents a large state and he is identified as a liberal. Kennedy and Dirksen differed from other senators not only because of the large number of comments they evoked but also because a greater proportion were directed toward personal characteristics. Kennedy was readily associated with his brothers and family. Dirksen was seen as a nice man with a certain flair for showmanship. He was famous for giving impromptu speeches on the virtues of marigolds and presenting bouquets to Senator Smith of Maine.

Each of the six senators singled out has distinct reasons for gaining popular attention that mirror the three explanations of senatorial notoriety. Clearly, Kennedy, Goldwater, and McCarthy fit the presidential explanation. Dirksen and Fulbright are members of the Senate leadership, and Fulbright and Javits have gained attention because of their policy positions.

Partisanship and the Salience of Senators

If the partisan values of a respondent play a role in shaping responses to any public institution, then the effect on perceptions of United States senators should be profound. Every explanation of why a senator becomes known is tied to partisan-based differences. Senators are known because they seek a party nomination for the presidency, or because they are members of the party leadership in the Senate, or because they take policy stands that are usually associated with one party or another. Thus, the most well-known senators become so because of party-oriented activity.

As a result, Republican respondents reacted differently to senators than Democratic ones. Republicans were more likely to mention Dirksen, Goldwater, and other Republicans as "best known." Democrats were most knowledgeable about Kennedy. Independents responded most often about McCarthy and other Democratic senators.

Respondents not only differed on which senators they were most attentive to but also on the characteristics they selected. Table 7-3 shows how Kennedy, Dirksen, and other senators were viewed by each party's respondents. The body of the table shows the most frequently mentioned characteristics for each senator. Only those characteristics that were mentioned more often than average are listed.

Senator Kennedy's personal characteristics—namely, his youth, good looks, and family connections—were mentioned by all respondents, but Republicans were much more likely to identify him as a presidential aspirant and as the Senate's Democratic whip. Senator Dirksen, in addition to his personal characteristics, was known best for his position as Senate minority leader, but Republicans were much more likely to see him in his party role. The other members of the Senate were best known for their representation of "home" state interests, and Republican senators were more often identified by all respondents for their party and ideological positions than Democratic senators were. Overall, there is a general tendency for Republican respondents to associate partisan and presidential characteristics with individual senators more often than either Democrats or Independents do.

Table 7–3

Effects of Respondent's Party Identification on Perceived Characteristics* of Selected Senators

	Republican	Independent	Democrat
Kennedy	Personal characteristics Presidential activity Senate leadership role	Personal characteristics	Personal characteristics
Dirksen	Personal characteristics Party and ideological label Senate leadership role	Personal characteristics Senate leadership role	Personal characteristics Senate leadership role Other leadership role
Other Republican senators	Home state senator Party and ideological label Presidential activity Other office holding	Home state senator Party and ideological label	Home state senator Party and ideological label
Other Democratic senators	Home state senator Other office holding Policy positions	Home state senator Policy positions Other office holding Presidential activity	Home state senator Policy positions Other office holding

*The characteristics are in order of frequency of response. Only characteristics with a higher-than-average response rate are listed.

Public Evaluations of Congress

The average citizen views the performance of his national legislature with a general feeling of dissatisfaction. Even though the Congress is the only popularly elected body at the national level, Davidson and Parker (1972) found that many Americans had a low opinion of how well Congress performs its tasks. Similar conclusions are supported by the Harris Poll (see Figure 7–1) for the period 1963 to 1975. Except for a period after the death of President Kennedy, less than half of Americans rated Congress in favorable terms. Since the middle 1960s, there has been a steady decline in the proportion of positive evaluations.

Other poll results reported by Louis Harris provide some perspective on the magnitude of this decline in popularity. Table 7–4 reports the levels of confidence Americans place in the various branches of the federal government. These comparative data suggest two trends. First, all institutions—executive, legislative, and judicial—experienced a relative decline in confidence from 1966 to 1972. From 1972 to 1973, all but the executive branch showed a slight upturn in public confidence.

Figure 7-1
The Public's Evaluation of Congress, 1963-75

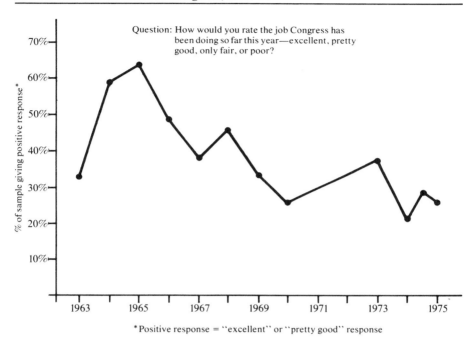

Question: How would you rate the job Congress has been doing so far this year—excellent, pretty good, only fair, or poor?

*Positive response = "excellent" or "pretty good" response

Source: Louis Harris and Associates

The second trend is the comparatively low ratings given Congress. Confidence in the Supreme Court never dropped to the level of the Congress and presidency, but it is a striking fact that the Congress did not generate signifi-

Table 7-4

Comparisons of Level of Public Confidence in Selected Institutions, 1966-73

Question: As far as the people in charge of running (institution) are concerned, would you say you have a great deal of confidence, only some confidence, or hardly any confidence at all in them?

Institution	1966	1972	1973
The U.S. House of Representatives	42%*	21%	29%
The U.S. Senate	42	21	30
The U.S. Supreme Court	51	28	33
The Executive branch of government	41	27	19

Source: U.S. Senate (1973), Part I, 33.
*% responding "great deal."

cantly more confidence than the executive branch, which was then mired down in the Watergate mudhole. Comparing the performance rating given Congress in 1973 (see Figure 7–1) with the confidence levels expressed in both Houses of Congress in that same year (see Table 7–4), one must conclude that the 29 to 30 percent who had a "great deal of confidence" represented only a short-term gain.

Several polls show that the Congress fared little better than the president during the height of the Watergate investigations. For example, Gallup asked the question "Do you approve or disapprove of the way [name of institution] is handling its/his job?" in April, 1974, for both the U.S. Congress and Nixon. Twenty-five percent approved of Nixon's performance, and only 30 percent approved of the Congress's behavior (Gallup Index No. 107). If one compares these results with public response to two specific Watergate-related events involving both the president and Congress, the enigma becomes more complex. These two events are the 1973 Senate Watergate Committee hearings (Ervin Committee) and the 1974 House Judiciary Committee hearings. A Harris Poll in September, 1973, showed a generally favorable response to individual members of the Ervin Committee and an increase in popularity between July and August of that year, when the Committee held public hearings. In August of that year, the "good" or "excellent" ratings for individual committee members were Ervin (63 percent), Baker (61 percent), Inouye (56 percent), Weicker (45 percent), Gurney (43 percent), Talmadge (43 percent), and Montoya (41 percent). The senators with less than 50 percent approval ratings received over 30 percent "not sure" ratings, suggesting that the lower ratings were partly the result of poor name-identification. A year later in August, 1974, Harris again measured public response to the House Judiciary Committee (Rodino Committee) proceedings. He reported that only 36 percent of the American people gave postitive ratings and 48 percent gave negative ratings in July, 1974, before the hearings started. By August, 1974, the approval rate was up 26 percent from July. In sum, almost half of those polled prior to the committee hearings were unfavorable to the proceedings. Harris notes that "credit for bringing about this dramatic change in public expectations and attitudes can be traced directly to the sharp rise in public respect for the behavior of the House Judiciary Committee and its chairman, Rep. Peter Rodino, in the way the impeachment proceedings were handled." Nonetheless, more citizens initially judged a fundamental constitutional inquiry conducted only weeks before the president resigned in unfavorable terms.

In an attempt to sum up the public's overall evaluation of Watergate, Harris asked (February, 1975) the question:

With the conclusion of the Watergate cover-up trial, there will be almost no other new cases to be tried in connection with Watergate. How would you rate the way the U.S. system of justice has worked in the case of (referent)—excellent, pretty good, only fair, or poor?

The response to the list is a revealing picture of the status of Congress in the public's mind. The following is a description of the "excellent–pretty good" ratings of several principal actors:

	Excellent— Pretty Good
—The way Judge John Sirica handled the Watergate case	71%
—The way Leon Jaworski handled the job of Special Prosecutor	67
—The House Judiciary Committee vote on impeachment of President Nixon	66
—The U.S. Senate Watergate hearings	61

Although a majority of citizens gave the principal actors favorable ratings, the congressional proceedings again received lower ratings.

Even though the Watergate period presented unusual circumstances from which to generalize about public attitudes toward Congress, placing the evidence collected during that period into a broader context permits several observations to be drawn. It is clear that Congress as a body gained little in public evaluation from the Watergate period. Although individual members—Senators Ervin, Baker, and Inouye and Congressman Rodino—greatly enhanced their name recognition and standing, the body as a whole did not reap many collective benefits. By January, 1975, a time when President Ford had held office for only five months, the public's ratings of Congress had dropped again to pre-Watergate levels. Although all institutions declined in their public ratings in the early 1970s, Congress maintained a consistently lower standing than other institutions —especially the Supreme Court.

Although it is now obvious that Congress is not viewed in favorable terms by the average American, I have established a few reasons why this is so. Davidson and Parker (1972) argue that the Congress suffers the fate of all politicians: in the eyes of the public it does not perform essential tasks. Its rules, procedures, and organizational structure defy public understanding and many times invite the conclusion that Congress "does nothing." In 1970 Harris asked for specific reasons why respondents evaluated Congress positively or negatively (Harris, 1971). One-fifth of respondents who rated Congress could give no particular reason for their feelings. Most individuals who gave reasons expressed only vague feelings devoid of specific policy content. The respondents with positive feelings most often expressed the feeling that "they are trying, doing the best they can." Citizens with negative judgments most often felt that "they aren't getting enough done, dragging their feet." In general, there is evidence that most Americans have little understanding of or appreciation for the discussion, delay, and compromise inherent to the American legislative process. At later points in time (1974 and 1975) Harris conducted polls in which he asked respondents to rate specific policy actions of Congress. It is fair to conclude that most Americans were not aware of these specific actions but were quick to express opinions regarding Congress's performance when asked about specific actions. As one can see below, the evaluations were overwhelmingly negative and consistent across the period 1974 to 1975:

Policy	Positive	Negative
Controlling inflation		
January, 1975	7%	86%
January, 1974	6	88
Handling the energy shortage		
January, 1975	17	77
January, 1974	10	82
Inspiring confidence in government		
January, 1975	18	73
January, 1974	10	82
Handling taxes and spending		
January, 1975	12	80
January, 1974	—	—
Providing adequate health insurance		
January, 1975	16	68
January, 1974	—	—

Though these judgments may reflect the public's frustration with these serious problems, it is obvious that most citizens have expectations that Congress can and should act to solve the problems.

Partisanship and Evaluations of Congress

In addition to lack of information about congressional activity, the generally low visibility of most members, and a failure to appreciate the give and take of the legislative process, partisan considerations also affect how Congress is judged. Harris (1971) reported strong differences in the percent positive ratings of Congress in 1970 based on the party identification of the respondent: Democrats, 37 percent positive; Republicans, 33 percent; and Independents, 30 percent. A Gallup Poll in April, 1974, also found a similar partisan spread on evaluations of Congress: Democrats, 38 percent approval; Independents, 27 percent; and Republicans, 23 percent approval. Undoubtedly, Republicans were influenced during this period by congressional inquiries into President Nixon's affairs. In a study of the Iowa legislature, party identification was a major factor in the level of support expressed by Iowans (Boynton et al., 1968; Patterson et al., 1969), but Davidson and Parker (1972) found little relationship between a respondent's party identification and specific support for the legislature. Thus, there is some evidence pointing toward the conclusion that party loyalties color specific judgments about Congress.

Individual members also are evaluated in highly partisan terms. After collecting information regarding what respondents perceived about the senator nominated as "best known" to them, each respondent was asked to record an overall assessment of the senator's performance.[3]

Table 7–5 suggests a pronounced effect of party identification on specific evaluations of a senator's performance. For all senators taken together, Democrats (80 percent) were most supporting, followed next by Republicans (73 percent) and Independents (68 percent). A closer examination of individual senators, however, indicates a clear partisan effect on evaluations. Generally speaking, Republicans were more supporting of Republican senators, and Democrats preferred Democratic ones. Independents fell in-between the two extremes. The pattern for Senator Dirksen (R-Ill.) illustrates the relationship for Republican senators. Senator Dirksen received 89 percent approval from Republicans, 80 percent from Independents, and 78 percent from Democrats. Senator Kennedy is an example of the pattern for Democratic senators. He received 90 percent approval from Democrats, 68 percent from Independents, and 56 percent from Republicans.

Table 7–5
The Effects of Respondent's Party Identification on the Approval of Selected U.S. Senators in 1969

	Republican	*Independent*	*Democrat*
Kennedy (D-Mass.)	56%*	68%	90%
Dirksen (R-Ill.)	98	80	78
Javits (R-N.Y.)	78	70	59
Fulbright (D-Ark.)	88	**	**
Goldwater (R-Ariz.)	66	**	**
McCarthy (D-Minn.)	**	7	31
Other Republican senators	92	75	61
Other Democratic senators	46	80	83
All senators	73	68	80

*The percentage is the net approval rating defined as: % Net Approval = % Approve −% Disapprove. A negative percentage means more respondents "disapproved" than "approved."
**Less than 10 respondents identified senator as "best known."

Two other interesting facts should be noted about Table 7–5. First, Senator McCarthy had significantly less approval, even among Democrats, than other senators. Second, Republicans were much less approving of Democratic senators than Democrats were of Republican ones. Republicans gave "Other Democrats" a rating of 46 percent, while Democrats evaluated "Other Republicans" at 61 percent.

During the Watergate days, Republicans were consistently more critical of Congress than Democrats or Independents. Among Republicans, Senator Ervin's rating dropped from 77 percent to 52 percent approval during his committee's hearings. Independents remained stable in their approval (62–63 percent) and Democrats, as expected, increased their positive ratings of the senator by 6 percent to 71 percent positive. A year later Harris found that 65 percent of the total public favored the impeachment vote of the House Judiciary Committee, but only 40 percent of Republicans did. In sum, the effects of a citizen's party loyalties on evaluations of individuals and Congress are strongly related to party label.

Public Expectations about Congressional Performance

The expectations the public has regarding the job of a legislator are focused primarily on his service to the people of the constituency and not so much on broad policy issues. In regard to the legislator's relationship to the constituency, two general models are presented—the instructed-delegate model and the representative model. When a national sample was asked to evaluate these alternate roles, the instructed-delegate role received more support, as measured by the following two statements:

a. A U.S. senator ought to think like people of his state so he can react to proposed legislation the way they would.
b. A U.S. senator should usually vote in the interest of the entire nation even if it might hurt his state.

The agreement rate was 74 percent for the instructed-delegate model and 64 percent for the representative model (U.S. Senate, 1973, Part II).

Americans also feel strongly that the Congress should play a "watchdog" role. In regard to feelings about the relationship of the Congress to the presidency, two questions demonstrated the strong desire of most citizens to keep presidential power in rein:

a. Congress should serve as a check over the president and his executive agencies.
b. Congress should always cooperate with the president and not oppose his proposals.

Eighty-nine percent believed Congress should oversee the president's actions, and 84 percent disagreed that Congress should always cooperate with the White House.[4] But the most strongly articulated attitude regarding a legislator's role concerned the statement, "An important part of an elected congressman's job should be to help the people in dealing with governmental agencies." An overwhelming 93 percent of the public agreed with this statement. The fact that a congressman, and to a lesser extent a U.S. senator, is thought to be a source of assistance in dealing with governmental problems is also illustrated by the data summarized in Table 7–6. Respondents were asked to select what individuals or organizations, both public and private, they would go to for help. Although the type of problem presented affected the public's choice for assistance, the local congressman and U.S. senator were consistently perceived as a source of aid. Respondents were especially oriented toward the Congress, where questions about civil liberties were raised. The president and governor were generally not thought of as possible sources of assistance.

The special place that congressmen and senators hold in the public's mind

Table 7–6

Institutions from Which the Public Would Seek Assistance in Solving Selected Problems

	a. Income Tax Problem	*b.* Invasion of Privacy	*c.* Unfair Treatment by Army	*d.* Nuisance from Airplanes
Your U.S. senator	11%	16%	27%	8%
Your congressman	22	26	46	18
State legislator	3	4	4	13
The president	21	1	6	21
Your governor	3	3	6	6
Top local official's office	13	15	5	30
A lawyer	35	21	7	3
A local citizens group of active citizens	2	7	2	16

Source: U.S. Senate, 1973, Part II.
a. If on your federal income tax return you asked for a refund and were turned down unfairly, which of these people or organizations would you turn to for help?
b. If an investigator from the federal government came around to your house to ask about your personal political beliefs or political activities, in a way you thought was not justified, who on the list would you turn to for help?
c. If you had a son in the army who told you he was being treated unfairly, who on the list would you turn to for help?
d. If airplanes took a new route that made a lot of noise over where you live, who on the list would you go to to make the planes change their route?

when some assistance is needed in obtaining a service is also corroborated by other findings. When asked "Would you do any of the following to change things you don't like about government?" respondents selected their representatives in Washington as the source of assistance. Here is a selected list of actions people were questioned about and the percentage indicating they would "certainly do that" (U.S. Senate, 1973, Part II):

	Certainly Do That
Vote against a public official	78%
Write to your congressman	52
Write to your U.S. senator	50
Contact local law enforcement officials	44
Write letters to the newspapers	29
Join a political party group and work to make changes	27
Do nothing	3

In the eyes of their constituents, congressmen, and to a lesser extent senators, are representatives not of policy views but of needs arising from interaction with governmental institutions. They serve as watchdogs and facilitators as much as policy planners debating broad questions pertaining to the public interest.

The Effects of Social Background on Perceptions

Previous studies of the effects of social background characteristics have found that these attributes shape a citizen's view of the legislative process (cf. Boynton et al., 1968; Patterson et al., 1969; Davidson and Parker, 1972). Yet these studies suggest that social background attributes such as race, sex, income education, and occupation do not produce as systematic differences in the public's summary of the overall rating of Congress as they do for other institutions. Gallup (Index No. 107), for example, reports approval and disapproval rates for Congress for April, 1974, by various background characteristics. The Gallup data reveal that the largest differences on the sex, race, and status dimensions are for response versus nonresponse. Females, blacks, and grade-school educated respondents most often give "no opinion" responses to Gallup's rating question. When the approval rates are adjusted for the levels of nonresponse, there is little or no difference in the approval ratings between whites and blacks, males and females, and among occupation and income categories. College-educated respondents, however, are much more likely to approve of the Congress (forty-nine adjusted approval rate) than noncollege respondents. The low saliency of Congress, its lack of issues, and few publicly recognized members contribute to a blurring of distinctions commonly found with other institutions.

The Effects of Sex

If the collective rating of Congress is not as strongly influenced by the familiar background conditions, one might expect ratings of individual members to show some variations. Table 7–7, for the most part, does not confirm this expectation in the case of U.S. senators.[5] With the exception of Senator Kennedy, the differences by sex in the percentage selecting a senator as "best known" are not large. Kennedy, however, has a high salience level among female respondents.

Respondents were also asked to evaluate their "best known" senator by responding to the question, "Do you approve, or not approve of the way (he/she)

Table 7–7
The Effects of Sex on Salience and Approval of Selected U.S. Senators

	Selecting as "Best Known"		Net Approval	
	Males	*Females*	*Males*	*Females*
Kennedy	20%[a]	33%	73%[b]	81%
Dirksen	18	17	85	83
Javits	7	4	71	89
Fulbright	2	1	85	[c]
Goldwater	3	2	61	61
McCarthy	3	3	−12	55
Other Republicans	15	14	78	78
Other Democrats	29	21	71	73

[a]These percentages are based on the subset of respondents who identified at least one senator and not the entire sample.
[b]% Net Approval = % Approval − % Disapproval.
[c]Less than twenty respondents identified Senator Fulbright.

is handling (his/her) job?" The "net approval" rates, representing the difference between the percent approving and not approving, show considerable variation. Thus, Senators Kennedy, Javits, and McCarthy received much more favorable ratings from women than from men; the difference is especially pronounced for McCarthy. Women were also slightly more approving of senators generally than men were.

The Effects of Race

The race of the interviewee plays an important role in determining which senators are salient and how they are evaluated. Senator Kennedy inherited the favorable public image held by black people of his brothers John and Robert, since he was selected as "best known" by 42 percent of all black respondents (Table 7–8). Generally, black respondents were more aware of Democratic senators than white interviewees, and whites distributed their comments more among other senators (such as Dirksen, Javits, Goldwater, and McCarthy) in addition to Kennedy.

Table 7–8
The Effects of Race on Salience and Approval of Selected U.S. Senators

	Selecting as "Best Known"		Net Approval	
	Whites	Blacks	Whites	Blacks
Kennedy	25%	42%	76%	90%
Dirksen	19	7	85	*
Javits	6	4	77	*
Fulbright	<2	<2	77	*
Goldwater	2	<1	61	*
McCarthy	3	2	19	*
Other Republicans	15	11	80	44
Other Democrats	24	30	72	66

*Less than ten respondents identified these senators.

Blacks and whites did not differ on the overall net approval of senators, but they differed markedly on individuals. Senator Kennedy was highly approved by black respondents (90 percent), but other senators, regardless of party and with the exception of Kennedy, were evaluated more favorably by whites. Republican senators also fared better in the eyes of white respondents than Democrats. Blacks, in comparison, rated Democrats higher.

The Effects of Social Status

Sociostatus—the combined effects of a respondent's education, income, and occupation—does not have any pronounced and systematic effect on the salience of individual senators. It does, however, affect respondents' judgments about individual senators. Republican senators as a group receive increasing approval from higher status individuals, whereas Democrats have their greatest support among the middle and lower classes (Table 7–9). Looking at individual senators, one finds such senators as Kennedy with their greatest support among the middle classes. Senators Dirksen and McCarthy show opposite patterns, Dirksen receiving more approval from higher status individuals and McCarthy receiving his greatest support from lower status citizens.

Table 7–9
The Effects of Status on the Salience and Approval of Selected U.S. Senators

| | Selecting as "Best Known" | | | Net Approval | | |
	Low	Medium	High	Low	Medium	High
Kennedy	24%	28%	27%	78%	82%	71%
Dirksen	17	19	17	79	77	93
Javits	4	6	6	52	100	72
Fulbright	1	2	2	*	*	*
Goldwater	1	2	4	*	*	*
McCarthy	3	3	2	32	23	12
Other Republicans	15	14	15	65	71	88
Other Democrats	25	20	24	70	75	64

*Less than ten respondents identified these senators.

Although the differences in perceptions attributed to sex, race, and status are not as large as with other institutions, the variations associated with individuals such as Senators Kennedy and Dirksen suggest one thing: that the few individuals who develop name recognition nationally speak to distinctly different publics and receive support from different sectors. To understand the components of the remaining ninety or more senators would require data from their specific geographical constituencies, their home states, where their recognition rate is higher and public evaluations of their performances are undoubtedly more structured. It is an unusual senator who gains the national reputation of a Kennedy or a Dirksen. In many ways, they are each one-of-a-kind, even though the their popularity may flow from a common set of circumstances.

In summary, we should note that the specific support for Congress as an institution has been low during the last decade. This fact results mainly from its organizational complexity and its use of delay and compromise to achieve legislative consensus. Both characteristics are only partially understood by most Americans, and these conditions no doubt contribute to negative feelings toward Congress.

Yet Congress is a relatively salient institution as embodied in the incumbent representative who comes home to seek re-election. His name and party identification are generally known facts, and the individual citizen also has rather well-defined notions about what his representative ought to do in Washington. The incumbent congressman is expected to protect the interests of the citizen from the other branches of government and especially the bureaucracy, and more importantly, he is expected to give assistance whenever the constituent faces a problem involving bureaucratic red tape.

The citizen does not see his congressman as a spokesman for specific policy positions. In fact, the citizen has little perception of the policy-related activities of Congress and tends to view the policy performance of Congress in extremely negative terms. This pattern is in marked contrast to the attentive publics associated with the executive and judicial branches. The theoretical idea of a legislative body as a source of and soundboard for policy disputes is not mirrored by public opinion.

Most congressmen and senators have local reputations for hard work, competence, and experience. They labor to maintain this image, because incumbency and the associated image of competence are the main reasons for their re-election. Party business in the Halls of Congress, great legislative debates, and national images must take second place. The constituent expects a congressmen or senator to help at critical periods—break a bureaucratic logjam or fight an individual case of injustice. The role of policy leadership must be played elsewhere or be accomplished in addition to service to the constituency.

Notes

[1]In the Miller and Stokes study the Independent category excludes respondents who indicated a leaning toward the Republican or Democratic parties. The proportion of Independents in midterm congressional elections, including party leaners, is closer to 25 percent. See Figure 3–1 for a text of the party identification question.

[2]The data were collected prior to Senator Kennedy's automobile accident on Chappaquiddick Island.

[3]The question was: Do you approve or not approve of the way (he/she) is handling (his/her) job?

[4]This poll was taken in the fall, 1973.

[5]Since a few senators are the only members of Congress who gain wide public recognition, this analysis will be limited to them. The small sample sizes for individual senators prevented the analysis of sex and race effects, controlled for status, as done in previous chapters.

Political Action: Modes of
Overt Citizen Participation

Historically, the emphasis on citizen participation in political matters has always had strong normative overtones. Many people—whether they be elected officials, scholars, active or inactive citizens—believe that personal involvement in public affairs is extremely important. Presidential elections, for example, take on a larger-than-life dimension. Media commentators make sweeping interpretations of the meaning of high (or low) voter turnout. Citizens groups urge people, "Regardless of how you vote, be sure to vote." And election surveys show that people in overwhelming numbers believe they ought to vote even if they do not. An interesting by-product of this feeling is that election polls consistently overestimate voter turnout because respondents are hesitant to admit to an interviewer that they probably will not take time to vote (Clausen, 1968–69). For example a study conducted by the Bureau of the Census on voting turnout in the 1972 presidential election estimated a turnout rate 9 percent above the actual vote (U.S. Bureau of the Census, 1973).

Not all actions are considered politically relevant ones; rather, only a small set of societal actions have been judged important to the political process. A well-known scholar has defined political participation to be "those activities by private citizens that are more or less directly aimed at influencing the selection of governmental personnel and/or the decisions they make" (Verba et al., 1971). This definition is somewhat too restrictive for my purposes because it excludes strictly psychological, private forms of participation by emphasizing only those acts that determine who shall govern and that influence what decisions elites make. Thus, activities such as voting, campaigning, and contacting officials have received the most attention.

An expanded definition of participation must include those activities that are of relevance to the actor (citizen) and have political implications for him as well as those activities that affect the operation of government. A single participatory activity may be relevant at both the individual and the system levels. Take voting as an example: voting meets the Verba definition because it affects the selection of leaders and to a limited extent the execution of policy, but it also has important private effects on the individuals who participate. Rose and Mossawir (1967) note the symbolic and expressive effects of this activity on citizens, in addition to any instrumental or policy-determining consequences. They suggest that elections are especially important emotional experiences for Americans, much more so than in other Western societies. One can use the Verba definition with its emphasis on activities by private citizens but expand its meaning to include those actions that affect individuals in a politically relevant way.

Three dimensions are critical for determining what activities are politically relevant and thus treated as forms of participation: (1) the intent of the private actor and the consequences to him; (2) the interpretations made by elites of the political act and the consequences resulting for the political system; and (3) the context in which the action occurs. The first dimension simply summarizes the need to re-emphasize individual consequences of political behavior. These consequences may be psychological—feelings of support, efficacy toward government, or alienation—but they are nonetheless as real as consequences such as determining who wins an electoral contest. It is important to clarify the implications of the second dimension—that elites also define what is politically relevant. The urban disorders of the 1960s created extreme political reactions among elites. Most officials judged these acts to be politically motivated and directed toward public officials, although most studies of riot behavior confirmed the contrary conclusion that little planning or political intent was present in these acts.

Similarly, sky-jacking was viewed initially as a politically motivated act to embarrass the government and promote a cause. Yet the profile of known sky-jackers reveals the opposite: the typical sky-jacker is an apolitical, psychologically unstable person who has experienced repeated failures in life and who desires a sense of success and recognition. The publicity associated with the attempt is actually a cry for help. These are two examples of how elites can place political meanings on essentially nonpolitical (for the individual involved) activities. Thus, actions have no inherent meaning; they must be interpreted and have meanings assigned them. The criteria described above provide a means for classifying which actions are political participation.

The third dimension relevant for interpreting political acts is the context in which they occur. The political culture of a society provides the reference points by which an act is judged political. In Communist China, for example, many actions defined as private, nonpolitical behavior in Western societies are judged to be highly relevant to the collectivity, and thus political. A worker who produces well in a factory is engaging in political activity (cf. Townsend, 1969). In Western societies many more activities are deemed nonpolitical and thus the scope of participation is relatively limited.

The same act may also have different political meanings in different cultures. Rose and Mossawir (1967) note the British are much less emotionally concerned with elections than Americans. A cross-cultural study of various kinds of participation, which compared Austria, India, Japan, Nigeria, and the United States, found considerable variation in the styles of participation. The authors, however, cautioned against attributing the same meaning to a given act across cultures (Kim et al., 1974). Another example is the attempt to introduce elections into South Vietnam to legitimate its government. It failed in part because the political act was devoid of its Western cultural context. The values and interpretations most Vietnamese placed on their electoral process were quite distinct from American interpretations. Thus, two distinct political cultures produced two distinct interpretations of the same event.

Some Types of Participation

In the context of American political culture, several forms of behavior are politically significant. They include political interest, electoral behavior, contact with officials, protest behavior, and group involvement. Political interest is a form of awareness. Political awareness includes the activities necessary to be cognizant of political matters—for example, a willingness to acquire political information and learn differing points of view. The appeal to be informed about your public officials is a manifestation of the values placed on political awareness. Electoral behavior includes voting as well as more active forms of campaign involvement, such as contributing money, attending rallies, and working for a candidate.

Another significant form of political action is citizen contact with government officials. This contact takes many forms. It may include writing or calling an elected or appointed official, and it also encompasses the day-to-day interactions citizens have with their elected and appointed officials. The appeals to write your congressman or call City Hall represent encouragements to have contact. Several writers stress the importance of citizen-initiated as contrasted with involuntary contacts (cf. Verba and Nie, 1972). Such a conceptual limitation unnecessarily excludes contact behavior that may have significant political consequences for the individual. Walker and others (1972) demonstrate that involuntary contacts with the police and courts have important attitudinal consequences. The major contributing factor is the satisfaction participants had in dealing with these public officials, and such satisfaction may not be directly related to whether the contact was voluntary or not. People called for jury duty, for example, varied on their support for the courts depending on their satisfaction (cf. Walker et al., 1972; Walker and Richardson, 1974).

Protest behavior has received renewed interest in the past few years. During the 1960s many forms of extreme political action occurred—demonstrations, sit-ins, marches, riots, protests, and organized violence. Though they vary widely with respect to purposes and consequences, those actions share a common theme. The motivations of many participants were intense and the reactions of many observers were equally so. Many political cultures experience sustained and systematically organized political activity of this type; Ireland, Israel, and Chile are three current examples.

Americans are reluctant to engage in unconventional political acts. A recent national study asked whether the respondents had ever engaged in various kinds of political acts. Although a large number of respondents reported signing a petition (69 percent), attending a speech or rally for a political candidate (50 percent), and writing letters to congressmen (33 percent), a much smaller number reported picketing or taking part in a street demonstration (11 percent) and taking part in a demonstration where violence occurred (2 percent) (U.S. Senate, 1973, Part II). The final form of participation listed above is group involvement. Although the other forms of of participation discussed previously involve individual citizens acting alone and interrelating with officials, the central idea of group involvement is that individuals work through local organizations and influence-groups to participate. Much of this activity is community-oriented and locally based, but it need not be limited to this level. For example, 36 percent of a national sample said they would "join a citizens group to take action" to change "things they didn't like about government" (U.S. Senate, 1973, Part II).

Every type of political act has a threshold that determines the likelihood of participation. This threshold is determined by three factors: the initiative required to participate; the range of interpersonal interaction encountered; and the potential for conflict and violence associated with the act. Table 8–1 presents a summary of the various kinds of political actions characterized by these three descriptive dimensions. For participatory behavior such as political involvement and voting the threshold is relatively low, whereas campaigning and protest behavior have high ones.

Table 8–1
Description of Selected Types of Political Participation

	Psychological Involvement	Voting	Cam-paigning	Contact	Protest	Community and Group Involvement
Initiative required to participate	low	low to medium	high	medium	high	medium to high
Range of interpersonal interactions	limited	limited	wide	usually limited	limited to wide	wide
Potential for conflict and violence	low	low	medium	low to medium	low to high	medium to high

Political actions that allow for little initiative and privacy, and lw levels of conflict have the lowest thresholds for participation. In contrast, high initiative, public, and conflict-laden activities have high thresholds. Some studies of political participation have argued that the types of participation were ordered according to difficulty of involvement. Milbrath's (1965) early study of participation focused on political awareness, voting, and campaigning. He saw these activities as ordered along a continuum from a low to a high threshold. A later in-depth study of participation (Verba and Nie, 1972) included all the activities summarized in Table 8–1 except protest behavior. Their study suggests that activity cannot be ordered along a single dimension. Thus, contact behavior could require a high degree of initiative or a low one. It is, therefore, not possible to establish a single order or hierarchy in the Milbrath sense for participatory actions. Verba and Nie suggest the notion of styles of participation. For them citizens may engage in mixed forms of participation based on combinations of activities.

The Degree of Participation

Involvement in Politics

Being "interested" in politics is one activity that requires relatively little for a citizen to participate. As Table 8–2 shows, such involvement can be measured in six different ways, indicating the customary high rates of participation. Thus, 91 percent agreed with the statement "I like to hear about what's going on in politics." Almost everybody is "interested," in this sense. There is some important variation in the responses which suggests the passive nature of this form of participation. Some opinion researchers believe that disagreement is harder to express than agreement, and they therefore include questions that must be answered "disagree" as well as "agree" to provide a check on this bias. Significantly, the items in Table 8–2 requiring a disagree response all have lower rates of participation than those items requiring agree responses.

Table 8–2
Selected Indicators of Citizen Involvement in Politics

Statement Measuring Involvement in Politics	*Sample Giving "Participatory" Response**
I like to hear about what's going on in politics.	91 % Agree
It makes a lot of difference to me who wins a presidential election.	89 % Agree
It makes a lot of difference to me who represents me in Congress.	86 % Agree
A good many elections for state offices aren't important enough to bother with.	75 % Disagree
A good many local elections aren't important enough to bother with.	73 % Disagree
I find most campaigns silly and ridiculous.	57 % Disagree

*Respondents answering "no opinion" were excluded before computing percentages.

Societies differ in how participation is distributed. Three hypothetical patterns of participation are the uniform, selective, and intense. Figure 8–1 pictures these three hypothetical distributions of participation. The uniform pattern shows the situation where the degree of participation is the same across the intensity scale. In this case, the same proportions of people have low levels of intensity as have high levels. The selective pattern shows a large proportion of people with low levels of participation and only a small proportion highly involved. The intense pattern shows the opposite case—many people have high involvement and there

Figure 8-1
Hypothetical Patterns of Political Participation

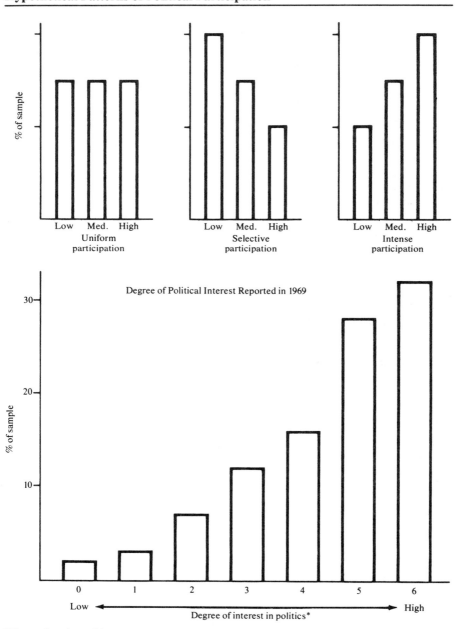

*The number of ''participatory'' responses given to questions are listed in Table 8-2

are relatively few uninvolved citizens. It is important to recognize that Figure 8–1 presents ideal situations, never perfectly duplicated in practice. The three patterns, however, may be taken as useful standards from which to evaluate the distribution of political interest.

To create an overall summary of each respondent's degree of political involvement, each person was assigned an index score from 0 to 6 according to the number of statements reported in Table 8–2 as answered in a "participatory" manner. Thus, a score of 6 means that the respondent gave responses indicating an interest in political matters to all six statements, and a score of 0 means no responses indicating interest were given. The distribution of this involvement index is summarized in Figure 8–1. Almost one-third (32 percent) of the sample have a high interest in politics; at the other extreme, only 2 percent have low interest. The overall shape of the distribution suggests a pattern of intense participation (see Figure 8–1), because a substantial proportion of the sample fell at the high end of the index. This pattern is not entirely unpredicted, since it has been noted previously that being interested in politics requires minimal initiative and has little potential for conflict. Yet relative to other societies, such as Austria, India, Italy, Mexico, Nigeria, the United Kingdom, and West Germany, the levels of mass participation by comparison are intense in the United States (Almond and Verba, 1965; Kim et al. 1974; Rose and Mossawir, 1967). Finally, it is especially important to remember that measures of political involvement are not absolute measures—no one is absolutely uninvolved politically, except possibly a deceased participant. "Low" involvement does not mean no, but rather less, involvement. Thus, most Americans are relatively intense in their interests, especially in comparison to other cultures.

Electoral Participation

Voting and campaigning activities are the major expressions of electoral participation. An important means of political involvement, they constitute widely varied degrees of participation. Table 8–3, which summarizes reported rates of electoral participation, shows that voting in presidential elections has a degree of involvement comparable to being "interested" in politics (see Table 8–2), but campaigning is a much more limited form of participation. The most frequent form of campaign behavior, wearing a button or displaying a sticker, occurs only among one-quarter of the population, whereas voting is reported by over three-quarters.

There is important evidence to suggest that this 79 percent figure reported for 1968 is inflated. The Bureau the of Census estimates a 68 percent voter turnout figure for the 1968 election (U.S. Bureau of the Census, 1973). Although there is some question about the exact validity of both sources (cf. Clausen, 1968–69), one can safely say that the inflation in the voting figure reported in Table 8–3 is in excess of 5 percent.

Electoral activity presents a higher threshold for participation. Even a rel-

Table 8–3
Report of Electoral Participation (1968)

	Sample Reporting Activity
Voted in 1968 election	79%
Campaign Activities:	
Wore campaign buttons or displayed bumper sticker	24
Went to campaign rally, meeting, etc.	21
Gave money to a candidate	18
Worked for a political party passing out literature,	
addressing letters, or contacting voters	12

atively common act such as voting has large proportions of people who are prevented from participating. These restrictions fall into several categories: lack of political interest, technical and legal barriers, and social-economic background considerations. Although the last factor will be discussed in a later section, we can gain some insight into the role political interest, technical, and legal hurdles play in disenfranchising individuals. Table 8–4 summarizes a

Table 8–4
Summary of Turnout and Voting in 1972 Presidential Election

Registered and voted in 1972 presidential election		63.0% (85.8 million)
Registered but did not vote in 1972 presidential election		9.3%* (12.7 million)
Reasons for not voting:		
-unable to get to polls	3.2%	
-out of town; away from home	1.0	
-machines not working, long lines, etc.	4	
-not interested	1.4	
-dislike politics, candidates	1.1	
-other reasons, DK, and NA	2.3	
Subtotal	9.4	
Not registered to vote in 1972 presidential election		27.7% (37.7 million)
Reasons for not registering:		
-not a citizen	2.9%	
-residence requirements	1.7	
-unable to register	3.5	
-not interested	11.9	
-dislike politics, candidates	2.1	
-other reasons, DK, and NA	5.6	
Subtotal	27.7	
Total noninstitutionalized population 18 years and older residing in the 50 states and the District of Columbia in November, 1972		100% (136.2 million)

Source: U.S. Bureau of the Census, 1973.
*This figure is smaller than the one in the previous column due to rounding.

report provided by the Bureau of the Census (1973) on participation in the 1972 presidential election. Sixty-three percent reported voting; 9 percent were registered but did not vote; and the remaining 28 percent were not registered. If one examines the reasons why people did not vote, almost 13 percent of the eligible voters were disenfranchised for technical and legal reasons; over 16 percent did not vote because of lack of interest and dissatisfaction with the candidates and politics; and 8 percent gave other reasons or their feelings were not recorded. The technical and legal limitations included such barriers as being unable to register (3.5 percent), being unable to get to the polls (3.2 percent), not having citizenship (2.9 percent), failing residence requirements (1.7 percent), being out of town during election (1.0 percent), and encountering long lines and malfunctioning voting machines (.4 percent). People who were unable to register or get to the polls were often working, ill, or lacking adequate transportation. But a still larger proportion (16.5 percent) of potential voters were simply turned off by the political process. This group of disenfranchised people numbered over 22 million people who did not vote for lack of interest and another 17 million who did not vote for known technical reasons. The peculiar circumstances of the 1972 campaign did not create an abnormal election on which to make comparisons. Adjusting for the influx of new voters (eighteen to twenty years old) in 1972, the turnout rate was not dramatically lower than in 1968 and 1964 (U.S. Bureau of the Census, 1973). In sum, the number of people disenfranchised in the United States is greater than the entire voting populations of many Western nations.

Campaigning, in contrast to voting, is an activity limited to smaller groups of people. An index of campaign activity, similar to that constructed for political involvement, indicates a pattern of selective involvement (see Figure 8–1).[1] Sixty percent of the sample reported no (0) campaign actions. Of the remaining 40 percent, half of those respondents (20 percent) participated in only one activity. Thus, the proportion of the sample involved rapidly declines as the amount of involvement increases. Table 8–3 shows that the relatively passive actions—displaying a bumper sticker or wearing a button—were the activities most commonly engaged in, whereas the more active behavior—talking to voters and passing out campaign literature—was less common. In sum, one finds electoral activity—especially campaigning—to be highly selective and not as frequent as participation requiring only a psychological commitment.

Citizen Contacts with Government

Agency contacts are important because they provide individual citizens the opportunity for obtaining specific remedies and for providing input into the political system. They are also a means of interfacing agencies with their respective clienteles and thus providing output and feedback to their publics. During nonelectoral periods these interactions represent a critical channel of communication of public wants and needs to elected and appointed officials. They also provide a means whereby public agencies can communicate with their clientele to provide information, influence public behavior, and otherwise implement policy.

The manner in which these functions are performed can vary along several dimensions. First, the object of the contact can vary greatly. The agencies may range from regulatory to social-welfare organizations. The role of the citizen in the exchange is important. Citizens may act privately or as agents of some public or private institution. In other words, not all citizen interactions are in the role of private citizen to public official. The initiation of the contact is of interest also. Citizens may initiate the interaction, but public agencies also may do so. Even if a citizen acts in a nonvoluntary capacity, the interaction with its resultant consequences nonetheless occurs. The reasons or purposes of the interaction also are important for revealing the nature of participation. Citizens may seek or give information; they may have a complaint; or they may simply consume the service of the agency in question. Finally, the consequences of the interactions are important. Citizens carry something away from the exchange— an impression, a feeling, or a judgment. They also leave a residue of information, impressions, and reactions with the public official contacted. In sum, the object, role, initiation, purpose, and consequences are important aspects for further understanding the nature of public interactions with government.

In an overall context, citizen contact with public officials regardless of circumstances is less likely—that is, has a higher threshold—than political involvement and voting. There is, however, considerable variation in the rates of contact with specific agencies. Table 8–5 summarizes the rate of contact for eleven agencies and functional areas.[2] The taxing agencies lead the list in rate of contact with 42 percent of the sample reporting some form of interaction with either the Internal Revenue Service or local tax assessor. This figure is inflated no doubt, because the interviewing was done in late spring, close to the filing deadline for tax returns. The educational and police agencies also show relatively high rates of interaction. These three represent high consumption services.

A second group of agencies is headed by social security. In this group one finds elected public officials such as mayor, councilmen, and commissioners, the courts, and many routine service departments. Elected officials received only an average rate of contact, substantially less than taxing, educational, and law enforcement agencies. This pattern reinforces the argument that contact with administration as contrasted with elected officials is an important source of public input. Welfare and agriculture are at the bottom of the list. Their position reflects the relatively limited size of their clienteles in these functional areas.

In a citizen contact study conducted in Milwaukee, Jacob (1972) also found police and social security to be agencies with high rates of contact,[3] and Walker et al. (1972) in a study of North Carolinians reported high rates of contact with the police and courts.

The distribution of the number of contacts with the eleven agencies in Table 8–5 reveals a selective pattern of interaction, similar to the one found for campaign activities. Twenty-eight percent of the sample had no contacts, or in

Table 8–5

Rates of Citizen Interaction with Selected Public Agencies and Officials

Had Contact with Agency in Last Year or So	(a) Contact	(b) "Most Important"	(c) (b) Divided by (a)
The Internal Revenue Service or local property tax assessor (Tax)*	43%	13%	30%
A teacher, principal, or other school official (Education)	39	17	43
The police, sheriff, or highway patrol (Police)	32	6	19
The social security office (Social Security)	20	8	40
The sanitation or trash pick-up agency (Sanitation)	19	2	11
The mayor's office, a city councilman, county commissioner, or city manager (Elected Officials)	17	4	14
The street department (Streets)	16	1	6
A local judge, justice of the peace, or police magistrate (Courts)	15	2	13
The employment or unemployment compensation office (Employment)	12	2	17
The soil conservation or county agricultural agent or agricultural stabilization people (Agriculture)*	10	2	20
The welfare department (Welfare)	9	2	22

*The tax and agriculture estimates were constructed by combining the responses to two separate questions in each case in order to produce a grouped estimate.
(a) % answering "yes"
(b) % selecting agency as "most important" contact
(c) % having contact who selected agency as "most important" contact: column (b) divided by column (a)

other words, 72 percent of the sample reported at least one agency interaction, and less than one-third of the sample reported three or more contacts. Thus, the probability of some citizen contact with a public agency is approximately equal to the likelihood of voting in a presidential election. The pattern of involvement, though, is selective. People are much more likely to have a small number of contacts (one or two) than a large number. This pattern reinforces the Verba and Nie (1972) finding that citizen contacts are often specific and restricted kinds of political participation, even though one expects about 70 percent to have at least one of these restricted contacts.

The data on citizen contacts reported in Table 8–5 provided an overview of all reported public contacts with officials. The rates of contact may be viewed as gross rates because no effort was made to determine the circumstances surrounding each contact. Every respondent who reported more than one contact was asked a series of follow-up questions about which contact was most important and what transpired during the interaction.[4] These interactions with public officials nominated as most important by the respondents represent a subset of all contacts that were most intense. A series of follow-up questions were then administered to respondents selecting a most important contact to gather information about the role of the citizen, who initiated the contact, and the purpose of the interaction.

Table 8–6 shows the role the citizen played in the contact—either private or

Table 8–6
Distribution of Most Important Contacts by Citizen Role in Contact

Citizen acted as private citizen:	
a. Citizen initiated contact	30%
b. Government initiated contact	6
c. Initiation of contact NA	23
Subtotal	59
Citizen acted as agent of a government or	
private agency in the contact	6%
Role citizen played in contact NA	7
Subtotal	13
Total having some contact with government	72%
Total respondents having no reported contacts	28
	100%

public—and the source of the initiation—either citizen or government. One finds that most intense contacts were by citizens acting in a private capacity and initiated by them (30 percent); only 6 percent of all citizens reported their most important contact as being in a private capacity but initiated by government. In 23 percent of the cases reported, the citizen was acting as a private person but the source of initiation was not given.[5] In sum, 59 percent of all citizens acted in a private capacity with respect to contacts they termed most important, and private initiation was about five times as frequent as governmental initiation (30 percent versus 6 percent). An additional 6 percent of the sample reported their most important contact as occurring while acting as a business agent of a private or public concern. Another 7 percent had multiple contacts but did not provide sufficient information or did not select a most important contact.

One can infer how citizens evaluate the significance of governmental outputs by looking at the proportion of most important selections received by the eleven agencies listed in the questionnaire. Table 8–5 (column b) lists the percentage of people reporting contact who selected the agency as most important. The order is somewhat different from the one provided by the rate of gross contact (column a of Table 8–5). Although contact with education and tax agencies received a high proportion of the most important selections, contacts with welfare and social security agencies were considered quite important in comparison to the other agencies. Thus, one can conclude that the education, tax, and social security agencies receive high proportions of intense contacts.

Another way of examining the intensity of citizen contact is to consider the proportion of people having contact who selected the agency as most important. This is a more accurate measure of intensity because agencies differ in the size of their clienteles. Thus, an agency with a large number of contacts would be expected to receive a large number of "most important" selections. One can think of this proportion as an adjusted intensity contact measure. Table 8–5 summarizes the intensity measures as adjusted for size of clientele for eleven agencies (column c). One finds significant differences in the ordering of the agencies from that given for gross contact. Although education leads the list, social security, taxes, and elected officials also receive a higher proportion of intense contacts. At the other extreme, one finds police, employment, courts, sanitation, and streets. Clearly, social services—education, social security, and welfare—take on new significance when the intensity of the contact, as judged by the respondents, is also considered.

The information provided on the gross rates of citizen contact and the adjusted intensity of contact measures permit one to classify public agencies by two dimensions: (1) the range of contact experienced by the agency and (2) the intensity of contact. The range of contact is an indication of the size of an agency's clientele—that is, approximately what proportion of adult Americans, regardless of circumstances, will come in contact with that agency. We know that the police are an agency with a relatively wide range of contact and agriculture is not. The second dimension, intensity, considers what proportion of the clientele has intense interactions with the agency. These two dimensions give rise to a four-way typology:

Range of Contact	*Intensity of Contact*
I. Wide	High
II. Wide	Low
III. Narrow	High
IV. Narrow	Low

The terms "wide" and "high" refer to an agency that is in the upper half of the eleven agencies classified. Thus, category III is for agencies in the lower half on the range dimension and the upper half on the intensity dimension. An agency in category III would have a small but intense clientele.

In Category I (Wide, High) one finds the taxing, educational, and social security agencies; Category II (Wide, Low) contains the police and sanitation agencies; Category III (Narrow, High) are agriculture and welfare; and Category IV (Narrow, Low) includes streets, courts, and employment, and elected officials.

The Category I agencies have large clienteles and many intense contacts; thus, these agencies would be subjected to a high degree of public awareness. At the other extreme are the small clientele, low intensity agencies (Category IV). These agencies create little public concern. Category III is of interest because of the small but intense clienteles served by these officials. It should be noted that agriculture and welfare are found here.

Considering the wide range of public services provided by the eleven agencies examined, the reasons why citizens engaged in the contact can be quite varied. One particular type of contact having special interest is the interaction rising out of some dispute or grievance. These contacts were of particular importance because a citizen acting in a private capacity sought to correct some situation he felt was inappropriate or to solicit some action to solve a problem. In examining the data on why people had contact, the dispute and grievance contact was not commonly encountered. In fact, only 12 percent of all "important" contacts by citizens acting privately could be classified as such. A much more common type of contact by private citizens was for consuming the service offered by the agency. Sixty-three percent of all "important" contacts were service-oriented. Many citizens (18 percent of those selecting "most important" contacts) sought neither to obtain a service nor to solve a conflict. They were either obtaining or providing information. Three agencies—courts, police, end elected officials—were the most likely to engage in conflict-related interactions. Forty-six percent ofall important contacts with courts and with elected officials related to disputes and grievances and 23 percent of those with the police. Because it is partly the function of enforcement and adjudicatory bodies to deal with conflict, one would expect the courts and police to have a greater proportion of this type of contact. It is interesting to see that elected officials also serve this role of adjudicating disputes. Contacts for the consumption of normal services are most common for the street, employment, welfare, and sanitation agencies. Roads and garbage do not provoke much controversy. Information seeking and giving contacts are most common for schools and social security. The former creates a large number of contacts because parents are seeking information about a child's performance. Most of these contacts do not involve criticisms of the school or attempts to correct some aspect of school policy. Social security contacts are primarily about benefits. elected officials have the most variation in the reasons poeple contact them about important business. In one sense, this is understandable because of the variety of officials included under this heading. In another sense, the data suggest that elected officials are simply serving the general purpose of political communication, while individual agencies deal primarily with a more restricted clientele in their functional jurisdictions. The data reported in chapter 7 on the Congress revealed that next to a national legislator, local officials were considered a possible source of assistance whenever problems arose (U.S. Senate, 1973, Part II).

To summarize, interaction with elected and appointed public officials provides an important means of political involvement for the average citizen. He is as likely to contact at least one official as he is to vote in a presidential election. The majority of the interactions involve the private citizen initiating the action to give or obtain information. Few of these contacts are related to grievances and disputes. Citizens evaluate their contacts with service agencies most highly— namely, those with the schools, the social security office, and taxing agencies. Elected officials, in comparison to these agencies, have relatively low rates of interaction with the public, but the evidence shows that contacts with elected officials are much more likely to be conflictual.

Styles of Participation

Although I have established the thresholds for various types of participatory actions, I have not considered the combinations of political activity. Verba and

Nie (1972) emphasize the point that citizens differ in their patterns or styles of political participation. They classified citizens into six types, based on electoral behavior, contact with government and community activity. Accordingly, they found the following distribution:

Inactives: no political participation	22%
Voting Specialists: vote only	21
Parochial Participants: only contact with government and may vote	4
Communalists: voting and community-related activity	20
Campaigners: voting and compaigning	15
Complete Activists: At least voting, campaigning, and community-related activity	11
	93%
Unclassified:	7
Total	100%

Verba and Nie's classification of styles of participation clearly points out the range of citizen participation. Excluding psychological behavior, they found about one-fifth of all citizens were inactive and only 11 percent were complete activists. Most citizens have participatory patterns in between these two extremes. Verba and Nie, for example, observe the varied nature of contact with government. For some citizens, contact is part of a mixed scenario of involvement, whereas for others, contact with government is a specialized activity pertaining to private and personal needs.[6] Group memberships and community-related actions are also part of the Verba and Nie classification. They summarize organizational involvement by noting that 62 percent reported belonging to an organization and 44 percent reported belonging to an organization active in community affairs, but only 31 percent reported belonging to an organization in which political discussion takes place. In other words, much group activity is nonpolitical. In another national study, three-quarters of all respondents said they were active in one or more of a wide range of religious, social, and professional groups; but only 12 percent reported belonging to a political group, and 14 percent said they were active in a civic group (U.S. Senate, 1973, Parts I and II). In general, the level of group activity is high, but the degree of membership in groups oriented to community and political goals is much more limited (Verba and Nie, 1972).

Table 8–7 presents a summary of styles of participation based on electoral and contact behavior. It differs in two ways from the Verba and Nie classification presented above: (1) the definition of governmental contact is not limited to citizen-initiated contacts and (2) it does not incorporate group membership in community-oriented organizations. In spite of the differences in definition, there are some strong similarities in the findings. The percentage of citizens who limit their participation to voting is estimated to be 21 percent by Verba and Nie and 23 percent in Table 8–7; the electorally active group are estimated to be 15 and 12 percent respectively. Verba and Nie, however, report twice as many

Table 8–7
Distribution of Styles of Participation

Voted?	Campaigned?	Contacted More than One Agency?	Classification of Participation	High Political Sample	High Political Interest
No	No	No	Inactive	10%	44%
No	No	Yes	Parochial contact	7	62
Yes	No	No	Voter	23	68
Yes	Yes	No	Electoral active	12	83
Yes	No	Yes	General contact	20	87
Yes	Yes	Yes	General active	24	89
				96%	
—	—	—	Unclassified	4	—
				100%	

*The distributions of the total sample for the three participatory activities are as follows: Voted, 79% Yes; Campaigned, 40% Yes; Contacted More than One Agency, 53% Yes.

inactive citizens as Table 8–7 (22 percent versus 10 percent) and a correspondingly smaller proportion of complete activists (11 percent versus 24 percent). These variations result from the definitional variations noted above.

One manifestation of the different styles of participation is the corresponding levels of political interest associated with each style (Table 8–7). As one might guess, the inactive citizen has relatively low interest. Citizens who engage in at least two of the three types of activities mentioned have generally high levels of interest also. There is little variation in levels of interest among the electoral active, general contact, and general active styles. Thus, citizens who have crossed the threshold of two participatory acts manifest a correspondingly high degree of psychological involvement.

Some Causes of Political Participation

Most studies on participation show the importance of social and psychological conditions on shaping a citizen's involvement in the political arena. These theories of participation point to the conclusion that characteristics of respondents often shape behavior as much as conditions external to the respondents. As a case in point, Matthews and Prothro (1966) observed that many legal voting restrictions (external constraints) on Southerners had been removed, but people, especially blacks, continued to participate at lower levels than would be expected (cf. Kelley et al., 1967). Conditions such as education, income, occupation, race, and sex contribute to the ability of an individual to actively engage in politics. Verba and Nie (1972) refer to this prevailing explanation of participation as the social status theory of participation. They hypothesize that conditions determining one's social status—education, income, and occupation— are controlling conditions affecting levels of participation. They serve as barriers in the same sense as legal restrictions. Other factors such as sex, race, and age may affect participation, but the effects of these attributes must be studied in the context of social status characteristics. One method for accomplishing this end is to look at the effects of attributes such as sex, race, and age for people having the *same* social status. One therefore can examine the effects of an attribute under constant (social status) conditions. If social status is the only cause, then the second attribute would show no difference.

The Effects of Sex

Table 8–8 presents the effects of a respondent's sex on political participation for each of three levels of social status.[7] Within each of these three levels of status, one can examine whether being male or female makes a difference in the level of participation. Table 8–8 shows that men are more active than women, as a general rule; they show more political participation than women on all four participation indicators. This difference between men and women is present despite the strong effects of status. The campaign measure, for example, increases from 28 percent, to 45 percent, to 57 percent for males and from 24 percent, to 35 percent, to 55 percent for females. For every level of status, however, men report more campaign activity than women. In sum, Table 8–8 confirms the social status explanation of participation—that increased social status enhances participation. Women, however, regardless of their status, are usually less involved.

Styles of political participation can be expected to vary, based on the sex and social status of the participant, since the underlying indicators have shown some marked variation. Table 8–9 summarizes the impact of sex controlled for status on participatory style. Women show different combinations of activity than men do, especially those in the upper status ranks. These women are more involved in the electoral process, especially campaign activity, than men, but men show a predominance in the general active category. At the other end of the status continuum, women are more likely to be inactive, but they also show a greater likelihood to contact government. Overall, the effects of status and sex roles provide a mixed picture of participatory styles. When the styles of activity

Table 8–8
The Effects of Sex on Political Participation, with Socioeconomic Status Controlled

	Low Status		Medium Status		High Status	
	Male	Female	Male	Female	Male	Female
Political Participation						
Having high interest in politics	62%	62%	81%	74%	91%	84%
Voting (1968)	72	64	77	76	92	89
Campaigning (1968)	29	24	45	35	57	55
Having two or more contacts with public agencies	37	42	59	48	72	60

Table 8–9
The Effects of Sex on Style of Political Participation, with Socioeconomic Status Controlled

	Low Status		Medium Status		High Status	
	Male	Female	Male	Female	Male	Female
Style of Political Participation						
Inactive	18%	23%	8%	9%	1%	4%
Parochial contact	8	10	9	11	4	3
Voter	32	25	20	30	15	19
Electoral active	12	11	14	12	11	18
General contact	17	20	21	19	24	20
General active	13	11	28	19	45	36
	100%	100%	100%	100%	100%	100%

are examined, women are more active than men in some modes of participation, but for single forms of participation, they are consistently less active in all phases.

The Effects of Race

Many previous studies exploring the effects of race on political participation show, contrary to initial expectations, that blacks and whites do not differ greatly in their degree of political involvement and that in some cases blacks are more politically involved than whites (cf. Matthews and Prothro, 1966). These seeming contradictions to conventional wisdom arise because the known effects of social status have been accounted for. Thus, many supposed differences between blacks and whites are simply the result of the hidden effects of status differences. When people of the same social status are compared, the observed differences in behavior resulting from racial characteristics often change or disappear entirely.

Table 8–10 presents such a comparison where the effects of status have been

Table 8–10
The Effects of Race on Political Participation, with Socioeconomic Status Controlled

	Low Status		Medium Status		High Status	
	White	Black	White	Black	White	Black*
Political Participation						
Having high interest in politics	66%	48%	79%	59%	88%	86%
Voting (1968)	72	54	77	75	92	85
Campaigning (1968)	27	21	39	51	56	66
Having two or more contacts with public agencies	40	37	54	42	67	45

*The percentages for high status blacks are based on eleven cases.

allowed for. Social status interacts with race to present varied differences. Among lower status people, whites are more likely to have interest in politics, vote, and campaign, but blacks are almost as likely to have contact with government officials as whites. As one moves up the status scale, the differences between rates of black and white participation diminish or reverse. At the high status levels, whites and blacks show nearly equal levels of interest and a similar likelihood of voting. Blacks report higher rates of campaign activity, but whites are more likely to interact with public officials.

Matthews and Prothro (1966) argue that many of the observed differences in participation result from a combination of two conditions. First, historical and legal restrictions on various types of participation have caused black Americans to develop different styles of participation to compensate for exclusion from some aspects of political life, especially voting. They note that increased levels of campaign activity and related work is one manifestation of this phenomenon. Second, psychological adjustments have not kept pace with recent legal changes lowering participation thresholds. People have learned to be nonparticipants, and they must now adapt to unfamiliar circumstances. Thus, black participation, especially in the area of voting, lags behind white levels. There is also the suggestion that lower status people find it more difficult to adapt to these changes than higher status individuals. Finally, one cannot ignore the usually subtle yet all too often blatant, community pressures against participation. It may be legally possible for blacks to vote, but it often is not socially acceptable (Kelley et al., 1967).

The data on styles of participation (Table 8–11) support these observations. Middle-class blacks are much more active in campaigning and voting than

Table 8–11

The Effects of Race on Style of Political Participation, with Socioeconomic Status Controlled

	Low Status		Medium Status		High Status	
	White	Black	White	Black	White	Black*
Style of Political Participation						
Inactive	17%	32%	8%	18%	2%	—
Parochial contact	8	11	11	3	17	—
Voter	30	23	26	17	14	—
Electoral active	12	10	12	23	4	—
General contact	20	16	20	14	22	—
General active	13	8	23	25	40	—
	100%	100%	100%	100%	100%	

*There were insufficient data to calculate the percentages for high status blacks (N = 10).

whites, but blacks also are more likely, regardless of status, to be inactive participants. Most situations where whites are more active than blacks occur in the low status categories. For middle status respondents, blacks show varied but not substantially less participation than whites.

The Effects of Age

The age of respondents has known effects on their political behavior. Probably the best documented pattern is the relationship between interest in elections voting, and the aging process. Many national studies have shown how participation is relatively low in early years, rises to a peak in the middle years, and then shows a decline in the later years. This form of a relationship is called "curvilinear" because the ideal line on a graph has a bend or curve in it, and in this case the curve is downward at both ends with a high point in the middle.

There are several explanations for observing the curvilinear effect of age on participation. These explanations focus on the lifestyle, social status, and consequences of political participation. Lifestyle varies greatly according to one's age. People under thirty usually are in the process of establishing their lifestyle and social status. Many are in school or temporary jobs. Decisions about marriage and family size have not been finalized. Thus, the life pattern of younger people is more mobile, less stable, and less permanent. These conditions contribute to lower degrees of involvement with community and political matters. By the middle years, people reach the height of permanence in their lifestyle. They have settled on employment, their status is relatively fixed, and decisions about family are past. People become more involved with the community, and the consequences of certain political decisions—say, to raise taxes—are more immediate. In the later years, one is again less tied to com munity. Family moves away and relatives pass on. The resources—material and physical—are not available to sustain a once active life. Thus, political activity declines.

Verba and Nie (1972) observed this general pattern of high political activity in the middle years, but also noted that status is related to age. Older people did not have the same opportunities for education and earning potential as people entering the labor market today. Aging often brings a real decline in status. Loss of income and unemployment often precede retirement. When Verba and Nie adjusted for the effects of status differences, they found the effects of aging to be substantially less than without the adjustment; nevertheless, they found a curvilinear relationship between aging and participation, with the peak levels of participation coming after thirty and before fifty-five.

Four figures depicting the relationship between age and four forms of participation with social status controlled are presented in Figure 8–2. Each line in Figure 8–2 represents the relationship of age to participation for one status level. In addition, the total line show the relationship between age and participation without adjusting for social status. In each of the four figures, the line marked "High SES" is generally above that marked "Med SES," which in turn appears above the "Low SES" line. The differences between these three lines show the size of the effect of social status on each form of participation. Figure 8–2, therefore, reaffirms the hypothesis that higher status individuals participate more.

The effects of age on participation are represented by the shape of the lines.

Figure 8-2
The Effects of Age on Political Participation, with Status Controlled

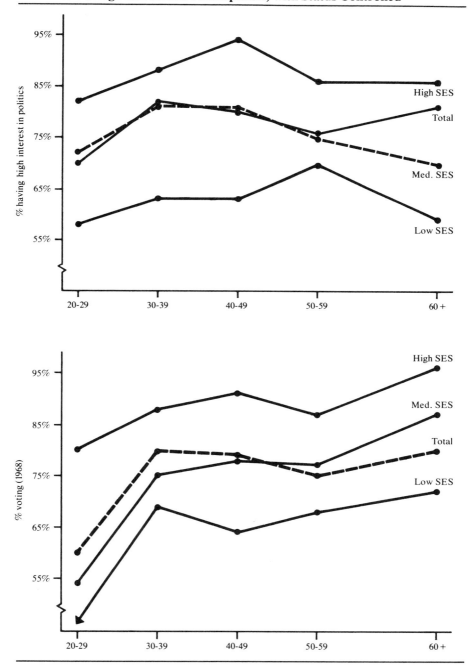

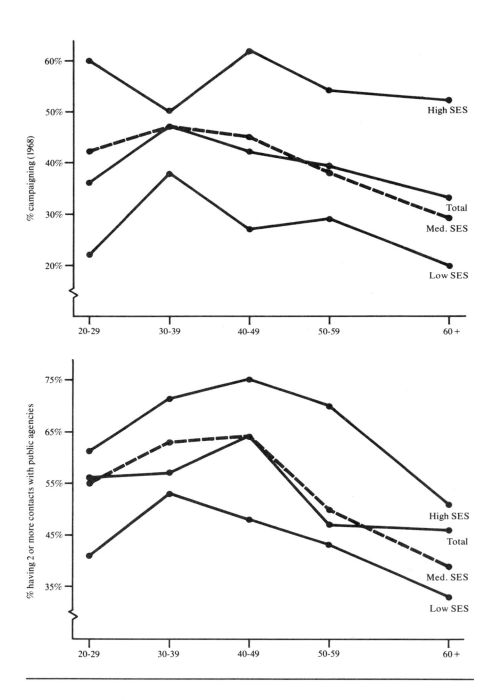

In most cases, the shape of each line is curvilinear—that is, highest in the center (middle years) and lower at each end (early and later years).

Each type of political activity has its own pattern. In the case of election campaigning, the peak activity comes from the thirty to thirty-nine age group and it falls off significantly among older persons. In contrast, voting activity appears to develop over the years and not decline with increasing age. In a strict sense, voting does not conform to the curvilinear hypothesis, because the elderly show as much tendency to vote as middle-aged citizens. Contact with governmental agencies and political interest come closest to conforming to expectations. The highest levels of participation are among forty-year-olds, with young people showing increasing levels and people past forty showing declining levels of involvement. The drop in citizen contact among the elderly is especially great.

The overall relationship of aging, status, and political participation is confirmed. The early years (twenty to twenty-nine) manifest low degrees of participation followed by a middle period (thirty to forty-nine) when political activity reaches its crest. After fifty, most rates of participation decline. This relationship is especially strong because the general pattern is present for each status level regardless of political activity.

Some Consequences of Participation

In considering the consequences of political participation, one needs to examine the way different styles of participation affect related political phenomena. There is a wide range of desirable characteristics one might attribute to a responsible citizen. Certainly, knowledge of political affairs and attentiveness to government are two attributes common to almost all lists of desirable characteristics.

Political knowledge represents the respondent's window to the political world. No respondent has an unrestricted view, but many people are better prepared to see and understand politics. Political knowledge is as much a consequence of political action as it is a stimulant of it. Citizens do not always need to fully understand the political circumstances that are a cause for action, but political action often changes a citizen's level of comprehension. These consequences are aptly demonstrated by Table 8–12, which summarizes five indicators of political knowledge by style of participation. These five indicators do not represent complete knowledge. They are only reference points from which to judge the level of difficulty in acquiring the information. For most people, identifying the location of their state capital is not as difficult as naming a Supreme Court justice. Yet all things considered, active citizens have a wider range of correct knowledge than less active ones. They are more likely to identify the names and the party of key officials, and this awareness is not limited to one level of government or to one political institution.

Table 8–12

The Consequences of Differing Styles of Political Participation on Levels of Political Knowledge

	Inactive	Parochial Contact	Voter	Electoral Active	General Contact	General Active
Correctly identifying one or more Supreme Court justices	22%	40%	51%	63%	59%	74%
Correctly identifying one or more U.S. senators	62	64	81	82	86	92
Correctly naming the political party having a majority in Congress	40	56	68	79	75	86
Correctly naming the political party of the state governor	68	72	86	90	86	96
Correctly identifying the location of their state capital	92	90	95	94	98	98

Another consequence of political involvement is enhanced awareness of the activities and policies associated with political institutions. The rate of nonresponse to questions pertaining to the actions of the president, state governors, Supreme Court, and U.S. senators is strongly related to style of participation. As the data below show, the inactive citizen more often fails to articulate any political judgments:

Style	Making No Comments
Inactive	23%
Parochial contact	18
Voter	7
Electoral active	6
General contact	5
General active	1

Voting is an especially important activity for stimulating evaluations and judgments about the political process. The nonvoters (inactive and parochial contact) show substantially higher levels of no comment about any aspect of the political process than citizens who report having voted.

Political participation not only affects the probability of making judgments, it also influences the content of these judgments. There is no reason to expect that a participatory experience will influence judgments about government either favorably or unfavorably. We have learned that other factors—social background, political party, and political attitudes—are the strongest determinants of political evaluations. There are, nevertheless, some differences in broad evaluations of government that are related to participation. Table 8–13 summarizes five standard questions about government by participatory style.

Table 8–13
The Consequences of Differing Styles of Political Participation on Evaluations of Governmental Performance

	Inactive	Parochial Contact	Voter	Electoral Active	General Contact	General Active
Disagreeing with statement "The government in this state capital wastes a lot of money we pay on taxes."	18%	22%	15%	22%	20%	27%
Agreeing with statement "The government in this state capital pays a lot of attention to what people think when it decides what to do."	37	32	30	33	37	42
Disagreeing with the statement "Quite a few of the people running the state government are at least a little crooked."	11	9	15	22	27	34
Agreeing with the statement "Almost all the people running the state government are intelligent."	68	68	66	56	66	67
Agreeing with the statement "Most politicians can be trusted to do what they think is best for the country."	40	52	50	56	61	60

Exposure to government creates more favorable attitudes toward government. The more active respondents are more likely to believe government "pays attention" and that politicians "can be trusted." They also are not as likely to think that taxes are wasted and that public officials are a "little crooked." Inactive citizens show the opposite pattern; they feel neglected by government and are suspicious of most politicans' motives. They also see more waste and corruption in government.

In sum, citizens with higher degrees of active involvement in political affairs are more knowledgeable about politics and more responsive to policies and programs of government. They are more trusting of officials and expect a higher degree of attentiveness than most people. Active citizens are also less suspicious about how tax money is spent and about dishonesty among governmental officials. Less active people do not have as much correct political knowledge, nor do they respond as readily to the day-to-day activities of government. To a greater degree they believe that public revenues are wasted and that officials are crooked. Although they are distrustful of politicians in general, they have reasonably high expectations that government "pays attention." Citizens with selective modes of participation generally fall between these two extremes, but the precise degree of their evaluations on specific characteristics cannot be predicted. The selective styles of participation, therefore, do not conform to any single order where political judgments are concerned.

The main points of this chapter can be summarized as follows. The United States has relatively high levels of participation in comparison to other countries. The rate of participation for specific forms of behavior varies considerably however, because the thresholds of participation—in other words, the costs of involvement—vary. The initiative, type of interpersonal interaction, and conflictual interactions required all contribute to the costs. Being interested in government and politics does not require much of the individual citizen, but acts such as voting, campaigning, and contacting officials place considerably more demands on the individual. More than 70 percent of the citizenry are interested, but only about one-quarter work in a campaign. Contacts with officials are especially important because they provide direct input between elections. Most contact behavior is initiated by citizens who are seeking or giving information. It is generally not related directly to conflict, except in the case of public officials.

Overt participation is influenced greatly by the socioeconomic status of the citizen, but race, sex, and age differences have important effects also. Lower status whites are more active than their black counterparts, but these differences disappear with increased status. For many kinds of participation, the differences are reversed. Women are less active than men, but again these differences are mediated with increased status. Finally, aging has an important influence on political participation. The citizen under thirty is consistently the least active, and the middle-aged person is the most active. Aging beyond fifty tends to reduce participation somewhat, except in the case of voting. In this instance, the elderly vote at the same or even higher levels than middle-aged people of equivalent status.

Participatory acts have important consequences for the involved individuals. We may summarize some of the more obvious ones here. Higher rates of participation are associated with more and broader political knowledge. Participatory citizens are also more likely to find the actions of political elites more salient and thus form judgments—attitudes of specific support—accordingly. Active participants are also more accepting, in a general sense at least, of government than are inactive citizens. Active people tend to trust officials slightly more, not to believe public officials to be wasteful, and to presume that they are honest.

In his study "Confidence and Concern: Citizens View American Government," Louis Harris observed that the American public was still trustful and confident in its government and did not desire basic structural change. He found a people deeply interested in a free and open society but also a people who were frustrated for their lack of involvement. Harris concluded, "If anything, the people opt for an even more pluralistic and responsibility-sharing system, involving more dialogue and more contact between leaders and led.

. . . Perhaps even more important, the people also want to see themselves and the citizens groups they feel could represent them have a much more important place in the governmental process. The public feels deeply that it can and would participate much more than now in a more open and inviting process" (U.S. Senate, 1973, Part I, 153).

This is the unfulfilled challenge of democracy. The problem is not that citizens do not desire more involvement but that they find the costs too high. The challenge, then, is to lower these thresholds, to bring more people into the active citizenry, for "if the preconditions to open government are not met, then frustration, alienation, and polarization are likely to proceed apace. And the distrust of the governed for those who govern is a dangerous development indeed" (U.S. Senate, 1973, Part I, 154).

Notes

[1]Respondents were scored according to how many (0 to 4) campaign activities they participated in.

[2]The rates of contact reported in Table 8–5 are gross rates not adjusted for the purpose of the interaction or the causes of the contact.

[3]Jacob did not include questions on taxing agencies.

[4]In the analysis that follows, respondents having only one reported contact had that agency defined as the "most important" contact.

[5]This lack of information resulted from a combination of complex questionnaire design and a failure of the field staff to follow instructions. The open-ended questions did not always elicit complete response, and interviewers were not always as careful as they might have been when administering the various follow-up questions.

[6]Verba and Nie limited their study of agency contact to citizen-initiated actions.

[7]The creation of the Social Status Index is described in Appendix E.

Part Three

Some Concluding Observations

The American Citizen and Participatory Democracy

Most contemporary arguments favoring a restricted participatory role for the average citizen are based on a critical premise. That premise is that classical democracy implies certain responsible actions by the participant; and, so the argument goes, modern social science tells us that most people fail to meet these requirements for participation. These tests are usually vague and loosely stated. The more explicit ones—such as the rational-activist model and selected aspects of the responsible party model—have usually been found either to be inadequate in conceptualization or largely irrelevant to modern situations. Yet many social scientists working during the 1950s and 1960s have suggested reasons to suspect the common man's capacities for democratic government.

The problems of interpretation and analysis concerning the citizen's proper Democratic role at the present time focus on one particular aspect of this debate: Do the findings of social scientists truly relegate the ideal that people are capable of sound, democratic behavior to the realm of utopian thought? In other words, is it impractical in the face of modern social science to trust in the basic goodness of each citizen to form the foundation of a democratic society? Even the classical democrat, who, morally speaking, desires to answer negatively must confront the implications of science.

The problem is akin to one faced by sixteenth century Christians after the research of Copernicus was published. Much of the Christian value system was based on the (mistaken) empirical presumption that the earth was the center of the universe and that the sun, planets, and stars revolved around it. Copernicus found a more simple explanation of celestial movements, but his system was not compatible with existing Christian values. What was one to do: (1) ignore scientific evidence and maintain the value system; or (2) adapt the value system in light of this new knowledge? During his lifetime Copernicus had to deny his findings, but the full implications of his work have been accepted today. No modern Christian would find knowledge that the earth is not the center of the universe incompatible with his moral value system. If the collective findings of modern social science are as challenging to classical democrats as Copernicus's system was to the Roman Catholic Church, then a similar revolution in thinking may be necessary. Is it possible that democratic elitism is the new value system for the future?

If we examine the core of the argument against the feasibility of man's participatory role, it centers on three crucial points. First, the average citizen is supposed to know little about day-to-day political disputes, called policy issues. Second, he seems to make decisions—specifically, electoral decisions—for "questionable" reasons, such as those based on party identification instead of policy attitudes. Third, his knowledge of government is limited and incomplete. Let me examine the question of policy beliefs first. I have looked in some detail at the nature of specific support given political leaders in the legislative, executive, and judicial branches. In every case I found a large attentive public —ranging from 40 to 60 percent of the total population—associated with any one institution. Less than one out of five people were unaware of any events associated with the president, state governors, or the Supreme Court. Except in the case of Congress, most of the opinions expressed by these attentive publics were about the issues and controversies of the time and not about such political irrelevancies as the politicians' pets, personal habits, and eccentricities. Furthermore, the policy content of these responses varied directly with the institution under study. I did not find, as a general rule, people blaming the Supreme Court for sending a half million troops to Vietnam or holding the president responsible for barring Bible recitation in the public schools or believing that governors were responsible for foreign policy. In other words, evidence was found indicating multiple, overlapping attentive publics who monitored key policy issues associa ted with each political institution.

If one were to replicate these results today, he would probably find few major differences. The relative size of the attentive publics would be the same and the proportion of issue-content would probably be similar. Certainly, the substance of the perceptions would change—depending on what spectacular issues were current and what cumulative issues had emerged into stage center. Yet the basic picture of attentive publics faced with complex, changing issues and limited information who, nevertheless, have managed to monitor the activities of elites and form judgments about them would still appear.

If we examine why people form their political judgments—pro and con— there is no reason to fear the common man's feelings. It would be tenuous indeed to say that a citizen was wrong because he favored or opposed a particular policy, since that would place every analyst in the position of interposing his judgment for all others. Yet the reasons behind these feelings are more suitable to scrutiny. The democratic elitists have argued that the causes of these judgments are not based on particular events. For example, voting is not based strongly on the issues of the campaign. Whenever I have examined the reasons for specific support for governmental authorities, the components of the individual (micro) behavioral model provided me useful guidelines. Political attitudes are structured along social background conditions encountered by the respondent, and his long range political beliefs and values enter the picture as well. For example, I found that blacks and whites saw two distinct Supreme Courts because their perspectives differed so greatly. I also learned that attitudes about Communism, law and order, race, and religion shaped policy attitudes. If this is not evidence that policy attitudes held by attentive publics are sensibly grounded in political interests, then what is? Should we strive for a society where people are homogeneous in their specific evaluations of political leaders, where regardless of social and psychological differences, their political views are the same?

A third point in the argument against the common man rests on the fact that he does not have wide-ranging textbook knowledge of political reality. The late E. E. Schattschneider (1975) stated an answer to this presumption that is worth repeating in some detail:

> One implication of public opinion studies ought to be resisted by all friends of freedom and democracy; the implication that democracy is a failure because the people are too ignorant to answer intelligently all the questions asked by the pollsters. This is a professorial invention for imposing professorial standards on the political system and deserves to be treated with extreme suspicion. Only a pedagogue would suppose that the people must pass some kind of examination to qualify for participation in a democracy. Who, after all, are these self-appointed censors who assume that they are in a position to flunk the whole human race? Their attitude would be less presumptuous if they could come up with a list of things that people must know. Who can say what the man on the street must know about public affairs? The whole theory of knowledge underlying these assumptions is pedantic. Democracy was made for the people, not the people for democracy. Democracy is something for ordinary people, a political system designed to be sensitive to the needs of ordinary people regardless of whether or not the pedants approve of them.

To base an argument about citizen participation on qualifications leads to one of two alternatives: (1) educate the citizenry in the art of citizenship or (2) restrict participation to the qualified. The second alternative is unacceptable and the first appears unworkable. What should a citizen know to participate? Is name identification of governmental leaders essential? Is awareness of current affairs essential? Clearly, one implication of the affirmation of the inherent worth of each citizen is the conclusion that he alone is the judge of his own interests. Furthermore, concluding whether he is correct about the collective or common interests is not a matter of scientific testing but one of persuasion. The American democracy is not built on a popular consensus based on failing the unqualified—that is, excluding those citizens who have deviant attitudes and beliefs. It begins with the premise that all opinions—reasoned or ridiculous—deserve the opportunity to be heard. What Americans disagree about will change from year to year, but the rules of fair play—the agreeing to disagree—should be protected. The principle of free exchange of opinions is the keystone in democracy's arch.

Democracy is a political system not only for the educated, refined, and rich; it is also for the ignorant, vile, and poor. As Schattschneider notes, people qualify to participate not because they received a college degree but simply because they are human beings (1967). He goes on to observe that democracy is based on ignorance. No one, from the president and elected officials to average citizens, possesses near complete knowledge. As Schattschneider concludes, "There is no escape from the problem of ignorance, because *nobody knows enough to run government.*" Throughout the middle section of this book, there is overwhelming evidence concerning our varying degrees of ignorance, but this fact in itself does not require us to reject our belief in the goodness of the average citizen.

It would leave the argument incomplete to end on a negative note—that is, to argue that citizens are not as incompetent as we first feared. There are many benefits that a participatory citizen contributes to the vitality of government and to his own personal public life. To the political system he provides the expression of loyalty and cooperation as well as the stamp of legitimacy. It has been shown how trusting and supportive Americans are of their public institutions. A relatively unknown congressman (Ford) can become president overnight and still receive the gift of trust necessary to govern, simply because Americans believe in their government. This is no small contribution to government, as societies torn by internal strife have learned. Yet as stated earlier, there is reason to endorse these high levels of diffuse support with caution. Diffuse support untempered by specific attitudes is a potential danger. Diffuse support poses an obligation to public leaders to earn and not abuse this trust; should elites fail to justify this trust, the mechanisms for public monitoring of specific actions become critical for the protection of individual interests.

This potential situation suggests why continued citizen interaction with government, in the overt sense, is also essential for a stable political system. Overt political actions provide some of the ways that citizens provide input into the system and monitor output. Being interested in politics, voting, campaigning, group activity, protest behavior, and contacting officials is not an idle, insignificant action. It is a complement to elite leadership for securing democratic government. By the decision to act (e.g., voting) or not to act (e.g., not voting) citizens can communicate broad trends, desires, and reactions to elites. Thus, an active citizenry (not frozen into predictable inaction) provides the constraints on elite action. There is no need, in other words, to abdicate to the experts the job of deciding what is good for you and me. Let the experts make their case and let each citizen judge it for himself.

Americans have rather varied styles of participation, yet nearly one-fifth cannot cross the lowest threshold to active participation. Furthermore, voting accounts for the sum of overt activity reported by a substantially large proportion of people. The electoral system though essential cannot be expected to carry the entire burden of communicating needs to elites and assessing their responses. Thus, it appears that some of the ideals of classical democracy have not yet been realized in practice.

Where, then, does the scientific study of public opinion fit into a picture of American democracy? It first provides a description of political characteristics of the American citizen—good and bad. It tells us about our ignorance and about our capabilities, but it does not tell us how to evaluate these capabilities. We can learn why people behave as they do, why some things happen and others do not, and why conflict exists in American politics. Finally, we can learn how democracy—as lived in the United States—is incomplete and imperfect. The science of public opinion does not provide the model, but it does provide a means for evaluating a model.

By the Schattschneider standard, the American democracy is imperfect. It disenfranchises over 40 million potential voters—*a number greater than the entire electorate of Great Britain.* It is a system where elites and quasi-elites have often failed to incorporate the opinions of attentive publics. Political parties, interest groups, community and civic associations, governmental agencies, and elected officials have not provided a sufficient basis for involvement in public affairs. In spite of these organizational failures, most Americans have definite, well-focused opinions about their political world, and furthermore, many actively participate by contacting officials, voting, and campaigning. If such modes of participation seem incomplete, the failure to be more involved is not simply a reflection of the citizen's inadequacies. Participation is a two-way street —the failure to represent adequately the opinions of the public is as much a shortcoming of our elite structures (organizations) as it is of the people. To fully realize the promise of American democracy the opportunity to participate must be secured for all citizens. In that way, the American experiment in government will become a system unique in man's political experience.

General Political Knowledge Index

Respondents were administered three questions pertaining to general political knowledge. These questions were:

Question 1: Can you tell me the name of the capital city here in [name of state]?

Question 2: Could you tell me what political party the governor here in [name of state] belongs to?

Question 3: Could you tell me which political party has a majority in the United States Congress?

Each of the three questions was scored as follows:

3 = correct
2 = attempted, but incorrect
1 = not attempted

In addition, each respondent had recorded the number of correct identifications to the following questions:

Question 4: Would you please tell me the names of any men now in the United States Senate that you have heard of? [number of correct identifications]

Question 5: Would you please tell me the names of any of the judges on the United States Supreme Court in Washington that you have heard of? [number of correct identifications]

The scores for these five questions were standardized according to the following formula:

$$Z_{ij} = \frac{X_{ij} - \bar{X}_i}{S.D._{\cdot i}}$$

where i = the question number (e.g., $i = 1,5$); j = the respondent. The means and standard deviations were:

Question	$\bar{X}_i$	$S.D._{\cdot i}$
$i = 1$	1.154	1.382
2	2.786	2.803
3	2.926	.359

4	2.766	.605
5	2.519	.798

The general political knowledge index KNOW is:

$$KNOW_j = Z_{1j} + Z_{2j} + Z_{3j} + Z_{4j} + Z_{5j}$$

The distribution of KNOW is:

Interval*	Midpoint	Frequency	Percent
−13.5 to −10.5	−12	13	<1
−10.5 to −7.5	−9	12	<1
−7.5 to −4.5	−6	115	8
−4.5 to −1.5	−3	264	18
−1.5 to +1.5	0	607	40
+1.5 to +4.5	+3	417	28
+4.5 to +7.5	+6	57	4
+7.5 to +10.5	+9	15	1
+10.5 to +13.5	+12	2	<1
+13.5 to +16.5	+15	1	<1
		1503	100

For some tables KNOW has been collapsed as follows:

Score	Interval	Frequency	Percent
−1	−13.5 to −1.5	404	27
0	−1.5 to +1.5	607	40
+1	+1.5 to +16.5	492	33
		1503	100

*Intervals are "closed" at the bottom and "open" at the top.

Construction of Indices for the Degree of Communist Threat (Comm), Need for International Cooperation (Coop), and Foreign Aid (Aid)

Two questions were administered for each of the three indices COMM, COOP, and AID. The text of these questions is found below. Each of the six individual questions was coded as follows:

 1   agree
 2   disagree
 9   not sure/no opinion

Each of the three indices was constructed using two questions in the following manner:

1	Support:	two agree responses
		one agree and one not sure/no opinion
2	Ambivalent or Mixed:	one agree and one disagree response
		one disagree and one not sure/no opinion
3	Opposition:	two disagree responses
99	Missing Data:	two not sure/no opinion responses

The Questions

Fear of Communism

International Communism is the greatest single cause of trouble inside countries throughout the world.

I think that Communist trained organizers working throughout the United States create most of the problems this country faces today.

International Cooperation

The United States and Communist countries should seek peaceful cooperation.

The United States and Russia should work together on such things as trade and nuclear agreements.

Foreign Aid

The government ought to give financial aid to countries that need help.

The government should spend some of my federal tax dollars to aid poorer countries in the world.

Definition of Law and Order Variables: The Construction of Police, Law, and Cause Variables*

POLICE:

		Question A2	
		Agree; Not Sure; No Opinion	*Disagree*
Question A1	Agree; not sure; no opinion	weak	mixed
	Disagree	weak	strong

LAW:

		Question B2	
		Object to Law	*No Objection to Law*
Question B1	Agree	strong	weak
	Disagree; not sure; no opinion	mixed	weak

CAUSES:

		Question C2		
		Agree	*Disagree*	*Not Sure; No Opinion*
Question C1	Agree	mixed	weak	mixed
	Disagree	strong	mixed	mixed
	Not sure; no opinion	mixed	mixed	missing data

*See Table 5–6 for the text of the question

Appendix D

Definition of Stereotyped Racial Attitute Index

A stereotyped racial response is defined as an "agree strongly" or "agree" response to any of the four questions:

Q1. White people work harder than Negroes.
Q2. Negroes are smarter than white people.
Q3. White people behave better than Negroes.
Q4. Negroes are more dependable than white people.

To measure the direction of stereotyped attitudes, a stereotyped response was scored as follows:

	Type of Response	
	Stereotyped	*Not Stereotyped*
Question (Q)		
1	$+1$	0
2	-1	0
3	$+1$	0
4	-1	0

The STEREO index was defined as:

$$\text{STEREO} = Q1 + Q2 + Q3 + Q4 \,(-2 \le \text{STEREO} \le +2)$$

The definition of the index is:

	STEREO
Stereotyped favoring Negroes over whites	-2 or -1
Mixed or not stereotyped	0
Stereotyped favoring whites over Negroes	$+2$ or $+1$

Appendix E

Socioeconomic Status Index

The Socioeconomic Status Index is based on three indicators: education, income, and occupation. The three variables were coded as follows:

Education (ED)

Less than high school	37
High school	75
Some college	100

Income (INC)

$0	to	$3999	22
$4000	to	$5999	35
$6000	to	$7999	51
$8000	to	$9999	67
$10,000	to	$11,999	80
$12,000	to	$14,999	91
$15,000	and above		100

Occupation (OC)

Laborers and tenant farmers	7
Unskilled blue collar	36
Skilled white collar	84
Professional	100

The scores assigned are the percentile rank for each distribution. The Status Index is:

$$\text{STATUS} = (ED + INC + OC)/D$$

where D is the number of variables without missing data (D > 1).

Bibliography

Commonly Used Abbreviations in the Bibliography:

APSR	*American Political Science Review*
BJPS	*British Journal of Political Science*
MWJPS	*Midwest Journal of Political Science*
JP	*Journal of Politics*
POQ	*Public Opinion Quarterly*

Aberbach, J.D. and J.L. Walker (1970). "Political Trust and Racial Ideology," *APSR* 64 (December): 1199–1219.

———— (1973). *Race in the City*. Boston: Little, Brown and Company.

Abrams, M. (1970). "The Opinion Polls and the 1970 British General Election," *POQ* 34 (Fall): 317–324.

Adamany, David (1972). "The Political Science of E.E. Schattschneider: A Review Essay," *APSR* 66 (December): 1321–1335.

Almond, G.A. (1950). *The American People and Foreign Policy*. New York: Praeger.

———— and S. Verba (1965). *The Civic Culture*. Boston: Little, Brown and Company.

Anderson, T.R. and M. Zelditch (1975). *A Basic Course in Statistics with Sociological Applications*. 3rd ed. New York: Holt, Rinehart and Winston.

Axelrod, R. (1967). "The Structure of Public Opinion on Policy Issues," *POQ* 31 (Spring): 51–60.

Bachrach, P. (1967). *The Theory of Democratic Elitism: A Critique*. Boston: Little, Brown and Comapny.

Berelson, B.R. (1952). "Democratic Theory and Public Opinion," *POQ* 16 (Fall): 313–330.

————, P. F. Lazarsfeld, and W.N. McPhee (1954). *Voting: A Study of Opinion Formation in a Presidential Campaign*. Chicago: University of Chicago Press.

Beyle, T. and J.O. Williams, eds. (1972). *The American Governor in Behavior Perspective*. New York: Harper & Row.

Birch, A.H. (1971). "Children's Attitudes and British Politics," *BJPS* 1 (October): 519–520.

Boyd, R.W. (1972). "Popular Control of Public Policy: A Normal Vote Analysis of the 1968 Election," *APSR* 66 (June): 429–449.

Boynton, G.R., S.C. Patterson and R.D. Hedlund (1968). "The Structure of Public Support for Legislative Institutions," *MWJPS* 12 (May): 163–180.

—— (1969). "The Missing Links in Legislative Politics: Attentive Constituents," *JP* 31 (August): 700–721.

Brown, S.R. (1970). "Consistency and the Persistence of Ideology: Some Experimental Results," *POQ* 34 (Spring): 60–68.

Budge, I. (1971). "Support for Nation and Government among English Children: A Comment," *BJPS* 1 (July): 389–392.

Campbell, A., P.E. Converse, W.E. Miller and D.E. Stokes (1960). *The American Voter.* New York: John Wiley & Sons.

—— (1966). *Elections and the Political Order.* New York: John Wiley & Sons.

Carroll, W.A. (1967). "The Constitution, the Supreme Court, and Religion," *APSR* 61 (September): 657–674.

Caspary, W.R. (1970). "The 'Mood Theory': A Study of Public Opinion & Foreign Policy," *APSR* 64 (June): 536–547.

Clausen, A.R. (1968–69). "Response Validity: Vote Report," *POQ* 32 (Winter): 588–606.

Clotfelter, J. and W.R. Hamilton (1972). "Electing a Governor in the Seventies," in T. Beyle and J.O. Williams, eds., *The American Governor in Behavioral Perspective.* New York: Harper & Row: 32–39.

Cohen, B.C. (1966). "The Military Policy Public," *POQ* 30 (Summer): 200–211.

Congressional Quarterly (1974). "Published Political Polls: Added Importance in '74," *CQ Weekly Report* 32, No. 17, 1029–1032.

Converse, P.E. (1964a). "The Nature of Belief Systems in Mass Publics," in D.E. Apter, ed., *Ideology and Discontent.* New York: Free Press. Chapter 6.

——(1964b). "New Dimensions of Meaning for Cross-Sectional Sample Surveys in Politics," *International Social Science Journal* 16: 19–34.

—— (1966). "Religion and Politics: The 1960 Election," in A. Campbell and others. *Elections and the Political Order.* New York: John Wiley & Sons.

—— (1974). "Comment: The Status of Nonattitudes," *APSR* 68 (June): 650–660.

——, A. Campbell, W.E. Miller and D.E. Stokes (1961). "Stability and Change in 1960: A Reinstating Election," *APSR* 55 (June): 269–280. Reprinted in A. Campbell and others (1966). Chapter 5.

——, W.E. Miller, J.G. Rusk and A.C. Wolfe (1969). "Continuity and Change in American Politics: Parties and Issues in the 1968 Election," *APSR* 63 (December): 1083–1105.

Cowart, A.T. (1973). "Electoral Choice in the American States: Incumbency Effects, Partisan Forces, and Divergent Partisan Majorities," *APSR* 67 (September): 835–853.

Dahl, R.A. (1967). "The City in the Future of Democracy," *APSR* 61 (December): 953–970.

Davidson, R.H. and G.R. Parker (1972): "Positive Support for Political Institutions: The Case of Congress," *Western Political Quarterly* (December): 660–612.

Dennis, J. (1966). "Support for the Party System by the Mass Public," *APSR* 60 (September): 600–615.

——, L. Lindberg and D. McCrone (1971). "Support for Nation and Government among English Children," *BJPS* 1 (January): 25–48.

Deutsch, K.W. and R.L. Merritt (1965). "Effects of Events on National and International Images," in H.C. Kelman, ed. *International Behavior.* New York: Holt, Rinehart and Winston. Chapter 5.

Devine, D.J. (1970). *The Attentive Public: Polyarchical Democracy.* Chicago: Rand McNally.

―――― (1972). *The Political Culture of the United States.* Boston: Little, Brown and Company.

Dolbeare, K.M. and P.E. Hammond (1968). "The Political Party Basis of Attitudes toward the Supreme Court," *POQ* 32 (Spring): 16–30.

Easton, D. (1965). *A Framework for Political Analysis.* Englewood Cliffs, N.J.: Prentice-Hall.

―――― and J. Dennis (1965). "The Child's Image of Government," *Annuals of the American Academy of Political and Social* Science 361: 40–57.

―――― (1965). "The Child's Acquisition of Regime Norms: Political Efficacy," *APSR* 61 (March): 25–38.

―――― (1969). *Children in the Political System: Origins of Political Legitimacy.* New York: McGraw-Hill.

Epstein, L.D. (1964). "Electoral Decision and Policy Mandate: An Empirical Example," *POQ* 28 (Winter): 564–572.

Erikson, R.S. (1971). "The Advantage of Incumbency in Congressional Elections," *Polity* (Spring): 395–405.

―――― (1972). "Malapportionment, Gerrymandering, and Party Fortunes in Congressional Elections," *APSR* 66 (December): 1234–1245.

Erskine, H. (1974a). "The Polls: Causes of Crime," *POQ* 38 (Summer): 288–298.

―――― (1974b). "The Polls: Control of Crime and Violence," *POQ* 38 (Fall): 490–502.

The "Federalist Papers" (1961), with introduction by C. Rossiter. New York: The New American Library, Mentor Books.

Field, J.O. and R.E. Anderson (1969). "Ideology in the Public's Conceptualization of the 1964 Election," *POQ* 33 (Fall): 380–398.

Finifter, A.W. (1970). "Dimensions of Political Alienation," *APSR* 64 (June): 389–410.

The Gallup Opinion Index. Princeton, N. J.: Princeton Opinion Press.

Glenn, N.D. (1972). "The Distribution of Political Knowledge in the United States," in D.D. Nimmo and C.M. Bonjean, eds. *Political Attitudes and Public Opinion.* New York: David McKay Company. Pp. 273–283.

Greenberg, B.S. and E.B. Parker (1965). *The Kennedy Assassination and the American Public Social Communication in Crisis.* Stanford: Stanford University Press.

Greenstein, F.I. (1961). "Sex-Related Political Differences in Childhood," *JP* 23 (May): 353–371.

―――― (1965). *Children and Politics.* New Haven: Yale University Press.

―――― (1966). "Popular Images of the President," *American Journal of Psychiatry* 122: 523–529.

Harris, L. (1959). "Why the Odds Are against a Governor's Becoming President," *POQ* 23 (Fall): 361–370.

―――― (1973). *The Anguish of Change.* New York: W.W. Norton.

―――― and Associates, Inc. (1971). *The Harris Survey Yearbook of Public Opinion* 1970. New York: Louis Harris and Associates.

Hennessy, B. (1970). *Public Opinion.* 2nd ed. Belmont, Calif.: Wadsworth.

―――― (1972). "A Headnote on the Existence and Study of Political Attitudes," in D.D. Nimmo and C.M. Bonjean, eds. *Political Attitudes and Public Opinion.* New York: David McKay Company. Pp. 27–40.

Hero, A.O., Jr. (1969). "Liberalism-Conservatism Revisited: Foreign vs. Domestic Federal Policies, 1937–67," *POQ* 33 (Fall): 399–408.

Hess, R.D. and J.V. Torney (1967). *The Development of Political Attitudes in Children.* Chicago: Aldine Publishing Company.

Hinckley, B. (1970). "Incumbency and the Presidential Vote in Senate Elections: Defining Parameters of Subpresidential Voting," *APSR* 64 (September): 836–842.

Huitt, R.K. (1961). "The Outsider in the Senate: An Alternative Role," *APSR* 55 (September): 566–575.

Jacob, H. (1972). "Contact with Government Agencies: A Preliminary Analysis of the Distribution of Governmental Service," *MWJPS* 16 (February): 123–146.

Jennings, M.K. (1967). "Pre-Adult Orientations to Multiple Systems of Government," *MWJPS* 11 (August): 291–317.

—— and H. Zeigler, (1970). "The Salience of American State Politics," *APSR* 64 (June): 523–535.

Jewell, M.E. and S.C. Patterson (1973). *The Legislative Process in the United States.* 2nd ed. New York: Random House.

Jones, C.O. (1966). "The Role of the Campaign in Congressional Politics," in M.K. Jennings and L.H. Zeigler, eds. *The Electoral Process.* Englewood Cliffs, N.J.: Prentice-Hall.

Katz, D. (1960). "The Functional Approach to the Study of Attitudes," *POQ* 24 (Summer): 163–204.

Kelley, S., Jr., R. E. Ayres and W. G. Bowen (1967). "Registration and Voting: Putting First Things First," *APSR* 61 (June): 359–379.

Kessel, J.H. (1966). "Public Perceptions of the Supreme Court," *MWJPS* 10 (May): 167–191.

—— (1972). "Comment: The Issues in Issue Voting," *APSR* 66 (June): 459–465.

Key, V.O., Jr. (1961). *Public Opinion and American Democracy.* New York: Alfred A. Knopf.

—— (1966). *The Responsible Electorate.* New York: Vintage Books.

Kim, J., N.H. Nie and S. Verba (1974). "The Amount of Concentration of Political Participation," *Political Methodology* 1 (Spring): 105–132.

Kostroski, W.L. (1973). "Party and Incumbency in Postwar Senate Elections: Trends, Patterns, and Models," *APSR* 67 (December): 1213–1234.

Leege, D.C. (1972). "Communications," *APSR* 66 (September): 1008–1009.

Lehnen, R.G. (1967). "Behavior on the Senate Floor: An Analysis of Debate in the US Senate," *MWJPS* 11 (November): 505–521.

—— (1971–72). "Assessing Reliability in Sample Surveys," *POQ* 35 (Winter): 578–592.

—— (1972). "Public Views of State Governors," in T. Beyle and J.O. Williams, eds. *The American Governor in Behavioral Perspective.* New York: Harper & Row. Pp. 258–269.

—— and G.G. Koch (1974). "The Analysis of Categorical Data from Repeated Measurement Research Designs," *Political Methodology* 1 (Fall): 103–123.

Luttbeg, N.R., ed. (1968). *Public Opinion and Public Policy: Models of Political Linkage.* Homewood, Ill.: Dorsey.

—— (1971). "The Structure of Public Beliefs on State Policies: A Comparison with Local and National Findings," *POQ* 35 (Spring): 114–116.

Matthews, D.R. (1959). "The Folkways of the United States Senate: Conformity to Group Norms and Legislature Effectiveness," *APSR* 53 (September): 1064–1089.

––––––– (1960). *U.S. Senators and Their World.* New York: Vintage Books.

––––––– and J.W. Prothro (1963a). "Political Factors and Negro Voter Registration in the South," *APSR* 57 (June): 355–367.

––––––– (1963b). "Social and Economic Factors and Negro Voter Registration in the South," *APSR* 57 (March): 24–44.

––––––– (1966). *Negroes and the New Southern Politics.* New York: Harcourt Brace Jovanovich.

Milbrath, L.W. (1965). *Political Participation.* Chicago: Rand McNally and Company.

Miller, W.E. and D.E. Stokes (1963). "Constituency Influence in Congress," *APSR* 57 (March): 45–56. Reprinted in Campbell and others (1966). Chapter 16.

Mueller, J.E. (1970). "Presidential Popularity from Truman to Johnson," *APSR* 64 (March): 18–34.

––––––– (1971). "Trends in Popular Support for the Wars in Korea and Vietnam," *APSR* 65 (June): 358–375.

––––––– (1973). *War, Presidents and Public Opinion.* New York: John Wiley & Sons.

Murphy, W.F. and J. Tanenhaus (1968). "Public Opinion and Supreme Court: The Goldwater Campaign," *POQ* 32 (Spring): 31–50.

––––––– (1968). "Public Opinion and the United States Supreme Court," *Law and Society Review* 2: 357–384.

––––––– (1972). *The Study of Public Law.* New York: Random House.

Nagel, S. and R. Erikson (1966–67). "Editorial Reaction to Supreme Court Decisions on Church and State," *POQ* 30 (Winter): 647–655.

Pateman, C. (1970). *Participation and Democratic Theory.* New York: Cambridge University Press.

Patterson, S.C., G.R. Boynton and R.D. Hedlund (1969). "Perceptions and Expectations of the Legislature and Support for It," *American Journal of Sociology* 75 (July): 62–76.

Pierce, J.C. (1970). "Party Identification and the Changing Role of Ideology in American Politics," *MWJPS* 14 (February): 25–42.

––––––– and D.D. Rose (1974). "Nonattitudes and American Public Opinion: The Examination of a Thesis," *APSR* 68 (June): 626–649.

Pomper, G.M. (1968). *Elections in America: Control and Influence in Democratic Politics.* New York: Dodd, Mead and Company.

––––––– (1972a). "From Confusion to Clarity: Issues and American Voters, 1956–1968," *APSR* 66 (June): 415–428.

––––––– (1972b). "Rejoinder to 'Comments' by Richard A. Brody and Benjamin I. Page and John H. Kessel," *APSR* 66 (June): 466–467.

Prewitt, K. and A. Stone (1973). *The Ruling Elites: Elite Theory, Power, and American Democracy.* New York: Harper & Row.

Prothro, J. W. and C.W. Grigg (1960). "Fundamental Principles of Democracy: Bases of Agreement and Disagreement," *JP* 22 (May): 276–294.

RePass, D.E. (1971). "Issues Salience and Party Choice," *APSR* 65 (June): 389–400.

––––––– (1972). "Communications," *APSR* 66 (September): 1010–1012.

Robinson, J.P. (1970). "Public Reaction to Political Protest: Chicago 1968," *POQ* 34 (Spring): 1–9.

Rockefeller, N.A. (1973). "Address at the 69th Annual Meeting of the American Political Science Association, New Orleans, Louisiana." New York: Third Century Corp. Pp. 1–28.

Rogers, W.C., B. Stuhler and D. Koenig (1967). "A Comparison of Informed and General Public Opinion on U.S. Foreign Policy," *POQ* (Summer): 242–252.

Roper Public Opinion Center (1974). *Survey Data for Trend Analysis: An Index to Repeated Questions in U.S. National Surveys Held by The Roper Public Opinion Research Center.* Williamstown, Mass.: Williams College, Roper Public Opinion Center.

Rose, D.D. and Pierce, J.C. (1974). "Rejoinder to 'Comment' by Philip E. Converse," *APSR* 68 (June): 661–666.

Rose, R. and H. Mossawir (1967). "Voting and Elections: A Functional Analysis," *Political Studies* 15 (June): 173–201.

Rosenau, J.N. (1974). *Citizenship between Elections.* New York: Free Press.

Schattschneider, E.E. (1967). *Two Hundred Million Americans in Search of a Government.* New York: Holt, Rinehart and Winston.

———— (1975). *The Semi-Sovereign People: A Realist's View of Democracy in America.* New York: Holt, Rinehart and Winston.

Schlesinger, J.A. (1970). "The Governor's Place in American Politics," *Public Administration Review* 30 (Jan. / Feb.): 2–10

Sigel, R.S. (1966). "Image of the American Presidency—Part II of an Exploration into Popular Views of Presidential Power," *MWJPS* 10 (February): 123–137.

———— and D.J. Butler (1964). "The Public and the No Third Term Tradition: Inquiry into Attitudes toward Power," *MWJPS* 8 (February): 39–54.

Stokes, D.E. and W.E. Miller (1962–63). "Party Government and the Saliency of Congress," *POQ* 26 (Winter): 531–546. Reprinted in Campbell and others (1966). Chapter 11.

Stouffer, S.A. (1955). *Cammunism, Conformity, and Civil Liberties: A Cross-Section of the Nation Speaks Its Mind.* New York: John Wiley & Sons.

Thompson, D.F. (1970). *The Democratic Citizen: Social Science and Democratic Theory in the Twentieth Century.* New York: Cambridge University Press.

Townsend, J.R. (1969). *Political Participation in Communist China.* Berkeley: University of California Press.

Turett, J.S. (1971). "The Vulnerability of American Governors: 1900–1969," *MWJPS* 15 (February): 108–132.

Verba, S. and R.A. Brody (1970). "Participation, Policy Preferences, and the War in Vietnam," *POQ* 34 (Fall): 325–332.

————, R.A. Brody, E.B. Parker, N.H. Nie, N.W. Polsby, P. Ekman and G.S. Block (1967). "Public Opinion and the War in Vietnam," *APSR* (June): 317–333.

———— and N.H. Nie (1972). *Participation in America: Political Democracy and Social Equality.* New York: Harper & Row.

————, H.H. Nie, and J. Kim (1971). *The Modes of Democratic Participation: A Cross-National Comparison.* Beverly Hills, Calif.: Sage Publications.

U.S. Bureau of the Census (1973). *Current Population Reports.* Series P-20, No. 253, "Voting and Registration in the Election of November 1972." Washington: Government Printing Office.

U.S. Senate, Committee on Government Operations, Subcommittee on Intergovernmental Relations (1973). *Confidence and Concern: Citizens View American Government, Parts I and 2.* Washington: Government Printing Office.

Wahlke, J.C. (1971). "Policy Demands and System Support: The Role of the Represented," *BJPS* 1 (July): 271–290.

Walker, D., J.R. Richardson, O. Williams, T. Denyer and S. McGaughey (1972). "Contact and Support: An Empirical Assessment of Public Attitudes toward the Police and the Courts," *North Carolina Law Review* 51 (December): 43–79.

Walker, N.D. and R.J. Richardson (1974). *Public Attitudes toward the Police.* Chapel Hill: University of North Carolina, Institute for Research in Social Sciences.

Webb, E.J., D.T. Campbell, R.D. Schwartz and L. Sechrest (1966). *Unobtrusive Measures: Nonreactive Research in the Social Sciences.* Chicago: Rand McNally and Company.

White, W.S. (1956). *Citadel: The Story of the U.S. Senate.* New York: Harper & Row.

Wilhoit, G.C. and K.S. Sherrill (1968). "Wire Service Visibility of U.S. Senators," *Journalism Quarterly* 45 (Spring): 42–48.

Zeisel, H. (1968). *Say It with Figures.* New York: Harper & Row.

Aberbach, J. D., 86
Abrams, M., 59
Almond, G. A., 17, 68, 86, 88, 183
Anderson, T. R., 10, 12, 75
Attentive publics, 17–21, 78, 100–101, 136–
140, 208–209
and the Supreme Court, 140–142
Awareness of government, 70–72, 79–80, 85–
89. *See also* Saliency of government
of Congress, 156–157
Axelrod, R., 8

Bachrach, P., 3–4
Berelson, B. R., 6, 39
Beyle, T., 105–106
Birch, A. H., 97
Boyd, R. W., 10
Boynton, G. R., 70, 156, 168, 172
Brody, R. A., 122
Brown, S. R., 11
Budge, I., 97
Bureau of the Census, U.S., 177, 183–184

Campbell, A., 6, 8, 39, 75
Carroll, W. A., 139
Civil rights, and attitudes toward Supreme
Court, 138, 148–150
Clausen, A. R., 177, 183
Clotfelter, J., 106
Cohen, B. C., 114
Cold War attitudes:
effects on perceptions of the President,
120–121
and antiballistic missiles, 123
Congress:
confidence in, 154–156, 164–168
knowledge of, 156–157
Converse, P., 8, 11, 29, 76, 118, 125, 145
Cowart, A. T., 117

Davidson, R. H., 164, 167–168, 172
Democratic theory:

classical, 3, 4, 40, 101, 210
elite, 3, 4, 208
grass-roots, 15, 88–91, 101
responsible party model of, 154–156
Dennis, J., 68, 70, 93, 97, 107, 156
Deutsch, K. W., 104
Devine, D. J., 17, 36, 68–69
Dolbeare, K. M., 137–138

Easton, D., 67–68, 86, 93, 107, 156
Epstein, L. D., 106, 112
Erikson, R. S., 157
Erskine, H., 128, 130, 139

Field, J. O., 11–12, 75
Finifter, A. W., 86, 98–99

Gallup Poll, 104, 107, 119, 128, 130, 132, 137,
139, 140, 142, 150, 152, 166, 168, 172
Glenn, N. D., 76–77
Government, effects of, 88–91, 98–100
Grass-roots democracy. *See* Democratic
theory, grass-roots
Greenberg, B. S., 37, 70
Greenstein, F. I., 68, 70, 93
Grigg, C. W., 69

Hamilton, W. R., 106
Hammond, P. E., 137–138
Harris, L., 106, 202
Harris Poll, 119, 128, 164, 166–169
Hedlund, R., 156
Hennessy, B., 12
Hero, A. O., Jr., 120
Hess, R. D., 68, 93
Hinckley, B., 157
House Judiciary Committee hearings, 166, 170
Huitt, R. K., 158

Institutional Saliency Index, 74–75, 101
Interest groups, 32
Involvement Index, 181

Jacob, H., 186
Jennings, M. K., 73, 101
Jewell, M. E., 155, 158
Jones, C. O., 154, 157, 162

Katz, D., 36
Kelley, S., Jr., 20, 38, 192, 195
Kessell, J. H., 138
Key, V. O., Jr., 10
Kim, J., 178, 183
Koch, G. G., 97
Kostroski, W. L., 157

Law and order:
    attitudes toward, 120–121, 144–148
    effects on attitudes, 129–130
    perception of courts, 129–130
    perception of police, 127–128
    perception of the Supreme Court, 138
Leege, D. C., 10
Lehnen, R. G., 11, 97, 158
Levels of government, citizen perceptions,
    72–74
Luttbeg, N. R., 6, 15

Matthews, D. R., 20, 38, 92, 157, 158, 192,
    194, 195
Measurement of opinion:
    card sort, 46–49
    closed questions, 44–46
    open questions, 44–46, 74, 89
Merritt, R.L., 104
Milbrath, L. W., 19, 21, 180
Miller, W. E., 154–156, 162, 175
Mossawir, H., 177–178, 183
Mueller, J. E., 104, 124
Murphey, W. F., 70, 82, 137, 140, 150

Nie N. H., 20–21, 179–180, 187, 191–192, 196

Opinion measurement. *See* Measurement of
    opinion
Opinions:
    definition of, 267–268
    centrality of, 31
    macro-view model of, 31–34
    micro-view model of, 34–36
    valence of, 27

Parker, E. B., 37, 70, 164, 167–168, 172
Participation of citizens:
    consequence of, 199–203
    contact with government, 179, 185–190
    effects of social background characteristics,
        193–199. *See also* Social background
        characteristics
    electoral behavior, 179, 183–185
    interest groups, 179, 211

political protest, 180
    psychological awareness, 172–179, 192–193
    styles of participation, 190–192
    voting, 177
Pateman, C., 12, 39
Patterson, S. C., 70, 155–156, 158, 168, 172
Pierce, J. C., 12
Policy events:
    cumulative, 104–105,109–115, 133, 208
    spectacular, 105, 108–115, 133, 208
Political culture,67–72, 91–93
Political ideology and attitudes toward the
    Supreme Court, 141–143
Political Involvement Index, 183
Political issues, effect of on voting, 10
Political knowledge, perceptions of, 71–72,
    111–115, 135, 140
Political Knowledge Index, 115
Political party identification and effects on
    attitudes toward:
    Congress, 154–156
    governmental policies, 118
    presidential policies, 111–115
    traditional loyalties, 115–119
Political theory:
    macro-model, 31–33
    micro-model, 35–37
Pomper, G. M., 11–12, 15, 106
Power of government, attitudes toward,
    85–88, 98–100
Presidential popularity, attitudes toward,
    98–100, 109
Pressure groups. *See* Interest groups
Prewitt, K., 3
Prothro, J., 20, 38, 69, 92, 192, 194–195

Racial Stereotype Index, 149–152
Rational-activist model, 6–18, 39
Religion and political attitudes toward the
    Supreme Court, 145–146
Repass, D. E., 10
Responsible party model. *See* Democratic
    theory, responsible party model
Richardson, R. J., 179
Robinson, J. P., 125
Rockefeller, N. A., 114
Rose, D. D., 177–178, 183
Rosenau, J. N., 17

Saliency of attitudes, 27. *See also* Awareness
    of government
    toward executives, 106–111
    toward institutions, 78
    toward political knowledge, 76
    toward United States Congress, 154–157
    toward United States senators, 168–170
    toward United States Supreme Court,
        136–140

Sampling:
 area probability samples, 52
 errors, 54–55, 58
 random sample, 51
 survey sample selection process, 50
Schattschneider, E. E., 3, 209. 211
Schlesinger, J. A., 106
School prayer, attitudes toward, 138, 145–148
Senate, U. S., 1973, 157, 165, 170–171, 180, 190–191, 203
Senate Watergate Committee Hearings, 166
Sherrill, K. S., 160
Sigel, R. S., 88
Social background characteristics, effects of, 35–36, 92, 98–100, 150–152, 208
 on age, 196–197
 on behavior, 37–38
 on Congress, 171–172
 on economic status, 96, 122, 131, 172–174, 192
 on formal education, 77, 92–93, 95, 122, 172, 192
 on perceptions of executives, 131–132
 on race, 92–93, 95, 122, 131–134, 149–152, 172–174, 193–195
 on religion, 97
 on sex, 36, 92–93, 122, 131–133, 150–151, 172, 193–194
Southeast Regional Survey, 42, 46, 49–50, 53, 73, 137
Statistical terms:
 complex tables, 61
 frequencies, 60
 mean score, 60
 net percentages, 60
 tables, bivariate, 61
 tables, univariate, 61
Stokes, D. E., 154–156, 162, 175
Stone, A., 3
Stouffer, S. A., 120
Support:
 diffuse, 67–72, 93–98

 relationship of diffuse and specific, 80–85
 specific, 79–85, 136
Support Saliency Index, 78
Supreme Court, attitudes toward justices, 136–141
Surveys:
 accuracy, 55–60
 coding, 55–56
 question construction, 42–44
 sample surveys, 41
 sampling error, 53–55
 sampling techniques, 50–53

Tables. *See also* Statistical terms
 bivariate, 61–62
 complex, 61
 univariate, 61
Tanenhaus, J., 70, 82, 137, 140, 143, 150
Taxes and spending, attitudes toward, 123–126
Torney, J. V., 68, 93
Turett, J. S., 106

Variables:
 dependent, 61
 independent, 61
Verba, S., 20–21, 36, 68–69, 86, 88, 122, 177–180, 183, 187, 191–192, 196
Vietnam, attitudes toward, 122

Wahlke, J. C., 67
Walker, J. L., 86, 95
Walker, N. D., 70, 179, 186
Watergate, 82–83, 85, 100, 119, 140, 166–167, 169
Webb, E. J., 49
White, W. S., 158
Wilhoit, G. C., 158, 160
Williams, O., 105–106

Zeisel, H., 73
Ziegler, H., 101